The Harcourt Brace Casebook Series in Literature

Hamlet

William Shakespeare

THE HARCOURT BRACE CASEBOOK SERIES IN LITERATURE
Series Editors: Laurie G. Kirszner and Stephen R. Mandell

DRAMA
Athol Fugard
"Master Harold" . . . and the boys

William Shakespeare
Hamlet

POETRY
Emily Dickinson
A Collection of Poems

Langston Hughes
A Collection of Poems

SHORT STORIES
Charlotte Perkins Gilman
"The Yellow Wallpaper"

John Updike
"A & P"

Eudora Welty
"A Worn Path"

The Harcourt Brace Casebook Series in Literature
Series Editors: Laurie G. Kirszner and Stephen R. Mandell

Hamlet

William Shakespeare

Contributing Editor

Scott Douglass
Chattanooga State Technical Community College

Harcourt Brace College Publishers

Fort Worth Philadelphia San Diego New York Orlando Austin San Antonio
Toronto Montreal London Sydney Tokyo

Publisher	Earl McPeek
Project Editor	Matt Ball
Production Manager	Linda McMillan
Art Director	Vicki Whistler

ISBN: 0-15-505480-5
Library of Congress Catalog Card Number: 97-80788

Address for Editorial Correspondence: Harcourt Brace College Publishers, 301 Commerce Street, Suite 3700, Fort Worth, TX 76102.

Address for Orders: Harcourt Brace & Company, 6277 Sea Harbor Drive, Orlando, FL 32887-6777. 1-800-782-4479.

(Copyright Acknowledgments begin on page 279, which constitutes a continuation of this copyright page.)

Web site address: www.hbcollege.com

Printed in the United States of America

7 8 9 0 1 2 3 4 5 6   066   10 9 8 7 6 5 4 3 2 1

ABOUT THE SERIES

The Harcourt Brace Casebook Series in Literature has its origins in our anthology *Literature: Reading, Reacting, Writing* (Third Edition, 1997), which in turn arose out of our many years of teaching college writing and literature courses. The primary purpose of each Casebook in the series is to offer students a convenient, self-contained reference tool that they can use to complete a research project for an introductory literature course.

In choosing subjects for the Casebooks, we draw on our own experience in the classroom, selecting works of poetry, fiction, and drama that students like to read, discuss, and write about and that teachers like to teach. Unlike other collections of literary criticism aimed at student audiences, The Harcourt Brace Casebook Series in Literature features short stories, groups of poems, or plays (rather than longer works, such as novels) because these are the genres most often taught in college-level Introduction to Literature courses. In selecting particular authors and titles, we focus on those most popular with students and those most accessible to them.

To facilitate student research—and to facilitate instructor supervision of that research—each Casebook contains all the resources students need to produce a documented research paper on a particular work of literature. Every Casebook in the series includes the following elements:

- A comprehensive **introduction** to the work, providing social, historical, and political background. This introduction helps students to understand the work and the author in the context of a particular time and place. In particular, the introduction enables students to appreciate customs, situations, and events that may have contributed to the author's choice of subject matter, emphasis, or style.

- A **headnote,** including birth and death dates of the author; details of the work's first publication and its subsequent publication history, if relevant; details about the author's life; a summary of the author's career; and a list of key published works, with dates of publication.

- The most widely accepted version of the **literary work,** along with the explanatory footnotes students will need to understand unfamiliar terms and concepts or references to people, places, or events.

- **Discussion questions** focusing on themes developed in the work. These questions, designed to stimulate critical thinking and discussion, can also serve as springboards for research projects.

- Several extended **research assignments** related to the literary work. Students may use these assignments exactly as they appear in the Casebook, or students or instructors may modify the assignments to suit their own needs or research interests.

- A diverse collection of traditional and non-traditional **secondary sources,** which may include scholarly articles, reviews, interviews, memoirs, newspaper articles, historical documents, and so on. This resource offers students access to sources they might not turn to on their own—for example, a popular song that inspired a short story, a story that was the original version of a play, a legal document that sheds light on a work's theme, or two different biographies of an author—thus encouraging students to look beyond the obvious or the familiar as they search for ideas. Students may use only these sources, or they may supplement them with sources listed in the Casebook's bibliography (see below).

- An annotated model **student research paper** drawing on several of the Casebook's secondary sources. This paper uses MLA parenthetical documentation and includes a Works Cited list conforming to MLA style.

- A comprehensive **bibliography** of print and electronic sources related to the work. This bibliography offers students an opportunity to move beyond the sources in the Casebook to other sources related to a particular research topic.

- A concise **guide to MLA documentation,** including information on what kinds of information require documentation (and what kinds do not); a full explanation of how to construct parenthetical references and how to place them in a paper; sample parenthetical reference formats for various kinds of sources used in papers about literature; a complete explanation of how to assemble a List of Works Cited, accompanied by sample works cited entries (including formats for documenting electronic sources); and guidelines for using explanatory notes (with examples).

By collecting all this essential information in one convenient place, each volume in The Harcourt Brace Casebook Series in Literature responds to the needs of both students and teachers. For students, the Casebooks offer convenience, referentiality, and portability that make the process of doing research easier. Thus, the Casebooks recognize what students already know: that Introduction to Literature is not their only class and that the literature research paper is not their only assignment. For instructors, the Casebooks offer a rare combination of flexibility and control in the classroom. For example, teachers may choose to assign one Casebook or more than one; thus, they have the option of having all students in a class write about the same work or having different groups of students, or individual students, write about different works. In addition, instructors may ask students to use only the secondary sources collected in the Casebook, thereby controlling students' use of (and acknowledgement of) sources more closely, or they may encourage students to seek both print and electronic sources beyond those included in the Casebook. By building convenience, structure, and flexibility into each volume, we have designed The Harcourt Brace Casebook Series in Literature to suit a wide variety of teaching styles and research interests. The Casebooks have made the research paper an easier project for us and a less stressful one for our students; we hope they will do the same for you.

Laurie G. Kirszner
Stephen R. Mandell
Series Editors

PREFACE

When Hamlet's companions are compelled to swear an oath of silence concerning their encounter with the Ghost, Horatio reflects on the fantastic events of the evening: "O day and night, but this is wondrous strange" (1.5.165). These words might be repeated by a modern reader who is acquainted with the performance and publication history of William Shakespeare's *The Tragedy of Hamlet, Prince of Denmark*. Although many readers and spectators regard it as the most complex and confusing among Shakespeare's dramatic pieces, *Hamlet* is revered as his most popular work in print, on film, and at the theatre. And, in spite of four centuries of critical attention, *Hamlet* continues to elicit literally hundreds of new articles annually. The volumes of investigation, analysis, and commentary illuminate the mystery surrounding *Hamlet*, but they also intensify the controversies. Among the countless questions that have been posed, these frequently recur:

- Is the Ghost actually Hamlet's murdered father returned to demand justice, or is it a demon determined to claim Hamlet's soul by tempting him to assassinate the king?
- Why does Hamlet delay avenging the murder of his father by Claudius, his father's brother?
- Was Gertrude unfaithful to her husband during his lifetime, and did she conspire with Claudius in the murder?
- Is Hamlet's madness genuine, or does he merely pretend to be mad, challenging us to distinguish between sanity and madness?
- Does Ophelia—crushed by Hamlet's cruel treatment and driven mad by Hamlet's murder of her father, Polonius—actually intend to drown herself?

Through these questions and many others, *Hamlet* the play and Hamlet the character retain their intrigue and command our attention. Although the extent of written critical study confirms this continued curiosity, more compelling evidence is provided in the release of two film versions during the closing decade of the twentieth century. One production, starring Mel Gibson, appeals to a large and varied audience with one of the screen's most handsome and engaging leading men. The other production features the leading Shakespearean entrepreneur of his day in Kenneth Branagh, who plays the title role and serves as the film's director. The present generation stands to benefit from these film interpretations, which permit Shakespeare and his *Hamlet* to speak to us in contemporary terms, just as they have addressed countless generations before us.

The sources included in this Casebook are intended to enlighten, stimulate, and encourage. Because of the limited nature of such an enterprise, though, no attempt has been made to achieve the impossible task of representing all points of view related to *Hamlet*. A brief glance at this Casebook's Bibliography—which itself has been distilled—indicates the complex challenge and utter frustration that awaits one who pursues such a venture. Nonetheless, the following sources have been selected for their general insights as well as their specific concerns.

- Jenkins, Harold. "Saxo, Belleforest, and *The Murder of Gonzago*." An examination of key elements of two early versions of the *Hamlet* story plus a source for the "play-within-the-play."
- Bligh, John. "The Women in the Hamlet Story." Bligh summarizes the Amleth story (a possible source of *Hamlet*) as told by Saxo and Belleforest and then examines Shakespeare's modification of a "success story" into a tragedy, focusing on his refashioning of the roles of the women and his transforming Hamlet into a misogynist.
- Zhang, Siyang. "Hamlet's Melancholy." An article that contends that Hamlet's melancholy—the mark of his character—stems from his realization of "the disparity between his environment and his version of life."
- Rose, Mark. "Reforming the Role." Because of Hamlet's disdain for "the usual style of the revenger" and his resolve to find a "satisfactory shape for his revenge," Rose asserts, *Hamlet* transcends the conventional "revenge play."
- Adelman, Janet. "'Man and Wife Is One Flesh': *Hamlet* and the Confrontation with the Maternal Body." In this largely psychological

assessment, Adelman contends that Hamlet's agenda of revenge is secondary to his desire to save his mother, to reform her, and to purify her by separating her from her sexuality.

- O'Brien, Ellen J. "Revision by Excision: Rewriting Gertrude." O'Brien traces the modifications in Gertrude's role made by editors and performers—especially during the nineteenth century—that ultimately have furnished the twentieth century with a Gertrude quite different from the role written in the Folio and Second Quarto texts.

- Schlueter, June, and James P. Lusardi. "The Camera in Gertrude's Closet." Schlueter and Lusardi concentrate on *Hamlet's* "Closet Scene" (3.4) to identify signals that the text provides for staging, and follow with an examination of interpretations in two acclaimed productions—the 1948 Olivier film and the 1980 BBC television presentation.

In addition to these sources, a student paper has been included in the Casebook. Its selection is based on its use of the sources also present in the Casebook, as well as its illustration of MLA documentation guidelines. The author, Afton Stinnett, evaluates Shakespeare's intentions for Gertrude as indicated in his text, while noting the role's modifications that have developed in recent film and stage productions.

Perhaps the most valuable aspect of this Casebook—indeed, of the entire series—lies in its inclusion of electronic sources in the Bibliography. Previous studies of this nature have not dealt with this aspect. How could they? Such did not exist until very recently. In the realm of the Internet and the World Wide Web, Shakespeare obviously has not been neglected. The options are numerous and varied—both in their content and value. For one turning to the Web sites listed in this Casebook's bibliography, an extremely important word of advice should be noted: as each day passes, the Web becomes even more complex—in a positive sense. While the electronic sources mentioned here are enlightening and intriguing, they should not be considered all-inclusive. Others of similar quality are only a matter of moments away.

Acknowledgments

Although the author receives credit for the product of such an undertaking, this project would not have been fruitful without the support of many persons, to whom I owe a large measure of gratitude.

- At Harcourt Brace College Publishers: Matt Ball, Katrina Byrd, Betsy Ener, Katie Frushour, Sam Gore, Laurie Kirszner, Stephen Mandell, Sheryl Nelson, Laura Newhouse, and Michael Rosenberg.

- At Chattanooga State Technical Community College: for support and encouragement, Dr. Fannie Hewlett and Dr. Don Andrews in the Liberal Arts Division; for "technical support," Debra Cross and Fay Ray in the Liberal Arts Division; for research assistance, Wiki Carter, Lee Hattabaugh, Tisa Houck, Vickie Leather, Steve Pec, and Joy Wooden in the Augusta J. Kolwicki Library; and for perseverance in honing their research skills, students in my Spring 1997 "Introduction to Shakespeare" course: Mary Afton, Michelle Allen, Christie Garner, Diane Gass, Shallena Russell, Andy Stewart, and Paula Stinnett.

- At home: Susan, Brian, and Beth—for understanding why I "camped out" at the computer and for giving me more than my share of computer time.

- And finally, those refreshing thirty seconds with a root beer proved invigorating as I prepared this manuscript during the warm months of late spring and early summer.

Contents

An annotated essay in which student Afton Stinnett evaluates Shakespeare's intentions for Gertrude as indicated in his text, while noting the role's modifications that have developed in recent film and stage productions.

Introduction

Shakespeare's Stage: *Hamlet* and the Theatre in Elizabethan England

SHAKESPEARE'S THEATER

Hamlet was first performed at the Globe Theatre, located on the south bank of the Thames River in an area known as Southwark. On this site, which was outside the City of London, the Globe's theatrical company was safely beyond the reach of London authorities, who often had Puritan sympathies and were opposed to theatrical performances. The Globe opened in 1599, and from then on Shakespeare's company principally performed there. As a shareholder, Shakespeare had a financial interest in the theatrical company and stood to profit from its success; consequently, during this period in his career, he wrote his plays intending for them to be produced at the Globe. (Specific references to the Globe are present in many of his plays. For instance, in the Prologue to *Henry V,* the Chorus refers to "this wooden O" [13], alluding to the Globe's polygonal shape and its construction materials.)[1]

On June 29, 1613, during the opening performance of *Henry VIII,* the Globe Theatre burned to the ground when a special effects device "misfired" and set the theatre ablaze. Excavations of the site where Shakespeare's Globe formerly stood have exposed its polygonal shape (with as many as twenty sides); its diameter was approximately one hundred feet. The inside gallery walls were about ten feet from the outer walls, so the "yard" was about eighty feet in diameter. Unfortunately, though, this investigation has provided few specific insights about other construction above ground level. Based on evidence provided by similar structures built during Shakespeare's day, however, some conclusions have been reached (see fig. 1). Like many of its counterparts, the polygonal Globe was constructed of wood and was several stories high. Performances, therefore, were "in the round," with only the area directly behind the stage inaccessible to the audience.

2

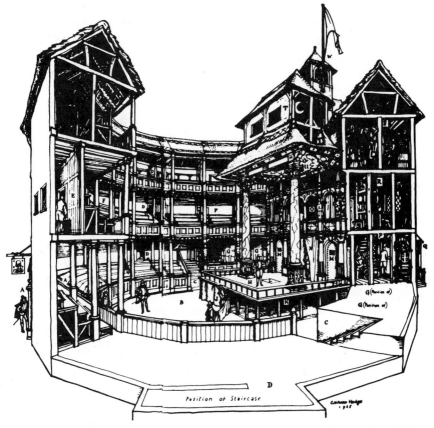

The Globe Playhouse,
1599-1613

A CONJECTURAL

RECONSTRUCTION

KEY

AA Main entrance
B   The Yard
CC Entrances to lowest gallery
D   Entrances to staircase and upper galleries
E   Corridor serving the different sections of the middle gallery
F   Middle gallery ('Twopenny Rooms')
G   'Gentlemen's Rooms' or 'Lords' Rooms'
H   The stage

J   The hanging being put up round the stage
K   The 'Hell' under the stage
L   The stage trap, leading down to the Hell
MM Stage doors
N   Curtained 'place behind the stage'
O   Gallery above the stage, used as required sometimes by musicians, sometimes by spectators, and often as part of the play
P   Back-stage area (the tiring-house)
Q   Tiring-house door
R   Dressing-rooms
S   Wardrobe and storage
T   The hut housing the machine for lowering enthroned gods, etc., to the stage
U   The 'Heavens'
W   Hoisting the playhouse flag

Estimates suggest that fifteen to twenty percent of the people living within a comfortable distance of the Globe and at other theatres in the area were "regular playgoers." Admission fees were paid in cash to "gatherers," equivalent to modern ushers or ticket takers. During Shakespeare's day, those closest to the stage were the poorest and paid the least. A modest fee of one penny provided access to the "yard," the flat ground near and around the stage where the "groundlings" stood to view the production. A spectator preferring a seat paid two pennies to gain access to the galleries (equivalent to modern balconies) that surrounded the yard, while three pennies purchased a seat in the higher galleries. For patrons who wanted to see and be seen, six pence gained admission to special areas of the galleries known as the *tarras* or the "lords' rooms," which were located near the stage and were comparable to the boxes in a modern theatre.

Public theatres like the Globe were very large by our standards for theatres. The yard, which was open to the sky, held as many as 800 spectators, and the galleries as many 1,500. Performances in public theatres occurred during the day, out of doors (no roof covered the yard), and without the effects of artificial lighting to which we are accustomed. The stage itself was a platform about forty feet wide extending at least as far out into the yard as it was wide. Consequently, the groundlings virtually surrounded the stage, while the audience in the galleries certainly did so. Because the stage placed the actors *among* the audience, the actor delivering one of Hamlet's soliloquies was provided a degree of intimacy uncommon among such a large group of people and difficult to create on most modern stages. By walking on stage to approach the middle of the yard, he could speak introspectively and be heard by the audience—perhaps as many 2,000 people—sitting and standing literally *around* him.

The thrust of Globe's stage prevented it from having a curtain similar to that so commonly associated with the modern stage. At the back of the stage, though, stood the gallery's wall, which served as a barrier to the audience's view and whose doors permitted actors to enter and exit from the stage. Behind this wall was the "tiring" house—the actors' dressing room, a name derived from the actors' attire. A balcony, located on the first gallery level above the tiring house, was considered part of the stage and figured prominently in the balcony scenes in *Romeo and Juliet,* as well as in the scene at Flint Castle in *Richard II* (3.3). Near the front of the stage was a large trapdoor which led to the "hell," a space below the stage and useful in *Hamlet*'s grave-digger's scene. Other clues indicate that this area played a prominent role in *Hamlet*: a stage direction in some editions of the play tells us, "Ghost cries under the stage" (1.5.168); and Hamlet refers to the Ghost as "this fellow in the cellarage" (1.5.152). Above a portion of the stage was a roof or covering called "the heavens." The theatre's construction, then, conveyed the idea that the stage represented a world with hell below and the heavens above. And in *As You Like It,* Jaques's reflection that begins "All the world's a stage" confirms the analogy (2.7.139).

No women performed on the Shakespearean stage. Throughout the sixteenth century and well into the seventeenth (until the closing of the theatres in 1642), women were excluded from the profession of acting. Consequently, female roles were played by adolescent boys whose voices had not yet deepened and whose beards had not yet grown. The fact that Shakespeare created relatively few female roles in his plays is explained, in part, by this restriction. But it is worth noting that many of Shakespeare's female creations—Portia, Lady Macbeth, and Rosalind—are among his most memorable characters.

PUBLICATION OF SHAKESPEARE'S PLAYS

In considering printed versions of Shakespeare's dramatic pieces, we must keep in mind that the plays were created primarily for performance, not publication. To that end, Shakespeare sold his plays to the theatrical company, deriving relatively little income from the deal. As a shareholder in the company, though, he realized greater earnings from the performances of successful plays. Indeed, his stagecraft and his knowledge of the audience enabled him to supply the Globe with plays that would "fill the house."

Publication began with Shakespeare's original manuscript, known as the "foul papers," which was written in longhand. To prepare the play for performance, the foul papers were transcribed—usually by a professional scribe—into a "fair copy" that would be suitable for theatrical use. In many instances, a fair copy often contains evidence of a copyist's work, such as consistent spelling and uniformity of proper names in speech headings and stage directions. For example, in some foul papers, an actor's name appears as a speech heading, indicating that Shakespeare had created the part with a particular member of the troupe in mind; the fair copy made the necessary correction for the sake of consistency. On some occasions, though, the scribe took his work too far, altering the foul papers by editing colloquialisms or contractions. Such editorial interventions, of course, further complicate the modern editor's work.

With a fair copy completed, the next step in the process of publication involved further editorial intrusion. A member of the theatrical company literally marked up the fair copy, specifying theatrical necessities (such as stage directions) that the author might not have clearly stated. To the theatrical company, this acting version, known as "the book of the play," was the most valuable form of the text. From these three manuscript versions—foul papers, fair copy, and the book of the play—the publisher selected his copy of the text for printing. Inherent to each text, of course, is its own unique set of problems.

The theatrical company, which owned the rights to Shakespeare's plays, did not necessarily rush to publish them. Copyright laws as we know them did not exist. Having the play circulating in print, therefore, was usually not in the best interest of the company, especially if the play were in the repertory. Indeed, publication permitted rival acting companies access to the script, and, therefore, threatened the commercial success of Shakespeare's company in producing the plays. On occasion, economic matters compelled the theatrical company to publish to help defray the cost of building the Globe Theatre.

Publication of the plays was not always under the control of the theatrical company, though. Publishers of the day had a variety of ways of "acquiring" plays and issuing them without authorization. In some instances, the publisher obtained a "copy" of the play through "memorial reconstruction," which was common in Shakespeare's day. The process probably went something like this: a rival group of actors sought to include a popular play (such as *Hamlet*) in their repertory. Without a printed copy of the play, though, they resorted to other means. Among their company, perhaps, was an actor who had performed in the play and who could recall significant portions. Accuracy was not necessary for such a version of the play. Presenting the play to lure the audience to their own playhouse was the ultimate goal. With the "reconstructed" version in hand, the rival company might then sell a copy to a publisher, who could print this corrupted version.

A play acquired in such a manner was usually issued in quarto format—as a cheaply printed paperback that sold for about six pence. The term *quarto*, which means "four," is derived from a printer's use of one large sheet of paper (approximately 18 by 14 inches), on which he printed eight pages; he then folded the sheet twice to make four leaves about 7 by 9 inches. These four leaves were then sewn together to form a gathering; and several gatherings were bound together to create a book about the size of a large modern paperback.

During Shakespeare's lifetime, eighteen of his plays appeared in quarto editions. Some of these plays appear in corrupted form because Shakespeare did not supervise—and in many cases did not authorize—their publication. Each play in this group is known as a "bad" quarto—a sign of its corrupted state. Another group is known as the "good" quartos, because the text printed may well be closer to Shakespeare's original. As we shall later see, *Hamlet*'s complex publication history places it in both of these categories.

A venture to publish a "complete works" version of Shakespeare's plays was undertaken seven years after his death (in 1623) by two of Shakespeare's fellow actors, John Heminges and Henry Condell, and two London publishers, Edward Blount and Isaac Jaggard. Rejecting the quarto format, they instead chose to issue the plays in the larger and more expensive folio format, which was associated with such noteworthy projects as Bibles and histories. The plays were arranged in double columns on the folio pages, which are nearly a foot high. The term *folio,* which means "leaf," is derived from a printer's use of one large sheet of paper, on which he printed four pages; he then folded the sheet only once to make two leaves, or four pages front and back. These two leaves were gathered "in sixes" (that is, three folded sheets were placed within one another at the fold), producing a gathering of six leaves or twelve pages. Scores of gatherings were then bound together to create the folio volume.

The collection of Shakespeare's plays issued in 1623 is called the First Folio to distinguish it from three other folio editions that appeared later in the seventeenth century (the Second Folio in 1632, the Third Folio in 1663–1664, and the Fourth Folio in 1685). When it first appeared, the First Folio is reputed to have sold for one pound—an extravagant sum indeed, in its day. But today its value to Shakespearean scholarship is priceless because it not only preserves the eighteen plays that had appeared in the quarto editions, but also includes eighteen others that had not previously been published and so might not otherwise have survived.

The most important point to be learned from this overview of the publication process is that for some plays—and *Hamlet* is among them—there is no single ideal text. We must consider that Shakespeare probably reworked and altered the text of the play during its life in the repertory. And modifications made by actors, prompters, scribes, compositors, and printers likely contributed to the text's development.

The Text of *Hamlet*

An editor of the text of *Hamlet* is confronted by an especially complicated problem. During Shakespeare's lifetime, *Hamlet* was printed in three different versions. In 1603, the play first appeared in a quarto version (known as Q1), and a second quarto (Q2) edition soon followed, with some copies dated 1604 and others dated 1605. A third version of *Hamlet* was included in the First Folio (F), which was published in 1623. As one might expect, this trio of versions complicates the task of determining a definitive text of the play.

The First Quarto (Q1), published in 1603, seems to be particularly corrupt and is known as one of the "bad" quartos. Radically different from the two subsequent versions, Q1 is slightly more than half as long as Q2 and F; it places scenes and speeches conspicuously out of sequence; it features omissions, mislinings, and paraphrases; and it distorts some well-known passages almost beyond recognition. For example, contrast the two versions of *Hamlet*'s most famous passage (perhaps the most famous in all of literature):

from Q1
To be, or not to be, I there's the point,
To Die, to sleepe, is that all? I all:
No, to sleepe, to dreame, I mary there it goes . . . .

from the First Folio
To be, or not to be, that is the Question:
whether 'tis Nobler in the minde to suffer
The Slings and Arrowes of outragious Fortune,
Or to take Armes against a Sea of troubles,
And by opposing end them: to dye, to sleepe
Nor more; and by a sleepe, to say we end
The Heart-ake, and the thousand Naturall shockes
That Flesh is heyre too? 'Tis a consummation
Devoutly to be wish'd. To dye to sleepe,
To sleepe, perchance to Dreame; I, there's the rub . . . .

Indeed, Q1 is not considered an original version of the play, but rather a reconstruction of Shakespeare's play. Such "memorial reconstructions," as noted earlier, were common in Shakespeare's day. Regarding the creation of the Q1 version of *Hamlet*, scholars have concluded that the actor who played the role of Marcellus recited the text to a scribe. The text's accuracy was of little concern. The "reconstructed" version of *Hamlet* need only be actable. It must have a coherent plot, of course, but details lost in the reconstruction could be overcome. It need only draw the audience.

The Second Quarto (Q2) appeared in 1604 and 1605, its title page bearing this claim: "Newly imprinted and enlarged to almost as much againe as it was, according to the true and perfect Coppie." This inscription seems a snub directed at Q1, whose corrupt text Q2 was obviously intended to supersede. Overall, Q2 is considered far more reputable than its predecessor. It is widely accepted as having been based on an authentic manuscript written by Shakespeare and sent—though not without annotation by a playhouse bookkeeper—to the printer. But the play's journey to the press was neither direct nor without intrusion. Evidence suggests, in fact, that Shakespeare delivered his own version of the play (called the "foul papers") to the acting company; the "foul papers" were transcribed to create the promptbook from which the actors rehearsed and performed; and the play—in Shakespeare's handwriting, but with annotations from another source or sources—was then sent to the press.

Yet another factor complicates the printing history of Q2. Although they had a copy of the play in Shakespeare's own handwriting, and despite the claim they placed on the title page, the printers of Q2 depended upon the "bad" quarto version of the play. The connection between the two quartos is most clear in the first act, while elsewhere it is not as obvious. The inevitable result of this "consultation" of Q1, of course, is that the authority of Q2 is undermined. Despite this series of events, however, Q2 is regarded as a "good" quarto.

The First Folio (F), which appeared in 1623 (seven years after Shakespeare's death), is based on a playhouse transcript of the play. Because F incorporates cuts and additions possibly made or authorized by Shakespeare (though they might have been made by someone else sometime before 1623), it may be even further removed from Shakespeare's original than is Q2. Similarly, as would be expected in a text based on a theatrical playbook, F also includes many more stage directions than are found in either of the quarto versions. Moreover, F includes about ninety lines not found in Q2, while Q2 includes about two hundred lines not in the F. Nevertheless, neither Q2 nor F can completely overshadow the other. In fact, modern editions of Hamlet usually present a combination of Q2 and F.

The most important point to be learned from *Hamlet*'s complicated publication history is that no single ideal text exists. We must consider that Shakespeare probably reworked and altered the text of the play during its life in the repertory. And modifications made by actors, prompters, scribes, and printers likely contributed to the text's development. Indeed, no modern version of *Hamlet*—in print and in performance—corresponds to the quartos or folio of the early seventeenth century. Perhaps even the Globe did not possess a stable text. As any acting troupe might do, including those that perform the play today, Shakespeare's company probably added and cut scenes when it went on the road or performed at court.

Shakespeare's Sources for *Hamlet*

As his primary source for *Hamlet*, Shakespeare likely depended upon a dramatic piece known as the *Ur-Hamlet* (*Ur* meaning "original"), a play on the same subject, and one known to have been popular in London in the 1580s. Unfortunately, no copy of the text has been discovered, so the connection cannot be made with certainty. Even the identity of its author is unknown, but many scholars have assigned the play to Thomas Kyd, who wrote *The Spanish Tragedy* (1588–1589), considered a probable companion piece to the *Ur-Hamlet*. The play's popularity on the London stage has led scholars to conclude that Shakespeare must have been aware of the *Ur-Hamlet*. Even more crucial is the fact that, for an element central to *Hamlet*, Shakespeare must certainly have turned to the *Ur-Hamlet*, which featured a Ghost who calls for revenge.

The *Ur-Hamlet* itself is derived from a tale in Francois Belleforest's collection *Histoires Tragiques*, which first appeared in 1570 and was issued in as many as eight editions before the end of the century. Such public demand might have encouraged the *Ur-Hamlet* author to develop one of its tales for the stage. Similarly, its popularity suggests that Shakespeare would have been aware of Belleforest's work.

Belleforest retold a story from the *Historiae Danicae*, by Saxo Grammaticus, written in the late twelfth century though not published until 1514.[2] Saxo provides the earliest complete account of a legendary tale of Amleth, a Danish nobleman who took revenge after his uncle killed his father and married his mother. The name Amleth (from the Old Norse) means "dim-witted" or "simpleton," and refers to his stratagem of feigning madness after his father's murder. Also in Saxo's account, Amleth and his mother share an emotional encounter, during which he kills a spy; he pursues a love affair with a beautiful woman; he sails to England and escapes death by altering the order for his execution; and he kills the usurper after changing swords with him.

In spite of these similarities, Shakespeare's direct indebtedness is improbable; it is unlikely that he read Saxo. These elements in Saxo's account are found in Belleforest's version as well, though the latter includes some conspicuous (and apparently influential) modifications. For example, during Amleth's conversation with his mother, Saxo conceals the spy under rushes, but Belleforest places him behind an arras. In other instances, Belleforest introduces new details to the story—most notably, the adultery of Amleth's mother. Although nothing in Saxo's account suggests this, Belleforest stipulates that before the usurper had murdered his brother, he had incestuously seduced his brother's wife. A great deal of controversy centers on the question of whether Shakespeare preserved this element in *Hamlet*.[3]

The evidence supports the idea that Belleforest serves as an important link between Saxo and Shakespeare. One must wonder, then, if all that Shakespeare inherited from Belleforest came to him through the *Ur-Hamlet*. Might Shakespeare also have looked beyond it and read Belleforest for himself? Unfortunately, these are questions which cannot be answered.

One other item must be mentioned as having influenced Shakespeare. Many scholars believe that Thomas Kyd's *The Spanish Tragedy*, also a revenge play, was itself a source for numerous elements in *Hamlet*. For instance, the procrastinating protagonist in Kyd's play chastises himself for talking instead of acting and later dies as he achieves his revenge; *The Spanish Tragedy* also features a play with a play, a heroine whose love is opposed by her family, and another woman who becomes insane and commits suicide. Some scholars suspect that Kyd borrowed at least some of these elements from the *Ur-Hamlet*, whether he wrote it or not. Could Shakespeare have done the same? This, too, is a question we cannot answer.

Hamlet's Niche

Shakespeare's audience would have recognized *Hamlet* as a "revenge tragedy." In a typical play of this type, the hero discovers that a close relative has been murdered, experiences considerable trouble in identifying the murderer, and, after overcoming numerous obstacles, avenges the death by killing the murderer. In many instances, other violent elements—such as mad scenes and ghosts—were included.

But *Hamlet* is a revenge tragedy with several significant distinctions. Because the Ghost has given him the necessary information, Hamlet has no need to investigate the cause of his father's death or seek the identity of the malefactor. In fact, the only serious obstacles in the way of Hamlet's revenge are those he creates himself. And by the time his delay has ended—when he has indeed avenged his father's death—the loss is immense: dead are his mother, the girl he loves, her father and brother, and himself. How much of this suffering and death could have been avoided if only Hamlet had acted promptly after the Ghost first informed him? The argument that we would have no play if not for the delay may be valid, but it fails to satisfy those who explore Hamlet's course of revenge.

But Hamlet's revenge is not the play's only issue, nor is Hamlet the only focus of our attention. Other characters capture our interest. His relationships with his mother, Gertrude, and with Ophelia provide further insights into human behavior. Hamlet's good-natured Gertrude is troubled by divided loyalties to her son and to her new husband. Ophelia, manipulated by those who love her, succumbs to the anguish of a broken heart and the murder of her father at the hands of her beloved. And her father, Polonius, displays a degree of dignity we tend to question when it appears in one so pretentious.

The key to the success of each of these characters is found in Shakespeare's language. The reader or spectator who encounters *Hamlet* for the first time is astonished that so many lines ring familiar. Such phrases as "To be, or not to be," "Frailty, thy name is woman!" and "to thine own self be true" remind us that no other Shakespearean work— indeed, no other work in the English language—rivals *Hamlet*'s universal appeal.

WORKS CONSULTED

Bligh, John. "The Women in the Hamlet Story." *Dalhousie Review* 53 (1973): 275–285.

Boyce, Charles. *Shakespeare A to Z: The Essential Reference to His Plays, His Poems, His Life and Times, and More.* New York: Dell-Doubleday, 1990.

Greenblatt, Stephen, et al., eds. *The Norton Shakespeare: Based on the Oxford Edition.* New York: Norton, 1997.

Gurr, Andrew. *The Shakespearean Stage, 1574–1642.* 3rd ed. Cambridge: Cambridge UP, 1992.

McDonald, Russ. *The Bedford Companion to Shakespeare: An Introduction with Documents.* Boston: Bedford-St. Martin's, 1996.

Schoenbaum, S. *Shakespeare's Lives.* New ed. Oxford: Oxford UP, 1991.

Shakespeare, William. *As You Like It.* Ed. Agnes Latham. Arden Edition of the Works of William Shakespeare. 1975. New York: Routledge, 1991.

---. *Hamlet, Prince of Denmark.* Douglass 19–139.

---. *Hamlet.* Ed. Harold Jenkins. Arden Edition of the Works of William Shakespeare. 1984. New York: Methuen, 1982.

---. *King Henry V.* Ed. J. H. Walter. Arden Edition of the Works of William Shakespeare. 1954. New York: Routledge, 1991.

---. *King Richard II.* Ed. Peter Ure. Arden Edition of the Works of William Shakespeare. 5th ed. 1961. New York: Routledge, 1991.

---. *The Tragedy of Hamlet, Prince of Denmark.* Eds. Barbara A. Mowat and Paul Werstine. New Folger Library Shakespeare. New York: Washington Square-Pocket, 1992.

NOTES

[1] An accurate reconstruction of the Globe Theatre opened during the spring of 1997. Further information is available at http://www.rdg.ac.uk/AcaDepts/ln/Globe/Globe.html.

[2] A detailed account of the transformation of Amleth to Hamlet is provided in John Bligh's "The Women in the Hamlet Story," found on pages 155–66 in this Casebook.

[3] For insights related to this controversy, consult the following items in this Casebook: the Student Essay on pages 235–43; and the articles by Bligh (155–66) and O'Brien (199–209).

Literature

About the Author

WILLIAM SHAKESPEARE (1564–1616) is universally recognized as the greatest of English authors, but unfortunately many "accepted" biographical details are based to a large degree on conjecture, legend, and tradition. The earliest dependable information concerning Shakespeare is found in the parish registers of Stratford-upon-Avon's Holy Trinity Church, where his baptism is recorded on April 26, 1564. Although his date of birth cannot be determined with certainty, tradition has assigned it to April 23, 1564, the day of St. George, England's patron saint.

Many admirers of Shakespeare are surprised to learn that little is known about his early life. Several factors suggest that he attended the Stratford "grammar school." His father's position as an alderman and bailiff in Stratford would have entitled William to attend the local school; and his writing indicates a familiarity with the Latin classics, which were fundamental texts in schools of the time. Reliable information about significant events in Shakespeare's young adult life is available, however. For example, his marriage to Anne Hathaway in 1582 and the births of their children—Susanna in 1583 and the twins Judith and Hamnet in 1585—are recorded in church documents. But the profession he chose to support his family is unknown.

We are confident, however, that soon after the birth of his children, Shakespeare left Stratford for London, although his reasons for leaving and precisely when he chose to move have not been determined. Upon his arrival in the capital, he set out to establish himself in London's literary world. His first step toward achieving this goal occurred in 1592, when he published his narrative poem, *Venus and Adonis;* in the following year, he further distinguished himself with the appearance of a second poem, *The*

Rape of Lucrece. And by 1594, Shakespeare had become quite involved in the London stage.

For approximately twenty years, Shakespeare enjoyed a successful professional career in London—as actor, playwright, and shareholder in an acting company. The income derived from these activities brought him significant wealth and enabled him, sometime between 1610 and 1613, to retire from the theatre and return to Stratford-upon-Avon, where he owned a large house and considerable property. On April 23, 1616, he died in Stratford; he was buried two days later in Holy Trinity Church.

Certainly Shakespeare is best known for his thirty-seven dramatic pieces, but we neglect a major part of his art if we fail to consider his verse productions. The two narrative poems are significant, if only for the role they played in establishing the aspiring young writer in London's literary world. Deserving even more attention, however, is Shakespeare's sequence of 154 sonnets, which he began writing as early as 1593 but did not intend for publication (although they circulated privately in manuscript form). Despite his wishes to the contrary, the sonnets were published without his approval in 1609.

By the last quarter of the sixteenth century, the Italian sonnet (also known as the Petrarchan sonnet, named for its consummate practitioner Francesco Petrarch) had been imported to England, where it underwent a slight modification. Writing sonnets soon became the fashion of the day, with most courtiers and authors participating. As one might expect, Shakespeare was among them. So exceptional were his sonnets, in fact, that the English sonnet is also known as the Shakespearean sonnet.

It is his collection of plays, though, that has secured Shakespeare's place of preeminence in the literary world. Virtually every high school graduate in the English-speaking world is familiar with at least one of Shakespeare's plays, which are traditionally arranged in four categories: Comedies, Tragedies, Histories, and Romances. These categories correspond fairly conveniently to the four phases of Shakespeare's career:

- His **apprenticeship** (1588–1593), during which he wrote some of his comedies [e.g., *A Comedy of Errors* (c. 1588–1594) and *The Taming of the Shrew* (c. 1590–1594)] and the early history plays [e.g., Parts 1, 2, and 3 of *Henry VI* (c. 1589–1592), and *Richard III* (c. 1592–1594)];
- The **second phase** (1593–1600), when he demonstrated his mastery of the comedy [*A Midsummer Night's Dream* (c. 1595–1596), *The Merry Wives of Windsor* (c. 1597–1601), *Much Ado about Nothing* (c. 1598–1600), and *As You Like It* (c. 1598–1600)] and the historic

[e.g., *Richard II* (c. 1595–1596), *I Henry IV* (c. 1596–1597) and *2 Henry IV* (c. 1597–1598), and *Henry V* (1599)];

- The **tragic period** (1600–1609), during which he produced many of his most celebrated plays [e.g., *Hamlet* (c. 1599–1601), *Othello* (c. 1603–1604), *King Lear* (c. 1605–1606) and *Macbeth* (c. 1606–1607)]; and

- The **last phase** (1609–1611), when he wrote spectacular romances [e.g., *Cymbeline* (c. 1608–1610), *The Winter's Tale* (c. 1609–1611), and *The Tempest* (1611)].

It is too much to expect that every play fits neatly into these niches. For instance, *Titus Andronicus* (1588–1594), Shakespeare's first tragedy and likely his first play, clearly belongs to the apprentice years. At the opposite end of Shakespeare's career stands *Henry VIII* (1613), which is considered Shakespeare's final play. (Without a doubt, it was the final play performed at The Globe Theatre, for, during its premiere, a special effects device "misfired," set the theatre ablaze, and burned it to the ground.)

Hamlet has been called Shakespeare's most complex and most confusing play, yet it is also the play most frequently performed, read, and written about. Why, then, does *Hamlet* command our attention? Many of us find the characters captivating. Others among us, confident about how we would react in such a situation, question Hamlet's delay in gaining revenge. Still others are intrigued by Hamlet's relationship with his father, with Gertrude, or with Ophelia. But the answer is far more complicated than any of these explanations provide. Indeed, as we return to *Hamlet* time after time, we find that a combination of factors—as complex as the play itself—has resulted in *Hamlet's* being celebrated as the greatest play by the world's foremost playwright.

Hamlet
Prince of Denmark*
(c. 1600)

CHARACTERS

CLAUDIUS, *King of Denmark*
HAMLET, *son to the former and*
  nephew to the present King
POLONIUS, *Lord Chamberlain*
HORATIO, *friend to Hamlet*
LAERTES, *son to Polonius*
VOLTIMAND ⎫
CORNELIUS   ⎪
ROSENCRANTZ ⎬ *courtiers*
GUILDENSTERN ⎪
OSRIC ⎭
A GENTLEMAN
A PRIEST
FRANCISCO, *a soldier*
MARCELLUS ⎫ *officers*
BERNARDO ⎭

REYNALDO, *servant to Polonius*
PLAYERS
TWO CLOWNS, *grave-diggers*
FORTINBRAS, *Prince of Norway*
A CAPTAIN
ENGLISH AMBASSADORS
GHOST OF HAMLET'S FATHER
GERTRUDE, *Queen of Denmark*
  and mother of Hamlet
OPHELIA, *daughter to Polonius*
LORDS, LADIES, OFFICERS,
SOLDIERS, SAILORS,
MESSENGERS, AND OTHER
ATTENDANTS

---

* Note that individual lines are numbered in the following play. When a line is shared by one or more characters, it is counted as one line.

ACT I SCENE I

Elsinore. A platform before the castle.

(Francisco at his post. Enter to him Bernardo.)

BERNARDO: Who's there?
FRANCISCO: Nay, answer me: stand, and unfold yourself.
BERNARDO: Long live the king!
FRANCISCO: Bernardo?
BERNARDO: He.
FRANCISCO: You come most carefully upon your hour.
5 BERNARDO: 'Tis now struck twelve; get thee to bed, Francisco.
FRANCISCO: For this relief much thanks: 'tis bitter cold,
    And I am sick at heart.
BERNARDO: Have you had quiet guard?
FRANCISCO: Not a mouse stirring.
BERNARDO: Well, good-night.
10   If you do meet Horatio and Marcellus,
    The rivals of my watch, bid them make haste.
FRANCISCO: I think I hear them.—Stand, ho! Who is there?

(Enter Horatio and Marcellus.)

HORATIO: Friends to this ground.
MARCELLUS: And liegemen to the Dane.
15 FRANCISCO: Give you good-night.
MARCELLUS: O, farewell, honest soldier:
    Who hath reliev'd you?
FRANCISCO: Bernardo has my place.
    Give you good-night.

(Exit.)

MARCELLUS: Holla! Bernardo!
BERNARDO: Say.
    What, is Horatio there?
HORATIO: A piece of him.
BERNARDO: Welcome, Horatio:—welcome, good Marcellus.
20 MARCELLUS: What, has this thing appear'd again to-night?
BERNARDO: I have seen nothing.
MARCELLUS: Horatio says 'tis but our fantasy,
    And will not let belief take hold of him

Touching this dreaded sight, twice seen of us:
25 Therefore I have entreated him along
With us to watch the minutes of this night;
That, if again this apparition come
He may approve our eyes and speak to it.
HORATIO: Tush, tush, 'twill not appear.
BERNARDO: Sit down awhile,
30 And let us once again assail your ears,
That are so fortified against our story,
What we two nights have seen.
HORATIO: Well, sit we down,
And let us hear Bernardo speak of this.
BERNARDO: Last night of all,
35 When yon same star that's westward from the pole
Had made his course to illume that part of heaven
Where now it burns, Marcellus and myself,
The bell then beating one,—
MARCELLUS: Peace, break thee off; look where it comes again!

(Enter Ghost, armed.)

40 BERNARDO: In the same figure, like the king that's dead.
MARCELLUS: Thou art a scholar; speak to it, Horatio.
BERNARDO: Looks it not like the king? mark it, Horatio.
HORATIO: Most like:—it harrows me with fear and wonder.
BERNARDO: It would be spoke to.
MARCELLUS: Question it, Horatio.
45 HORATIO: What art thou, that usurp'st this time of night,
Together with that fair and warlike form
In which the majesty of buried Denmark
Did sometimes march? by heaven I charge thee, speak!
MARCELLUS: It is offended.
BERNARDO: See, it stalks away!
50 HORATIO:. Stay! speak, speak! I charge thee, speak!

(Exit Ghost.)

MARCELLUS: 'Tis gone, and will not answer.
BERNARDO: How now, Horatio! you tremble and look pale:
Is not this something more than fantasy?
What think you on't?
55 HORATIO: Before my God, I might not this believe

Without the sensible and true avouch
Of mine own eyes.

MARCELLUS: Is it not like the king?

HORATIO: As thou art to thyself:
Such was the very armor he had on
60   When he the ambitious Norway combated;
So frown'd he once when, in an angry parle,[1]
He smote the sledded Polacks on the ice.
'Tis strange.

MARCELLUS: Thus twice before, and just at this dead hour,
65   With martial stalk hath he gone by our watch.

HORATIO: In what particular thought to work I know not;
But, in the gross and scope of my opinion,
This bodes some strange eruption to our state.

MARCELLUS: Good now, sit down, and tell me, he that knows,
70   Why this same strict and most observant watch
So nightly toils the subject of the land;
And why such daily cast of brazen cannon,
And foreign mart for implements of war;
Why such impress of shipwrights, whose sore task
75   Does not divide the Sunday from the week;
What might be toward, that this sweaty haste
Doth make the night joint-laborer with the day:
Who is't that can inform me?

HORATIO: That can I;
At least, the whisper goes so. Our last king,
80   Whose image even but now appear'd to us,
Was, as you know, by Fortinbras of Norway,
Thereto prick'd on by a most emulate pride,
Dar'd to the combat; in which our valiant Hamlet,—
For so this side of our known world esteem'd him,—
85   Did slay this Fortinbras; who, by a seal'd compact,
Well ratified by law and heraldry,
Did forfeit, with his life, all those his lands.
Which he stood seiz'd of,[2] to the conqueror:

---

[1] Parley, or conference.

[2] Possessed.

Against the which, a moiety competent[3]

90   Was gagéd[4] by our king; which had return'd

To the inheritance of Fortinbras,

Had he been vanquisher; as by the same cov'nant,

And carriage of the article design'd,

His fell to Hamlet. Now, sir, young Fortinbras,

95   Of unimproved mettle hot and full,

Hath in the skirts of Norway, here and there,

Shark'd up a list of landless resolutes,

For food and diet, to some enterprise

That hath a stomach in't: which is no other,—

100   As it doth well appear unto our state,—

But to recover of us by strong hand,

And terms compulsatory, those foresaid lands

So by his father lost: and this, I take it,

Is the main motive of our preparations,

105   The source of this our watch, and the chief head

Of this post-haste and romage[5] in the land.

Bernardo: I think it be no other, but e'en so:

Well may it sort that this portentous figure

Comes armed through our watch; so like the king

110   That was and is the question of these wars.

Horatio: A mote it is to trouble the mind's eye.

In the most high and palmy state of Rome,

A little ere the mightiest Julius fell,

The graves stood tenantless, and the sheeted dead

115   Did squeak and gibber in the Roman streets:

As, stars with trains of fire and dews of blood,

Disasters in the sun; and the moist star,

Upon whose influence Neptune's empire stands,

Was sick almost to doomsday with eclipse:

120   And even the like precurse of fierce events,—

As harbingers preceding still the fates,

And prologue to the omen coming on,—

---

[3]   A sufficient portion of his lands.

[4]   Engaged or pledged.

[5]   General activity.

Have heaven and earth together demonstrated
Unto our climature and countrymen.—
125   But, soft, behold! lo, where it comes again!

(Re-enter Ghost.)

I'll cross it, though it blast me.—Stay, illusion!
If thou hast any sound or use of voice,
Speak to me:
If there be any good thing to be done,
130   That may to thee do ease, and grace to me,
Speak to me:
If thou art privy to thy country's fate,
Which, happily,[6] foreknowing may avoid,
O, speak!
135   Or if thou has uphoarded in thy life
Extorted treasure in the womb of earth,
For which, they say, you spirits oft walk in death,

(Cock crows.)

Speak of it:—stay, and speak!—Stop it, Marcellus.
MARCELLUS: Shall I strike at it with my partisan?[7]
140   HORATIO: Do, if it will not stand.
BERNARDO: 'Tis here!
HORATIO: 'Tis here!
MARCELLUS: 'Tis gone!

(Exit Ghost.)

We do it wrong, being so majestical,
To offer it the show of violence;
For it is, as the air, invulnerable,
145   And our vain blows malicious mockery.
BERNARDO: It was about to speak when the cock crew.
HORATIO: And then it started like a guilty thing
Upon a fearful summons. I have heard,
The cock, that is the trumpet to the morn,
150   Doth with his lofty and shrill-sounding throat

---

6 Haply, or perhaps.

7 Pike.

Awake the god of day; and at his warning,
Whether in sea or fire, in earth or air,
The extravagant and erring spirit hies
To his confine: and of the truth herein
155 This present object made probation.[8]
MARCELLUS: It faded on the crowing of the cock.
Some say that ever 'gainst that season comes
Wherein our Saviour's birth is celebrated,
The bird of dawning singeth all night long:
160 And then, they say, no spirit can walk abroad;
The nights are wholesome; then no planets strike,
No fairy takes, nor witch hath power to charm;
So hallow'd and so gracious is the time.
HORATIO: So have I heard, and do in part believe.
165 But, look, the morn, in russet mantle clad,
Walks o'er the dew of yon high eastern hill:
Break we our watch up: and, by my advice,
Let us impart what we have seen to-night
Unto young Hamlet; for, upon my life,
170 This spirit, dumb to us, will speak to him:
Do you consent we shall acquaint him with it,
As needful in our loves, fitting our duty?
MARCELLUS: Let's do't, I pray; and I this morning know
Where we shall find him most conveniently.

(Exeunt.)

SCENE II

Elsinore. A room of state in the castle.

(Enter the King, Queen, Hamlet, Polonius, Laertes,
Voltimand, Cornelius, Lords, and Attendants.)

KING: Though yet of Hamlet our dear brother's death
The memory be green; and that it us befitted
To bear our hearts in grief, and our whole kingdom

---

[8] Proof.

To be contracted in one brow of woe;
5   Yet so far hath discretion fought with nature
That we with wisest sorrow think on him,
Together with remembrance of ourselves.
Therefore our sometime sister, now our queen,
The imperial jointress of this warlike state,
10   Have we, as 'twere with defeated joy,—
With one auspicious and one dropping eye,
With mirth and funeral, and with dirge in marriage,
In equal scale weighing delight and dole,—
Taken to wife: nor have we herein barr'd
15   Your better wisdoms, which have freely gone
With this affair along:—for all, our thanks.
Now follows that you know, young Fortinbras,
Holding a weak supposal of our worth,
Or thinking by our late dear brother's death
20   Our state to be disjoint and out of frame,
Colleagued with the dream of his advantage,
He hath not fail'd to pester us with message,
Importing the surrender of those lands
Lost by his father, with all bonds of law,
25   To our most valiant brother. So much for him.—
Now for ourself, and for this time of meeting:
Thus much the business is:—we have here writ
To Norway, uncle of young Fortinbras,—
Who, impotent and bed-rid, scarcely hears
30   Of this his nephew's purpose,—to suppress
His further gait herein; in that the levies,
The lists, and full proportions, are all made
Out of his subject:—and we here despatch
You, good Cornelius, and you, Voltimand,
35   For bearers of this greeting to old Norway;
Giving to you no further personal power
To business with the king more than the scope
Of these dilated articles allow.
Farewell; and let your haste commend your duty.
40   CORNELIUS and VOLTIMAND: In that and all things will we show our
duty.
KING: We doubt it nothing: heartily farewell.

(Exeunt Voltimand and Cornelius.)

And now, Laertes, what's the news with you?
You told us of some suit; what is't, Laertes?
You cannot speak of reason to the Dane,
45 And lose your voice: what wouldst thou beg, Laertes,
That shall not be my offer, nor thy asking?
The head is not more native to the heart,
The hand more instrumental to the mouth,
Than is the throne of Denmark to thy father.
50 What wouldst thou have, Laertes?
LAERTES: Dread my lord,
Your leave and favor to return to France;
From whence though willingly I came to Denmark,
To show my duty in your coronation;
Yet now, I must confess, that duty done,
55 My thoughts and wishes bend again toward France.
And bow them to your gracious leave and pardon.
KING: Have you your father's leave? What says Polonius?
POLONIUS: He hath, my lord, wrung from me my slow leave
By laborsome petition; and at last
60 Upon his will I seal'd my hard consent:
I do beseech you, give him leave to go.
KING: Take thy fair hour, Laertes; time be thine,
And thy best graces spend it at thy will!—
But now, my cousin Hamlet, and my son,—
65 HAMLET: [*Aside*] A little more than kin, and less than kind.
KING: How is it that the clouds still hang on you?
HAMLET: Not so, my lord; I am too much i' the sun.
QUEEN: Good Hamlet, cast thy nighted color off,
And let thine eye look like a friend on Denmark.
70 Do not for ever with thy vailed [1] lids
Seek for thy noble father in the dust:
Thou know'st 'tis common,—all that live must die,
Passing through nature to eternity.
HAMLET: Ay, madam, it is common.
QUEEN: If it be,
75 Why seems it so particular with thee?
HAMLET: Seems, madam! nay, it is; I know not seems.

---

[1] Downcast.

'Tis not alone my inky cloak, good mother,
Nor customary suits of solemn black,
Nor windy suspiration of forc'd breath,
80   No, nor the fruitful river in the eye,
Nor the dejected 'havior of the visage,
Together with all forms, moods, shows of grief,
That can denote me truly: these, indeed, seem;
For they are actions that a man might play:
85   But I have that within which passeth show;
These but the trappings and the suits of woe.
KING: 'Tis sweet and cómmendable in your nature, Hamlet,
To give these mourning duties to your father:
But, you must know, your father lost a father;
90   That father lost, lost his; and the survivor bound,
In filial obligation, for some term
To do obsequious sorrow: but to persever
In obstinate condolement is a course
Of impious stubbornness; 'tis unmanly grief:
95   It shows a will most incorrect to heaven;
A heart unfortified, a mind impatient;
An understanding simple and unschool'd:
For what we know must be, and is as common
As any the most vulgar thing to sense,[2]
100   Why should we, in our peevish opposition,
Take it to heart? Fie! 'tis a fault to heaven,
A fault against the dead, a fault to nature,
To reason most absurd; whose common theme
Is death of fathers, and who still[3] hath cried,
105   From the first corse till he that died to-day,
This must be so. We pray you, throw to earth
This unprevailing woe; and think of us
As of a father: for let the world take note
You are the most immediate to our throne;
110   And with no less nobility of love
Than that which dearest father bears his son
Do I impart toward you. For your intent

---

[2] Anything that is very commonly seen or heard.

[3] Ever, or always.

In going back to school in Wittenberg,
It is most retrograde to our desire:
115 And we beseech you bend you to remain
Here, in the cheer and comfort of our eye,
Our chiefest courtier, cousin, and our son.
QUEEN: Let not thy mother lose her prayers, Hamlet:
I pray thee, stay with us; go not to Wittenberg.
120 HAMLET: I shall in all my best obey you, madam.
KING: Why, 'tis a loving and a fair reply:
Be as ourself in Denmark.—Madam, come;
This gentle and unforc'd accord of Hamlet
Sits smiling to my heart: in grace whereof,
125 No jocund health that Denmark drinks to-day
But the great cannon to the clouds shall tell;
And the king's rouse[4] the heavens shall bruit[5] again,
Re-speaking earthly thunder. Come away.

(Exeunt all but Hamlet.)

HAMLET: O, that this too too solid flesh would melt,
130 Thaw, and resolve itself into a dew!
Or that the Everlasting had not fix'd
His canon 'gainst self-slaughter! O God! O God!
How weary, stale, flat, and unprofitable
Seem to me all the uses of this world!
135 Fie on't! O fie! 'tis an unweeded garden,
That grows to seed; things rank and gross in nature
Possess it merely. That it should come to this!
But two months dead!—nay, not so much, not two:
So excellent a king; that was, to this,
140 Hyperion[6] to a satyr: so loving to my mother,
That he might not beteem the winds of heaven
Visit her face too roughly. Heaven and earth!
Must I remember? why, she would hang on him
As if increase of appetite had grown

---

4 Drink.

5 Echo.

6 The Greek sun god, the brightest and most beautiful of the gods.

145 By what it fed on: and yet, within a month,—
Let me not think on't,—Frailty, thy name is woman!—
A little month; or ere those shoes were old
With which she follow'd my poor father's body
Like Niobe, all tears;—why she, even she,—
150 O God! a beast, that wants discourse of reason,
Would have mourn'd longer,—married with mine uncle,
My father's brother; but no more like my father
Than I to Hercules: within a month;
Ere yet the salt of most unrighteous tears
155 Had left the flushing in her galled eyes,
She married:—O, most wicked speed, to post
With such dexterity to incestuous sheets!
It is not, nor it cannot come to good;
But break, my heart,—for I must hold my tongue!

(Enter Horatio, Marcellus, and Bernardo.)

160 Horatio: Hail to your lordship!
Hamlet: I am glad to see you well:
Horatio,—or I do forget myself.
Horatio: The same, my lord, and your poor servant ever.
Hamlet: Sir, my good friend; I'll change that name with you:
And what make you from Wittenberg, Horatio?—Marcellus?
165 Marcellus: My good lord,—
Hamlet: I am very glad to see you.—Good even, sir.—
But what, in faith, make you from Wittenberg?
Horatio: A truant disposition, good my lord.
Hamlet: I would not hear your enemy say so;
170 Nor shall you do mine ear that violence,
To make it truster of your own report
Against yourself: I know you are no truant.
But what is your affair in Elsinore?
We'll teach you to drink deep ere you depart.
175 Horatio: My lord, I came to see your father's funeral.
Hamlet: I pray thee, do not mock me, fellow-student;
I think it was to see my mother's wedding.
Horatio: Indeed, my lord, it follow'd hard upon.
Hamlet: Thrift, thrift, Horatio! the funeral-bak'd meats
180 Did coldly furnish forth the marriage tables.

Would I had met my dearest foe[7] in heaven
Ere I had ever seen that day, Horatio!—
My father,—methinks I see my father.
HORATIO: Where, my lord?
HAMLET: In my mind's eye, Horatio.
185 HORATIO: I saw him once; he was a goodly[8] king.
HAMLET: He was a man, take him for all in all,
    I shall not look upon his like again.
HORATIO: My lord, I think I saw him yester-night.
HAMLET: Saw who?
190 HORATIO: My lord, the king your father.
HAMLET: The king my father!
HORATIO: Season your admiration[9] for awhile
    With an attent ear, till I may deliver,
    Upon the witness of these gentlemen,
    This marvel to you.
HAMLET: For God's love, let me hear.
195 HORATIO: Two nights together had these gentlemen,
    Marcellus and Bernardo, in their watch,
    In the dead vast and middle of the night,
    Been thus encounter'd. A figure like your father,
    Arm'd at all points exactly, cap-a-pe,[10]
200   Appears before them, and with solemn march
    Goes slow and stately by them: thrice he walk'd
    By their oppress'd[11] and fear-surprised eyes,
    Within his truncheon's length; whilst they, distill'd
    Almost to jelly with the act of fear,
205   Stand dumb, and speak not to him. This to me
    In dreadful secrecy impart they did;
    And I with them the third night kept the watch:
    Where, as they had deliver'd, both in time,

---

7 Worst enemy.

8 Handsome.

9 Astonishment.

10 *Cap-a-pie*, from head to toe.

11 Overwhelmed.

Form of the thing, each word made true and good,
210   The apparition comes: I knew your father;
These hands are not more like.
HAMLET: But where was this?
MARCELLUS: My lord, upon the platform where we watch'd.
HAMLET: Did you not speak to it?
HORATIO: My lord, I did;
But answer made it none: yet once methought
215   It lifted up its head, and did address
Itself to motion, like as it would speak:
But even then the morning cock crew loud,
And at the sound it shrunk in haste away,
And vanish'd from our sight.
HAMLET: 'Tis very strange.
220   HORATIO: As I do live, my honor'd lord, 'tis true;
And we did think it writ down in our duty
To let you know of it.
HAMLET: Indeed, indeed, sirs, but this troubles me.
Hold you the watch to-night?
225   MARCELLUS and BERNARDO: We do, my lord.
HAMLET: Arm'd, say you?
MARCELLUS and BERNARDO: Arm'd, my lord.
HAMLET: From top to toe?
MARCELLUS and BERNARDO: My lord, from head to foot.
230   HAMLET: Then saw you not his face?
HORATIO: O yes, my lord; he wore his beaver up.
HAMLET: What, look'd he frowningly?
HORATIO: A countenance more in sorrow than in anger.
HAMLET: Pale or red?
235   HORATIO: Nay, very pale.
HAMLET: And fix'd his eyes upon you?
HORATIO: Most constantly.
HAMLET: I would I had been there.
HORATIO: It would have much amaz'd you.
HAMLET: Very like, very like. Stay'd it long?
HORATIO: While one with moderate haste might tell[12] a hundred.
240   MARCELLUS and BERNARDO: Longer, longer.

---

[12] Count.

HORATIO: Not when I saw't.

HAMLET: His beard was grizzled,—no?

HORATIO: It was, as I have seen it in his life,
   A sable silver'd.

HAMLET: I will watch to-night;
   Perchance 'twill walk again.

HORATIO: I warrant it will.

245 HAMLET: If it assume my noble father's person
   I'll speak to it, though hell itself should gape
   And bid me hold my peace. I pray you all,
   If you have hitherto conceal'd this sight,
   Let it be tenable in your silence still;
250   And whatsoever else shall hap to-night,
   Give it an understanding, but no tongue:
   I will requite your loves. So, fare ye well:
   Upon the platform, 'twixt eleven and twelve,
   I'll visit you.

ALL: Our duty to your honor.

255 HAMLET: Your loves, as mine to you: farewell.

(Exeunt Horatio, Marcellus, and Bernardo.)

My father's spirit in arms; all is not well;
I doubt some foul play: would the night were come!
Till then sit still, my soul: foul deeds will rise,
Though all the earth o'erwhelm them, to men's eyes.

(Exit.)

SCENE III

A room in Polonius' house.

(Enter Laertes and Ophelia.)

LAERTES: My necessaries are embark'd: farewell:
   And, sister, as the winds give benefit,
   And convoy[1] is assistant, do not sleep,
   But let me hear from you.

---

[1] Means of conveyance.

OPHELIA: Do you doubt that?
5   LAERTES: For Hamlet, and the trifling of his favor,
        Hold it a fashion and a toy in blood:
        A violet in the youth of primy nature,
        Forward, not permanent, sweet, not lasting,
        The perfume and suppliance of a minute;
10   No more.
    OPHELIA: No more but so?
    LAERTES: Think it no more:
        For nature, crescent,[2] does not grow alone
        In thews and bulk; but as this temple[3] waxes,
        The inward service of the mind and soul
        Grows wide withal. Perhaps he loves you now;
15   And now no soil nor cautel[4] doth besmirch
        The virtue of his will: but you must fear,
        His greatness weigh'd, his will is not his own;
        For he himself is subject to his birth:
        He may not, as unvalu'd persons do,
20   Carve for himself; for on his choice depends
        The safety and the health of the whole state;
        And therefore must his choice be circumscrib'd
        Unto the voice and yielding of that body
        Whereof he is the head. Then if he says he loves you,
25   It fits your wisdom so far to believe it
        As he in his particular act and place
        May give his saying deed; which is no further
        Than the main[5] voice of Denmark goes withal.
        Then weigh what loss your honor may sustain
30   If with too credent ear you list his songs,
        Or lose your heart, or your chaste treasure open
        To his unmaster'd importunity.
        Fear it, Ophelia, fear it, my dear sister;
        And keep within the rear of your affection,

---

2   Growing.

3   Body.

4   Deceit.

5   Strong, or mighty.

35   Out of the shot and danger of desire.
     The chariest maid is prodigal enough
     If she unmask her beauty to the moon:
     Virtue itself scrapes not calumnious strokes:
     The canker galls the infants of the spring
40   Too oft before their buttons be disclos'd;
     And in the morn and liquid dew of youth
     Contagious blastments are most imminent.
     Be wary, then; best safety lies in fear:
     Youth to itself rebels, though none else near.
45 OPHELIA: I shall the effect of this good lesson keep
     As watchman to my heart. But, good my brother,
     Do not, as some ungracious pastors do,
     Show me the steep and thorny way to heaven;
     Whilst like a puff'd and reckless libertine,
50   Himself the primrose path of dalliance treads,
     And recks not his own rede.[6]
   LAERTES: O, fear me not.
     I stay too long:—but here my father comes.

(Enter Polonius.)

     A double blessing is a double grace;
     Occasion smiles upon a second leave.
55 POLONIUS: Yet here, Laertes! aboard, aboard, for shame!
     The wind sits in the shoulder of your sail,
     And you are stay'd for. There,—my blessing with you!

(Laying his hand on Laertes' head.)

     And these few precepts in thy memory
     See thou character.[7] Give thy thoughts no tongue,
60   Nor any unproportion'd thought his act.
     Be thou familiar, but by no means vulgar.
     The friends thou hast, and their adoption tried,
     Grapple them to thy soul with hoops of steel;
     But do not dull thy palm with entertainment
65   Of each new-hatch'd, unfledg'd comrade. Beware

---

[6] Counsel.

[7] Engrave in your mind.

Of entrance to a quarrel; but, being in,
Bear't that the opposèd may beware of thee.
Give every man thine ear, but few thy voice:
Take each man's censure,[8] but reserve thy judgment.
70   Costly thy habit as thy purse can buy,
But not express'd in fancy; rich, not gaudy:
For the apparel oft proclaims the man;
•   And they in France of the best rank and station
Are most select and generous chief in that.
75   Neither a borrower nor a lender be:
For a loan oft loses both itself and friend;
And borrowing dulls the edge of husbandry.
This above all,—to thine own self be true;
And it must follow, as the night the day,
80   Thou canst not then be false to any man.
Farewell: my blessing season this in thee!
LAERTES: Most humbly do I take my leave, my lord.
POLONIUS: The time invites you; go, your servants tend.[9]
LAERTES: Farewell, Ophelia; and remember well
85   What I have said to you.
OPHELIA: 'Tis in my memory lock'd,
And you yourself shall keep the key of it.
LAERTES: Farewell. [*Exit.*]
POLONIUS: What is't, Ophelia, he hath said to you?
OPHELIA: So please you, something touching the Lord Hamlet.
90   POLONIUS: Marry, well bethought:
'Tis told me he hath very oft of late
Given private time to you; and you yourself
Have of your audience been most free and bounteous:
If it be so,—as so 'tis put on me,
95   And that in way of caution,—I must tell you,
You do not understand yourself so clearly
As it behoves my daughter and your honor.
What is between you? give me up the truth.
OPHELIA: He hath, my lord, of late made many tenders

---

[8] Opinion.

[9] Wait.

100 Of his affection to me.

POLONIUS: Affection! pooh! you speak like a green girl,
Unsifted in such perilous circumstance.
Do you believe his tenders,[10] as you call them?

OPHELIA: I do not know, my lord, what I should think.

105 POLONIUS: Marry, I'll teach you: think yourself a baby;
That you have ta'en these tenders for true pay,
Which are not sterling. Tender yourself more dearly;
Or,—not to crack the wind of the poor phrase,
Wronging it thus,—you'll tender me a fool.

110 OPHELIA: My lord, he hath impórtun'd me with love
In honorable fashion.

POLONIUS: Ay, fashion you may call it; go to, go to.

OPHELIA: And hath given countenance to his speech, my lord,
With almost all the holy vows of heaven.

115 POLONIUS: Ay, springes to catch woodcocks. I do know,
When the blood burns, how prodigal the soul
Lends the tongue vows: these blazes, daughter,
Giving more light than heat,—extinct in both,
Even in their promise, as it is a-making,—

120 You must not take for fire. From this time
Be somewhat scanter of your maiden presence;
Set your entreatments at a higher rate
Than a command to parley. For Lord Hamlet,
Believe so much in him, that he is young;

125 And with a larger tether may he walk
Than may be given you: in few, Ophelia,
Do not believe his vows; for they are brokers,[11]—
Not of that die which their investments show,
But mere implorators of unholy suits,

130 Breathing like sanctified and pious bawds,
The better to beguile. This is for all,—
I would not, in plain terms, from this time forth,
Have you so slander any moment leisure
As to give words or talk with the Lord Hamlet.

---

[10] Offers.

[11] Procurers.

135   Look to't, I charge you; come your ways.
    OPHELIA: I shall obey, my lord.

(Exeunt.)

SCENE IV

The platform.

(Enter Hamlet, Horatio, and Marcellus.)

HAMLET: The air bites shrewdly; it is very cold.
HORATIO: It is a nipping and an eager air.
HAMLET: What hour now?
HORATIO: I think it lacks of twelve.
MARCELLUS: No, it is struck.
5   HORATIO: Indeed? I heard it not: then it draws near the season
    Wherein the spirit held his wont to walk.

(A flourish of trumpets, and ordnance shot off within.)

    What does this mean, my lord?
HAMLET: The king doth wake to-night, and takes his rouse,
    Keeps wassail, and the swaggering upspring[1] reels;
10   And, as he drains his draughts of Rhenish down,
    The kettle-drum and trumpet thus bray out
    The triumph of his pledge.[2]
HORATIO: Is it a custom?
HAMLET: Ay, marry, is't:
    But to my mind,—though I am native here,
15   And to the manner born,—it is a custom
    More honor'd in the breach than the observance.
    This heavy-headed revel east and west
    Makes us traduc'd and tax'd of other nations:
    They clepe us drunkards, and with swinish phrase
20   Soil our addition;[3] and, indeed, it takes
    From our achievements, though perform'd at height,

---

[1] A dance.

[2] The glory of his toasts.

[3] Reputation.

The pith and marrow of our attribute.
So oft it chances in particular men
That, for some vicious mole of nature in them,
25 As in their birth,—wherein they are not guilty,
Since nature cannot choose his origin,—
By the o'ergrowth of some complexion,
Oft breaking down the pales and forts of reason;
Or by some habit, that too much o'erleavens
30 The form of plausive[4] manners;—that these men,—
Carrying, I say, the stamp of one defect,
Being nature's livery or fortune's star,—
Their virtues else,—be they as pure as grace,
As infinite as man may undergo,—
35 Shall in the general censure take corruption
From that particular fault: the dram of evil
Doth all the noble substance of a doubt
To his own scandal.

HORATIO: Look, my lord, it comes!

(Enter Ghost.)

HAMLET: Angels and ministers of grace defend us!—
40 Be thou a spirit of health or goblin damn'd,
Bring with thee airs from heaven or blasts from hell,
Be thy intents wicked or charitable,
Thou com'st in such a questionable shape
That I will speak to thee: I'll call thee Hamlet,
45 King, father, royal Dane: O, answer me!
Let me not burst in ignorance; but tell
Why thy canóniz'd bones, hearsèd in death,
Have burst their cerements; why the sepulchre,
Wherein we saw thee quietly in-urn'd,
50 Hath op'd his ponderous and marble jaws
To cast thee up again! What may this mean,
That thou, dead corse, again in còmplete steel,
Revisit'st thus the glimpses of the moon,
Making night hideous and we[5] fools of nature
55 So horridly to shake our disposition

---

4 Pleasing.

5 Us.

With thoughts beyond the reaches of our souls?
Say, why is this? wherefore? what should we do?

(Ghost beckons Hamlet.)

HORATIO: It beckons you to go away with it,
  As if it some impartment did desire
60   To you alone.
MARCELLUS: Look, with what courteous action
  It waves you to a more removed ground:
  But do not go with it.
HORATIO: No, by no means.
HAMLET: It will not speak; then will I follow it.
HORATIO: Do not, my lord.
HAMLET: Why, what should be the fear?
65   I do not set my life at a pin's fee;
  And for my soul, what can it do to that,
  Being a thing immortal as itself?
  It waves me forth again;—I'll follow it.
HORATIO: What if it tempt you toward the flood, my lord.
70   Or to the dreadful summit of the cliff
  That beetles o'er his base into the sea,
  And there assume some other horrible form,
  Which might deprive your sovereignty of reason,
  And draw you into madness? think of it:
75   The very place puts toys of desperation,
  Without more motive, into every brain
  That looks so many fathoms to the sea
  And hears it roar beneath.
HAMLET: It waves me still.—
  Go on; I'll follow thee.
80 MARCELLUS: You shall not go, my lord.
HAMLET: Hold off your hands.
HORATIO: Be rul'd; you shall not go.
HAMLET: My fate cries out,
  And makes each petty artery in this body
  As hardy as the Némean lion's[6] nerve.—

---

6   The fierce lion that Hercules was called upon to slay as one of his "twelve labors."

(Ghost beckons.)

Still am I call'd;—unhand me, gentlemen;—[*Breaking from them*]
85   By heaven, I'll make a ghost of him that lets⁷ me.
I say, away!—Go on; I'll follow thee.

(Exeunt Ghost and Hamlet.)

HORATIO: He waxes desperate with imagination.
MARCELLUS: Let's follow; 'tis not fit thus to obey him.
HORATIO: Have after.—To what issue will this come?
90   MARCELLUS: Something is rotten in the state of Denmark.
HORATIO: Heaven will direct it.
MARCELLUS: Nay, let's follow him.

(Exeunt.)

SCENE   V

A more remote part of the platform.

(Enter Ghost and Hamlet.)

HAMLET: Where wilt thou lead me? speak, I'll go no further.
GHOST: Mark me.
HAMLET: I will.
GHOST: My hour is almost come,
   When I to sulphurous and tormenting flames
   Must render up myself.
HAMLET: Alas, poor ghost!
5   GHOST: Pity me not, but lend thy serious hearing
   To what I shall unfold.
HAMLET: Speak; I am bound to hear.
GHOST: So art thou to revenge, when thou shalt hear.
HAMLET: What?
GHOST: I am thy father's spirit;
10   Doom'd for a certain term to walk the night,
   And, for the day, confin'd to waste in fires

---

⁷ Hinders.

Till the foul crimes[1] done in my days of nature
Are burnt and purg'd away. But that I am forbid
To tell the secrets of my prison-house,

15   I could a tale unfold whose lightest word
Would harrow up thy soul; freeze thy young blood;
Make thy two eyes, like stars, start from their spheres;
Thy knotted and combined locks to part,
And each particular hair to stand on end,

20   Like quills upon the fretful porcupine:
But this eternal blazon[2] must not be
To ears of flesh and blood.—List, list, O, list!—
If thou didst ever thy dear father love,—

HAMLET: O God!

25   GHOST: Revenge his foul and most unnatural murder.

HAMLET: Murder!

GHOST: Murder—most foul, as in the best it is;
But this most foul, strange, and unnatural.

HAMLET: Haste me to know't, that I, with wings as swift

30   As meditation or the thoughts of love,
May sweep to my revenge.

GHOST: I find thee apt;
And duller shouldst thou be than the fat weed
That rots itself in ease on Lethe[3] wharf,
Wouldst thou not stir in this. Now, Hamlet,

35   'Tis given out that, sleeping in mine orchard,
A serpent stung me; so the whole ear of Denmark
Is by a forged process of my death
Rankly abus'd: but know, thou noble youth,
The serpent that did sting thy father's life

40   Now wears his crown.

HAMLET: O my prophetic soul! mine uncle!

GHOST: Ay, that incestuous, that adulterate beast,
With witchcraft of his wit, with traitorous gifts,—
O wicked wit and gifts that have the power

---

[1]   Rather, sins or faults.

[2]   Disclosure of information concerning the other world.

[3]   The river of forgetfulness of the past, out of which the dead drink.

So to seduce!—won to his shameful lust
45　The will of my most seeming virtuous queen:
O Hamlet, what a falling-off was there!
From me, whose love was of that dignity
That it went hand in hand even with the vow
I made to her in marriage: and to decline
50　Upon a wretch whose natural gifts were poor
To those of mine!
But virtue, as it never will be mov'd,
Though lewdness court it in a shape of heaven;
So lust, though to a radiant angel link'd,
55　Will sate itself in a celestial bed
And prey on garbage.
But, soft! methinks I scent the morning air;
Brief let me be.—Sleeping within mine orchard,
My custom always in the afternoon,
60　Upon my sécure hour thy uncle stole,
With juice of cursed hebenon[4] in a vial,
And in the porches of mine ears did pour
The leperous distilment; whose effect
Holds such an enmity with blood of man
65　That, swift as quicksilver, it courses through
The natural gates and alleys of the body;
And with a sudden vigor it doth posset[5]
And curd, like eager[6] droppings into milk,
The thin and wholesome blood: so did it mine;
70　And a most instant tetter bark'd about,
Most lazar-like,[7] with vile and loathsome crust,
All my smooth body.
Thus was I, sleeping, by a brother's hand,
Of life, of crown, of queen, at once despatch'd:
75　Cut off even in the blossoms of my sin,
Unhousel'd, unanointed, unanel'd;

---

[4]　Ebony.

[5]　Coagulate.

[6]　Acid.

[7]　Like a leper, whose skin is rough.

No reckoning made, but sent to my account
With all my imperfections on my head:
O, horrible! O, horrible! most horrible!
80   If thou hast nature in thee, bear it not;
Let not the royal bed of Denmark be
A couch for luxury[8] and damned incest.
But, howsoever thou pursu'st this act,
Taint not thy mind, nor let thy soul contrive
85   Against thy mother aught: leave her to heaven,
And to those thorns that in her bosom lodge,
To prick and sting her. Fare thee well at once!
The glowworm shows the matin to be near,
And 'gins to pale his uneffectual fire:
90   Adieu, adieu! Hamlet, remember me. [*Exit.*]
HAMLET: O all you host of heaven! O earth! what else?
And shall I couple hell?—O, fie!—Hold, my heart;
And you, my sinews, grow not instant old,
But bear me stiffly up.—Remember thee!
95   Ay, thou poor ghost, while memory holds a seat
In this distracted globe. Remember thee!
Yea, from the table of my memory
I'll wipe away all trivial fond[9] recórds,
All saws of books, all forms, all pressures past,
100   That youth and observation copied there;
And thy commandment all alone shall live
Within the book and volume of my brain,
Unmix'd with baser matter: yes, by heaven.—
O most pernicious woman!
105   O villain, villain, smiling, damned villain!
My tables,—meet it is I set it down,
That one may smile, and smile, and be a villain;
At least, I am sure, it may be so in Denmark:

(Writing)

So, uncle, there you are. Now to my word;
110   It is, *Adieu, adieu! remember me:*

---

8   Lechery.

9   Foolish.

I have sworn't.

HORATIO: [*Within*] My lord, my lord,—

MARCELLUS: [*Within*]   Lord Hamlet,—

HORATIO: [*Within*]   Heaven secure
   him!

MARCELLUS: [*Within*] So be it!

HORATIO: [*Within*] Illo, ho, ho, my lord!

115 HAMLET: Hillo, ho, ho, boy! come, bird, come.[10]

(Enter Horatio and Marcellus.)

MARCELLUS: How is't, my noble lord?

HORATIO: What news, my lord?

HAMLET: O, wonderful!

HORATIO: Good my lord, tell it.

HAMLET: No; you'll reveal it.

HORATIO: Not I, my lord, by heaven.

MARCELLUS: Nor I, my lord.

120 HAMLET: How say you, then; would heart of man once think it?—
   But you'll be secret?

HORATIO and MARCELLUS: Ay, by heaven, my lord.

HAMLET: There's ne'er a villain dwelling in all Denmark
   But he's an arrant knave.

125 HORATIO: There needs no ghost, my lord, come from the grave
   To tell us this.

HAMLET: Why, right; you are i' the right;
   And so, without more circumstance at all,
   I hold it fit that we shake hands and part:

130   You, as your business and desire shall point you,—
   For every man has business and desire,
   Such as it is;—and for mine own poor part,
   Look you, I'll go pray.

HORATIO: These are but wild and whirling words, my lord.

135 HAMLET: I'm sorry they offend you, heartily;
   Yes, faith, heartily.

HORATIO: There's no offence, my lord.

HAMLET: Yes, by Saint Patrick, but there is, Horatio,
   And much offence too. Touching this vision here,—

---

10 Hamlet used the word "bird" because this is a falconer's call.

It is an honest ghost, that let me tell you:

140   For you desire to know what is between us,

O'ermaster't as you may. And now, good friends,

As you are friends, scholars, and soldiers,

Give me one poor request.

HORATIO: What is't, my lord? we will.

145 HAMLET: Never make known what you have seen to-night.

HORATIO and MARCELLUS: My lord, we will not.

HAMLET: Nay, but swear't.

HORATIO: In faith,

My lord, not I.

MARCELLUS: Nor I, my lord, in faith.

HAMLET: Upon my sword.

MARCELLUS: We have sworn, my lord, already.

HAMLET: Indeed, upon my sword, indeed.

150 GHOST: [*Beneath*] Swear.

HAMLET: Ha, ha, boy! say'st thou so? art thou there, truepenny?—

Come on,—you hear this fellow in the cellarage,—

Consent to swear.

HORATIO: Propose the oath, my lord.

HAMLET: Never to speak of this that you have seen,

155   Swear by my sword.

GHOST: [*Beneath*] Swear.

HAMLET: *Hic et ubique?*[11] then we'll shift our ground.—

Come hither, gentlemen,

And lay your hands again upon my sword:

160   Never to speak of this that you have heard,

Swear by my sword.

GHOST: [*Beneath*] Swear.

HAMLET: Well said! old mole! canst work i' the earth so fast?

A worthy pioneer![12]—Once more remove, good friends.

165 HORATIO: O day and night, but this is wondrous strange!

HAMLET: And therefore as a stranger give it welcome.

There are more things in heaven and earth, Horatio,

Than are dreamt of in your philosophy.

But come;—

---

[11] Here and everywhere?

[12] A soldier who digs trenches and undermines fortresses.

170   Here, as before, never, so help you mercy,
    How strange or odd soe'er I bear myself,—
    As I, perchance, hereafter shall think meet
    To put an antic disposition on,—
    That you, at such times seeing me, never shall,
175   With arms encumber'd[13] thus, or this headshake,
    Or by pronouncing of some doubtful phrase,
    As, *Well, well, we know;*—or, *We could, an if we would;*—
    Or, *If we list to speak;*—or, *There be, an if they might;*—
    Or such ambiguous giving out, to note
180   That you know aught of me:—this not to do,
    So grace and mercy at your most need help you,
    Swear.
GHOST: [*Beneath*] Swear.
HAMLET: Rest, rest, perturbed spirit!—So, gentlemen,
185   With all my love I do commend to you:
    And what so poor a man as Hamlet is
    May do, to express his love and friending to you,
    God willing, shall not lack. Let us go in together;
    And still your fingers on your lips, I pray.
190   The time is out of joint:— O cursed spite,
    That ever I was born to set it right!—
    Nay, come, let's go together.

(Exeunt.)

ACT II SCENE I

A room in Polonius' house.

(Enter Polonius and Reynaldo.)

POLONIUS: Give him this money and these notes, Reynaldo.
REYNALDO: I will, my lord.
POLONIUS: You shall do marvelous wisely, good Reynaldo,
    Before you visit him, to make inquiry
5   On his behavior.
REYNALDO: My lord, I did intend it.

---

[13] Folded.

POLONIUS: Marry, well said; very well said. Look you, sir,
Inquire me first what Danskers[1] are in Paris;
And how, and who, what means, and where they keep,
What company, at what expense; and finding,
By this encompassment and drift of question,
That they do know my son, come you more nearer
Than your particular demands will touch it:
Take you, as 'twere, some distant knowledge of him;
As thus, *I know his father and his friends,*
And in part him;—do you mark this, Reynaldo?
REYNALDO: Ay, very well, my lord.
POLONIUS: *And in part him;*—*but,* you may say, *not well:*
But if 't be he I mean, he's very wild;
Addicted so and so; and there put on him
What forgeries you please; marry, none so rank
As may dishonor him; take heed of that;
But, sir, such wanton, wild, and usual slips
As are companions noted and most known
To youth and liberty.
REYNALDO: As gaming, my lord.
POLONIUS: Ay, or drinking, fencing, swearing, quarreling,
Drabbing:[2]—you may go so far.
REYNALDO: My lord, that would dishonor him.
POLONIUS: Faith, no; as you may season it in the charge.
You must not put another scandal on him,
That he is open to incontinency;
That's not my meaning: but breathe his faults so quaintly
That they may seem the taints of liberty;
The flash and outbreak of a fiery mind;
A savageness in unreclaimed blood,
Of general assault.
REYNALDO: But, my good lord,—
POLONIUS: Wherefore should you do this?
REYNALDO: Ay, my lord,
I would know that.
POLONIUS: Marry, sir, here's my drift;

10

15

20

25

30

35

---

[1] Danes.

[2] Going about with loose women.

And I believe it is a fetch of warrant:[3]
You laying these slight sullies on my son.
40 As 'twere a thing a little soil'd i' the working,
Mark you,
Your party in converse, him you would sound,
Having ever seen in the prenominate crimes
The youth you breathe of guilty, be assur'd
45 He closes with you in this consequence;
Good sir, or so; or *friend,* or *gentleman,*—
According to the phrase or the addition[4]
Of man and country.

REYNALDO: Very good, my lord.

POLONIUS: And then, sir, does he this,—he does,—
50 What was I about to say?—By the mass, I was
About to say something:—where did I leave?

REYNALDO: At *closes in the consequence,*
At *friend or so,* and *gentleman.*

POLONIUS: At—closes in the consequence,—ay, marry;
55 He closes with you thus:—*I know the gentleman;*
I saw him yesterday, or t'other day,
Or then, or then; with such, or such; and, as you say,
There was he gaming; there o'ertook in's rouse;
There falling out at tennis: or perchance,
60 *I saw him enter such a house of sale,*—
Videlicet, a brothel,—or so forth.—
See you now;
Your bait of falsehood takes this carp of truth:
And thus do we of wisdom and of reach,
65 With windlasses, and with assays of bias,
By indirections find directions out:
So, by my former lecture and advice,
Shall you my son. You have me, have you not?

REYNALDO: My lord, I have.

POLONIUS: God b' wi' you; fare you well.

70 REYNALDO: Good my lord!

POLONIUS: Observe his inclination in yourself.

---

[3] A good device.

[4] Form of address.

REYNALDO: I shall, my lord.
POLONIUS: And let him ply his music.
REYNALDO: Well, my lord.
POLONIUS: Farewell!

(Exit Reynaldo.)

(Enter Ophelia.)

75   How now, Ophelia! what's the matter?
OPHELIA: Alas, my lord, I have been so affrighted.
POLONIUS: With what, i' the name of God?
OPHELIA: My lord, as I was sewing in my chamber,
        Lord Hamlet,—with his doublet all unbrac'd;
80   No hat upon his head; his stockings foul'd,
        Ungarter'd, and down-gyved⁵ to his ankle;
        Pale as his shirt; his knees knocking each other;
        And with a look so piteous in purport
        As if he had been loosed out of hell
85   To speak of horrors,—he comes before me.
POLONIUS: Mad for thy love?
OPHELIA: My lord, I do not know;
        But truly I do fear it.
POLONIUS: What said he?
OPHELIA: He took me by the wrist, and held me hard;
        Then goes he to the length of all his arm;
90   And with his other hand thus o'er his brow,
        He falls to such perusal of my face
        As he would draw it. Long stay'd he so;
        At last,—a little shaking of mine arm,
        And thrice his head thus waving up and down,—
95   He rais'd a sigh so piteous and profound
        That it did seem to shatter all his bulk
        And end his being; that done, he lets me go:
        And, with his head over his shoulder turn'd,
        He seem'd to find his way without his eyes;
100   For out o' doors he went without their help,
        And to the last bended their light on me.

---

⁵ Dangling like chains.

POLONIUS: Come, go with me: I will go seek the king.
　　　This is the very ecstasy[6] of love;
　　　Whose violent property fordoes itself,[7]
105　　And leads the will to desperate undertakings,
　　　As oft as any passion under heaven
　　　That does afflict our nature. I am sorry,—
　　　What, have you given him any hard words of late?
OPHELIA: No, my good lord; but, as you did command,
110　　I did repel his letters, and denied
　　　His access to me.
POLONIUS:　　　　　That hath made him mad.
　　　I am sorry that with better heed and judgment
　　　I had not quoted him: I fear'd he did but trifle,
　　　And meant to wreck thee; but, beshrew my jealousy!
115　　It seems it is as proper to our age
　　　To cast beyond ourselves in our opinions
　　　As it is common for the younger sort
　　　To lack discretion. Come, go we to the king:
　　　This must be known; which, being kept close, might move
120　　More grief to hide than hate to utter love.

(Exeunt.)

SCENE II

A room in the castle.

(Enter King, Queen, Rosencrantz, Guildenstern, and Attendants.)

KING: Welcome, dear Rosencrantz and Guildenstern!
　　　Moreover that we much did long to see you,
　　　The need we have to use you did provoke
　　　Our hasty sending. Something have you heard
5　　　Of Hamlet's transformation; so I call it,
　　　Since nor the exterior nor the inward man
　　　Resembles that it was. What it should be,

---

[6] Madness.

[7] Destroys itself.

More than his father's death, that thus hath put him
So much from the understanding of himself,
10 I cannot dream of: I entreat you both,
That being of so young days brought up with him,
And since so neighbor'd to his youth and humor,
That you vouchsafe your rest here in our court
Some little time: so by your companies
15 To draw him on to pleasures, and to gather,
So much as from occasion you may glean,
Whether aught, to us unknown, afflicts him thus,
That, open'd, lies within our remedy.
QUEEN: Good gentlemen, he hath much talk'd of you;
20 And sure I am two men there are not living
To whom he more adheres. If it will please you
To show us so much gentry and good-will
As to expend your time with us awhile,
For the supply and profit of our hope,
25 Your visitation shall receive such thanks
As fits a king's remembrance.
ROSENCRANTZ: Both your majesties
Might, by the sovereign power you have of us,
Put your dread pleasures more into command
Than to entreaty.
GUILDENSTERN: We both obey,
30 And here give up ourselves, in the full bent,
To lay our service freely at your feet,
To be commanded.
KING: Thanks, Rosencrantz and gentle Guildenstern.
QUEEN: Thanks, Guildenstern and gentle Rosencrantz:
35 And I beseech you instantly to visit
My too-much-changed son.—Go, some of you,
And bring these gentlemen where Hamlet is.
GUILDENSTERN: Heavens make our presence and our practices
Pleasant and helpful to him!
QUEEN: Ay, amen!

(Exeunt Rosencrantz, Guildenstern, and some Attendants.)

(Enter Polonius.)

40 POLONIUS: The ambassadors from Norway, my good lord,
Are joyfully return'd.

KING: Thou still has been the father of good news.

POLONIUS: Have I, my lord? Assure you, my good liege,
    I hold my duty, as I hold my soul,
45   Both to my God and to my gracious king:
    And I do think,—or else this brain of mine
    Hunts not the trail of policy[1] so sure
    As it hath us'd to do,—that I have found
    The very cause of Hamlet's lunacy.
50 KING: O, speak of that; that do I long to hear.

POLONIUS: Give first admittance to the ambassadors;
    My news shall be the fruit to that great feast.

KING: Thyself do grace to them, and bring them in.

(Exit Polonius.)

He tells me, my sweet queen, that he hath found
55   The head and source of all your son's distemper.

QUEEN: I doubt it is no other but the main,—
    His father's death and our o'erhasty marriage.

KING: Well, we shall sift him.

(Re-enter Polonius, with Voltimand and Cornelius.)

                    Welcome, my good friends!
    Say, Voltimand, what from our brother Norway?

60 VOLTIMAND: Most fair return of greetings and desires.
    Upon our first, he sent out to suppress
    His nephew's levies; which to him appear'd
    To be a preparation 'gainst the Polack;
    But, better look'd into, he truly found
65   It was against your highness: whereat griev'd,—
    That so his sickness, age, and impotence
    Was falsely borne in hand,—sends out arrests
    On Fortinbras; which he, in brief, obeys;
    Receives rebuke from Norway; and, in fine,
70   Makes vows before his uncle never more
    To give the assay of arms against your majesty.
    Whereon old Norway, overcome with joy,
    Gives him three thousand crowns in annual fee;

---

[1] Statecraft.

And his commission to employ those soldiers,
75 So levied as before, against the Polack:
With an entreaty, herein further shown, [*gives a paper*]
That it might please you to give quiet pass
Through your dominions for this enterprise,
On such regards of safety and allowance
80 As therein are set down.

KING: It likes us well;
And at our more consider'd time we'll read,
Answer, and think upon this business.
Meantime we thank you for your well-took labor:
Go to your rest; at night we'll feast together:
85 Most welcome home!

(Exeunt Voltimand and Cornelius.)

POLONIUS: This business is well ended.—
My liege, and madam,—to expostulate
What majesty should be, what duty is,
Why day is day, night night, and time is time,
Were nothing but to waste night, day, and time.
90 Therefore, since brevity is the soul of wit,
And tediousness the limbs and outward flourishes,
I will be brief:—your noble son is mad:
Mad call I it; for to define true madness,
What is't but to be nothing else but mad?
95 But let that go.

QUEEN: More matter with less art.

POLONIUS: Madam, I swear I use no art at all.
That he is mad, 'tis true 'tis pity;
And pity 'tis 'tis true: a foolish figure;
But farewell it, for I will use no art.
100 Mad let us grant him, then: and now remains
That we find out the cause of this effect;
Or rather say, the cause of this defect,
For this effect defective comes by cause:
Thus it remains, and the remainder thus.
105 Perpend.
I have a daughter,—have whilst she is mine,—
Who, in her duty and obedience, mark,
Hath given me this: now gather, and surmise

(Reads)

To the celestial, and my soul's idol, the most beautified Ophelia,—

110   That's an ill phrase, a vile phrase,—*beautified* is a vile phrase: but
       you shall hear. Thus:

(Reads)

In her excellent white bosom, these, &c.

QUEEN: Came this from Hamlet to her?

POLONIUS: Good madam, stay a while; I will be faithful.

(Reads)

115   *Doubt thou the stars are fire;*
          Doubt that the sun doth move;
          Doubt truth to be a liar;
             But never doubt I love.
       O dear Ophelia, I am ill at these numbers,
120   *I have not art to reckon my groans: but that I love thee best, O most*
          best, believe it. Adieu.
             Thine evermore, most dear lady, whilst this machine is to him,
       Hamlet
       This, in obedience, hath my daughter show'd me:
       And more above, hath his solicitings,
125   As they fell out by time, by means, and place,
       All given to mine ear.

KING: But how hath she
       Receiv'd his love?

POLONIUS: What do you think of me?

KING: As of a man faithful and honorable.

POLONIUS: I would fain prove so. But what might you think,
130   When I had seen this hot love on the wing,—
       As I perceiv'd it, I must tell you that,
       Before my daughter told me,—what might you,
       Or my dear majesty your queen here, think,
       If I had play'd the desk or table-book; [2]
135   Or given my heart a winking, mute and dumb;
       Or look'd upon this love with idle sight;—
       What might you think? No, I went round to work,

---

[2] Memorandum pad.

And my young mistress thus I did bespeak:
Lord Hamlet is a prince out of thy sphere;
140   *This must not be:* and then I precepts gave her,
That she should lock herself from his resort,
Admit no messengers, receive no tokens.
Which done, she took the fruits of my advice;
And he, repulsed,—a short tale to make,—
145   Fell into a sadness; then into a fast;
Thence to a watch; thence into a weakness;
Thence to a lightness; and, by this declension,
Into the madness wherein now he raves
And all we wail for.

KING: Do you think 'tis this?

150 QUEEN: It may be, very likely.

POLONIUS: Hath there been such a time,—I'd fain know that,—
That I have positively said, *'Tis so,*
When it prov'd otherwise?

KING: Not that I know.

POLONIUS: Take this from this, if this be otherwise: [*Pointing to his head and shoulder*]
155   If circumstances lead me, I will find
Where truth is hid, though it were hid indeed
Within the center.

KING: How may we try it further?

POLONIUS: You know, sometimes he walks for hours together
Here in the lobby.

QUEEN: So he does, indeed.

160 POLONIUS: At such a time I'll loose my daughter to him:
Be you and I behind an arras[3] then;
Mark the encounter: if he love her not,
And be not from his reason fall'n thereon,
Let me be no assistant for a state,
165   But keep a farm and carters.

KING: We will try it.

QUEEN: But look, where sadly the poor wretch comes reading.

POLONIUS: Away, I do beseech you, both away:
I'll board[4] him presently:— O, give me leave.

---

3   Tapestry, hung some distance away from a wall.

4   Address.

(Exeunt King, Queen, and Attendants.)

(Enter Hamlet, reading.)

How does my good Lord Hamlet?

170 HAMLET: Well, God-a-mercy.

POLONIUS: Do you know me, my lord?

HAMLET: Excellent, excellent well; you're a fishmonger.

POLONIUS: Not I, my lord.

HAMLET: Then I would you were so honest a man.

175 POLONIUS: Honest, my lord!

HAMLET: Ay, sir; to be honest, as this world goes, is to be one man
picked out of ten thousand.

POLONIUS: That's very true, my lord.

HAMLET: For if the sun breed maggots in a dead dog, being a god

180 kissing carrion,—Have you a daughter?

POLONIUS: I have, my lord.

HAMLET: Let her not walk i' the sun: conception is a blessing; but
not as your daughter may conceive:—friend, look to't.

POLONIUS: How say you by that?—[*Aside*] Still harping on my

185 daughter:—yet he knew me not at first; he said I was a
fishmonger: he is far gone, far gone: and truly in my youth I
suffered much extremity for love; very near this. I'll speak to him
again.—What do you read, my lord?

HAMLET: Words, words, words.

190 POLONIUS: What is the matter, my lord?

HAMLET: Between who?

POLONIUS: I mean, the matter that you read, my lord.

HAMLET: Slanders, sir: for the satirical slave says here that old men
have gray beards; that their faces are wrinkled; their eyes purging

195 thick amber and plum-tree gum; and that they have a plentiful
lack of wit, together with most weak hams: all which, sir, though
I most powerfully and potently believe, yet I hold it not honesty
to have it thus set down; for you yourself, sir, should be old as I
am, if, like a crab, you could go backward.

200 POLONIUS: [*Aside*] Though this be madness, yet there is method
in't.—ill you walk out of the air, my lord?

HAMLET: Into my grave?

POLONIUS: Indeed, that is out o' the air.—[*Aside*] How pregnant⁵

---

5 Ready, and clever.

sometimes his replies are! a happiness that often madness hits on,
205 which reason and sanity could not so prosperously be delivered
of. I will leave him, and suddenly contrive the means of meeting
between him and my daughter.—More honorable lord, I will
most humbly take my leave of you.

HAMLET: You cannot, sir, take from me anything that I will more
210 willingly part withal,—except my life, except my life, except my
life.

POLONIUS: Fare you well, my lord.

HAMLET: These tedious old fools!

(Enter Rosencrantz and Guildenstern.)

POLONIUS: You go to seek the Lord Hamlet; there he is.

ROSENCRANTZ: [*To Polonius*] God save you, sir!

(Exit Polonius.)

215 GUILDENSTERN: Mine honored lord!

ROSENCRANTZ: My most dear lord!

HAMLET: My excellent good friends! How dost thou, Guildenstern?
Ah, Rosencrantz? Good lads, how do ye both?

ROSENCRANTZ: As the indifferent children of the earth.

220 GUILDENSTERN: Happy in that we are not overhappy; on fortune's cap
we are not the very button.

HAMLET: Nor the soles of her shoe?

ROSENCRANTZ: Neither, my lord.

HAMLET: Then you live about her waist, or in the middle of her
favors?

225 GUILDENSTERN: Faith, her privates we.

HAMLET: In the secret parts of fortune? O, most true; she is a
strumpet. What's the news?

ROSENCRANTZ: None, my lord, but that the world's grown honest.

HAMLET: Then is doomsday near: but your news is not true. Let me
230 question more in particular: what have you, my good friends,
deserved at the hands of fortune, that she sends you to prison
hither?

GUILDENSTERN: Prison, my lord!

HAMLET: Denmark's a prison.

235 ROSENCRANTZ: Then is the world one.

HAMLET: A goodly one; in which there are many confines, wards,
and dungeons, Denmark being one o' the worst.

Rosencrantz: We think not so, my lord.

Hamlet: Why, then, 'tis none to you; for there is nothing either
240   good or bad, but thinking makes it so: to me it is a prison.

Rosencrantz: Why, then, your ambition makes it one; 'tis too
      narrow for your mind.

Hamlet: O God, I could be bounded in a nutshell, and count
      myself a king of infinite space, were it not that I have bad dreams.

245 Guildenstern: Which dreams, indeed, are ambition; for the very
      substance of the ambitious is merely the shadow of a dream.

Hamlet: A dream itself is but a shadow.

Rosencrantz: Truly, and I hold ambition of so airy and light a
      quality that it is but a shadow's shadow.

250 Hamlet: Then are our beggars bodies, and our monarchs and
      outstretched heroes the beggars' shadows. Shall we to the court?
      for, by my fay, I cannot reason.

Rosencrantz and Guildenstern: We'll wait upon you.

Hamlet: No such matter: I will not sort you with the rest of my
255   servants, for, to speak to you like an honest man, I am most
      dreadfully attended. But, in the beaten way of friendship, what
      make you at Elsinore?

Rosencrantz: To visit you, my lord; no other occasion.

Hamlet: Beggar that I am, I am even poor in thanks; but I thank
260   you: and sure, dear friends, my thanks are too dear a halfpenny.
      Were you not sent for? Is it your own inclining? Is it a free
      visitation? Come, deal justly with me: come, come; nay, speak.

Guildenstern: What should we say, my lord?

Hamlet: Why, anything—but to the purpose. You were sent for;
265   and there is a kind of confession in your looks, which your
      modesties have not craft enough to color: I know the good king
      and queen have sent for you.

Rosencrantz: To what end, my lord?

Hamlet: That you must teach me. But let me conjure you, by the
270   rights of our fellowship, by the consonancy of our youth, by the
      obligation of our ever-preserved love, and by what more dear a
      better proposer could charge you withal, be even and direct with
      me, whether you were sent for or no?

Rosencrantz: What say you? [*To Guildenstern*]

275 Hamlet: [*Aside*] Nay, then, I have an eye of you.—If you love me,
      hold not off.

Guildenstern: My lord, we were sent for.

HAMLET: I will tell you why; so shall my anticipation prevent your
discovery, and your secrecy to the king and queen moult no
280   feather. I have of late,—but wherefore I know not,—lost all my
mirth, forgone all custom of exercises; and, indeed, it goes so
heavily with my disposition that this goodly frame, the earth,
seems to me a sterile promontory; this most excellent canopy, the
air, look you, this brave o'erhanging firmament, this majestical
285   roof fretted[6] with golden fire,—why, it appears no other thing to
me than a foul and pestilent congregation of vapors. What a piece
of work is man! How noble in reason! how infinite in faculties! in
form and moving, how express and admirable! in action, how like
an angel! in apprehension, how like a god! the beauty of the
290   world! the paragon of animals! And yet, to me, what is this
quintessence of dust? man delights not me; no, nor woman
neither, though by your smiling you seem to say so.

ROSENCRANTZ: My lord, there was no such stuff in my thoughts.

HAMLET: Why did you laugh, then, when I said, *Man delights not me?*

295   ROSENCRANTZ: To think, my lord, if you delight not in man, what
lenten entertainment[7] the players shall receive from you: we coted[8]
them on the way; and hither are they coming, to offer you service.

HAMLET: He that plays the king shall be welcome,—his majesty
shall have tribute of me; the adventurous knight shall use his foil
300   and target; the lover shall not sigh gratis; the humorous[9] man
shall end his part in peace; the clown shall make those laugh
whose lungs are tickled o' the sere;[10] and the lady shall say her
mind freely, or the blank verse shall halt[11] for't.—What players
are they?

ROSENCRANTZ: Even those you were wont to take delight in,—the
305   tragedians of the city.

HAMLET: How chances it they travel? their residence, both in
reputation and profit, was better both ways.

---

6   A roof with fretwork.

7   Poor reception.

8   Passed.

9   Eccentric.

10   Whose lungs, for laughter, are easily tickled.

11   Limp.

ROSENCRANTZ: I think their inhibition[12] comes by the means of the late innovation.

310 HAMLET: Do they hold the same estimation they did when I was in the city? Are they so followed?

ROSENCRANTZ: No, indeed, they are not.

HAMLET: How comes it? do they grow rusty?

ROSENCRANTZ: Nay, their endeavor keeps in the wonted pace; but
315 there is, sir, an aery[13] of children, little eyases,[14] that cry out on the top of question, and are most tyrannically clapped for't: these are now the fashion; and so berattle the common stages,—so they call them,—that many wearing rapiers are afraid of goose-quills, and dare scarce come thither.

320 HAMLET: What, are they children? who maintains 'em? how are they escoted?[15] Will they pursue the quality[16] no longer than they can sing? will they not say afterwards, if they should grow themselves to common players,—as it is most like, if their means are no better,—their writers do them wrong, to make them exclaim
325 against their own succession?

ROSENCRANTZ: Faith, there has been much to do on both sides; and the nation holds it no sin to tarre[17] them to controversy: there was for awhile no money bid for argument, unless the poet and the player went to cuffs in the question.

330 HAMLET: Is't possible?

GUILDENSTERN: O, there has been much throwing about of brains.

HAMLET: Do the boys carry it away?

ROSENCRANTZ: Ay, that they do, my lord; Hercules and his load[18] too.

HAMLET: It is not strange; for mine uncle is king of Denmark, and
335 those that would make mouths at him while my father lived, give

---

[12] Difficulty, preventing them from remaining in the capital.

[13] Aerie: brood of birds of prey.

[14] Young hawks; a reference to the boys' companies that became popular rivals of Shakespeare's company of players.

[15] Financially supported.

[16] Profession.

[17] Egg them on.

[18] The globe, or the world.

twenty, forty, fifty, an hundred ducats a-piece for his picture in little. 'Sblood, there is something in this more than natural, if philosophy could find it out.

(Flourish of trumpets within.)

GUILDENSTERN: There are the players.

340 HAMLET: Gentlemen, you are welcome to Elsinore. Your hands, come: the appurtenance of welcome is fashion and ceremony: let me comply with you in this garb; lest my extent[19] to the players, which, I tell you, must show fairly outward, should more appear like entertainment[20] than yours. You are welcome: but my
345 uncle-father and aunt-mother are deceived.

GUILDENSTERN: In what, my dear lord?

HAMLET: I am but mad north-north-west: when the wind is southerly I know a hawk from a handsaw.

(Enter Polonius.)

POLONIUS: Well be with you, gentlemen!

350 HAMLET: Hark you, Guildenstern;—and you too;—at each ear a hearer: that great baby you see there is not yet out of his swathing-clouts.

ROSENCRANTZ: Happily he's the second time come to them; for they say an old man is twice a child.

HAMLET: I will prophesy he comes to tell me of the players; mark it.
355 You say right, sir: o' Monday morning; 'twas so indeed.

POLONIUS: My lord, I have news to tell you.

HAMLET: My lord, I have news to tell you. When Roscius was an actor in Rome,—

POLONIUS: The actors are come hither, my lord.

360 HAMLET: Buzz, buzz!

POLONIUS: Upon mine honor,—

HAMLET: Then came each actor on his ass,—

POLONIUS: The best actors in the world, either for tragedy, comedy, history, pastoral, pastoral-comical, historical-pastoral, tragical-
365 historical, tragical-comical-historical-pastoral, scene individable,[21]

---

[19] Show of friendliness.

[20] Welcome.

[21] A play that observes the unities of time and place.

or poem unlimited:[22] Seneca cannot be too heavy nor Plautus too
light. For the law of writ and the liberty,[23] these are the only men.

HAMLET: O Jephthah, judge of Israel, what a treasure hadst thou!

POLONIUS: What a treasure had he, my lord?

370   HAMLET: Why—

> One fair daughter, and no more,
> The which he loved passing well.

POLONIUS: [*Aside*] Still on my daughter.

HAMLET: Am I not i' the right, old Jephthah?

375   POLONIUS: If you call me Jephthah, my lord, I have a daughter that I
love passing well.

HAMLET: Nay, that follows not.

POLONIUS: What follows, then, my lord?

HAMLET: Why—

380   > As by lot, God wot,

and then, you know,

> It came to pass, as most like it was,

the first row of the pious chanson will show you more; for look
where my abridgement comes.

(Enter four or five Players.)

385   You are welcome, masters; welcome, all:—I am glad to see thee
well:—welcome, good friends.—O, my old friend! Thy face is
valanced since I saw thee last; comest thou to beard me in
Denmark?—What, my young lady and mistress! By'r lady, your
ladyship is nearer heaven than when I saw you last, by the altitude

390   of a chopine.[24] Pray God, your voice, like a piece of uncurrent
gold, be not cracked within the ring.—Masters, you are all
welcome. We'll e'en to't like French falconers, fly at anything we
see: we'll have a speech straight: come, give us a taste of your
quality; come, a passionate speech.

395   1ST PLAYER: What speech, my lord?

HAMLET: I heard thee speak me a speech once,—but it was never
acted; or, if it was, not above once; for the play, I remember,

---

[22] A typical multiscened Elizabethan type of drama, not restricted by the unities. Examples
are *Hamlet, Macbeth, King Lear,* and virtually any other play by Shakespeare.

[23] For the laws of the unities and for playwriting that is not so restricted.

[24] A wooden stilt more than a foot high used under a woman's shoe; a Venetian fashion
introduced into England.

pleased not the million; 'twas caviare to the general: but it was,—
as I received it, and others whose judgments in such matters cried

400 in the top of mine,—an excellent play, well digested in the scenes,
set down with as much modesty as cunning. I remember, one said
there were no sallets in the lines to make the matter savory, nor no
matter in the phrase that might indite the author of affectation;
but called it an honest method, as wholesome as sweet, and by

405 very much more handsome than fine. One speech in it I chiefly
loved: 'twas Aeneas' tale to Dido; and thereabout of it especially
where he speaks of Priam's slaughter: if it live in your memory,
begin at this line;—let me see, let me see:—
The rugged Pyrrhus, like the Hyrcanian beast,[25]

410 —it is not so:—it begins with Pyrrhus:—
The rugged Pyrrhus,—he whose sable arms,
Black as his purpose, did the night resemble
When he lay couched in the ominous horse,—
Hath now this dread and black complexion smear'd

415 With heraldry more dismal; head to foot
Now is he total gules; horridly trick'd
With blood of fathers, mothers, daughters, sons,
Bak'd and impasted with the parching streets,
That lend a tyrannous and damned light

420 To their vile murders: roasted in wrath and fire,
And thus o'er-sized with coagulate gore,
With eyes like carbuncles, the hellish Pyrrhus
Old grandsire Priam seeks.—
So proceed you.

425 Polonius: 'Fore God, my lord, well spoken, with good accent and
good discretion.

1st Player: Anon he finds him
Striking too short at Greeks; his antique sword,
Rebellious to his arm, lies where it falls,

430 Repugnant to command: unequal match'd,
Pyrrhus at Priam drives; in rage strikes wide;
But with the whiff and wind of his fell sword
The unnerved father falls. Then senseless Ilium,

---

[25] This speech is an example of the declamatory style of drama, which Shakespeare surely
must have considered outmoded.

Seeming to feel this blow, with flaming top
435 Stoops to his base; and with a hideous crash
Takes prisoner Pyrrhus' ear: for, lo! his sword,
Which was declining on the milky head
Of reverend Priam, seem'd i' the air to stick:
So, as a painted tyrant, Pyrrhus stood;
440 And, like a neutral to his will and matter,
Did nothing.
But as we often see, against some storm,
A silence in the heavens, the rack stand still,
The blood winds speechless, and the orb below
445 As hush as death, anon the dreadful thunder
Doth rend the region; so, after Pyrrhus' pause,
A roused vengeance sets him new a-work;
And never did the Cyclops' hammers fall
On Mars his armor, forg'd for proof eterne,
450 With less remorse than Pyrrhus' bleeding sword
Now falls on Priam.—
Out, out, thou strumpet, Fortune! All you gods,
In general synod, take away her power;
Break all the spokes and fellies from her wheel,
455 And bowl the round knave down the hill of heaven,
As low as to the fiends!
POLONIUS: This is too long.
HAMLET: It shall to the barber's, with your beard.—Pr'ythee, say
on.—He's for a jig, or a tale of bawdry, or he sleeps:—say on;
460 come to Hecuba.
1ST PLAYER: But who, O, who had seen the mobled queen,—
HAMLET: *The mobled queen?*
POLONIUS: That's good; *mobled queen* is good.
1ST PLAYER: Run barefoot up and down, threatening the flames
465 With bissom rheum; a clout upon that head
Where late the diadem stood; and, for a robe,
About her lank and all o'er-teemed loins,
A blanket, in the alarm of fear caught up;—
Who this had seen, with tongue in venom steep'd,
470 'Gainst Fortune's state would treason have pronounc'd:
But if the gods themselves did see her then,
When she saw Pyrrhus make malicious sport
In mincing with his sword her husband's limbs,

The instant burst of clamor that she made,—
475   Unless things mortal move them not at all,—
Would have made milch the burning eyes of heaven,
And passion in the gods.

POLONIUS: Look, whether he has not turn'd his color, and has tears
in's eyes.—Pray you, no more.

480 HAMLET: 'Tis well; I'll have thee speak out the rest soon.—Good my
lord, will you see the players well bestowed? Do you hear, let them
be well used; for they are the abstracts and brief chronicles of the
time; after your death you were better have a bad epitaph than
their ill report while you live.

485 POLONIUS: My lord, I will use them according to their desert.

HAMLET: Odd's bodikin, man, better: use every man after his desert,
and who should scape whipping? Use them after your own honor
and dignity: the less they deserve the more merit is in your
bounty. Take them in.

490 POLONIUS: Come, sirs.

HAMLET: Follow him, friends: we'll hear a play to-morrow.

(Exit Polonius with all the Players but the First.)

Dost thou hear me, old friend; can you play the Murder of
Gonzago?

1ST PLAYER: Ay, my lord.

HAMLET: We'll ha't to-morrow night. You could, for a need, study a
495   speech of some dozen or sixteen lines which I would set down
and insert in't? could you not?

1ST PLAYER: Ay, my lord.

HAMLET: Very well.—Follow that lord; and look you mock him not.

(Exit First Player.)

—My good friends, [*to Rosencrantz and Guildenstern*] I'll leave
500   you till night: you are welcome to Elsinore.

ROSENCRANTZ: Good my lord!

(Exeunt Rosencrantz and Guildenstern.)

HAMLET: Ay, so God b' wi' ye!—Now I am alone.
O, what a rogue[26] and peasant slave am I!

---

[26] Wretched creature.

Is it not monstrous that this player here,
505   But in a fiction, in a dream of passion,
Could force his soul so to his own conceit[27]
That from her working all his visage wan'd;
Tears in his eyes, distraction in's aspéct,
A broken voice, and his whole function suiting
510   With forms to his conceit? And all for nothing!
For Hecuba?
What's Hecuba to him or he to Hecuba,
That he should weep for her? What would he do,
Had he the motive and the cue for passion
515   That I have? He would drown the stage with tears,
And cleave the general ear with horrid speech;
Make mad the guilty, and appal the free;
Confound the ignorant, and amaze, indeed,
The very faculties of eyes and ears.
520   Yet I,
A dull and muddy-mettled rascal, peak,
Like John-a-dreams, unpregnant of my cause,
And can say nothing; no, not for a king
Upon whose property and most dear life
525   A damn'd defeat was made. Am I a coward?
Who calls me villain? breaks my pate across?
Plucks off my beard and blows it in my face?
Tweaks me by the nose? gives me the lie i' the throat,
As deep as to the lungs? who does me this, ha?
530   'Swounds, I should take it: for it cannot be
But I am pigeon-liver'd, and lack gall
To make oppression bitter; or ere this
I should have fatted all the region kites
With this slave's offal:—bloody, bawdy villain!
535   Remorseless, treacherous, lecherous, kindless villain!
O, vengeance!
Why, what an ass am I! This is most brave,
That I, the son of a dear father murder'd,
Prompted to my revenge by heaven and hell,
540   Must, like a whore, unpack my heart with words,

---

[27] Conception.

And fall a-cursing like a very drab,
A scullion!
Fie upon't! foh!—About, my brain! I have heard
That guilty creatures, sitting at a play,
545 Have by the very cunning of the scene
Been struck so to the soul that presently
They have proclaim'd their malefactions;
For murder, though it have no tongue, will speak
With most miraculous organ. I'll have these players
550 Play something like the murder of my father
Before mine uncle: I'll observe his looks;
I'll tent[28] him to the quick: if he but blench,
I know my course. The spirit that I have seen
May be the devil: and the devil hath power
555 To assume a pleasing shape; yea, and perhaps
Out of my weakness and my melancholy,—
As he is very potent with such spirits,—
Abuses me to damn me: I'll have grounds
More relative than this:—the play's the thing
560 Wherein I'll catch the conscience of the king. [*Exit.*]

ACT III SCENE I

A room in the castle.

(Enter King, Queen, Polonius, Ophelia, Rosencrantz, and Guildenstern.)

KING: And can you, by no drift of circumstance,
Get from him why he puts on this confusion,
Grating so harshly all his days of quiet
With turbulent and dangerous lunacy?
5 ROSENCRANTZ: He does confess he feels himself distracted;
But from what cause he will by no means speak.
GUILDENSTERN: Nor do we find him forward to be sounded;
But, with a crafty madness, keeps aloof
When we would bring him on to some confession
10 Of his true state.

---

[28] Probe.

QUEEN: Did he receive you well?

ROSENCRANTZ: Most like a gentleman.

GUILDENSTERN: But with much forcing of his disposition.

ROSENCRANTZ: Niggard of question; but, of our demands,
        Most free in his reply.

QUEEN: Did you assay him

15   To any pastime?

ROSENCRANTZ: Madam, it so fell out that certain players
        We o'er-raught on the way: of these we told him;
        And there did seem in him a kind of joy
        To hear of it: they are about the court;

20   And, as I think, they have already order
        This night to play before him.

POLONIUS: 'Tis most true:
        And he beseech'd me to entreat your majesties
        To hear and see the matter.

KING: With all my heart; and it doth much content me

25   To hear him so inclin'd.
        Good gentlemen, give him a further edge,
        And drive his purpose on to these delights.

ROSENCRANTZ: We shall, my lord.

(Exeunt Rosencrantz and Guildenstern.)

KING: Sweet Gertrude, leave us too;
        For we have closely sent for Hamlet hither

30   That he, as 'twere by accident, may here
        Affront Ophelia:
        Her father and myself,—lawful espials,[1]—
        Will so bestow ourselves that, seeing, unseen,
        We may of their encounter frankly judge;

35   And gather by him, as he is behav'd,
        If't be the affliction of his love or no
        That thus he suffers for.

QUEEN: I shall obey you:—
        And for your part, Ophelia, I do wish
        That your good beauties be the happy cause

40   Of Hamlet's wildness: so shall I hope your virtues

---

[1] Spies.

Will bring him to his wonted way again,
To both your honors.

OPHELIA: Madam, I wish it may.

(Exit Queen.)

POLONIUS: Ophelia, walk you here.—Gracious, so please you,
We will bestow ourselves.—[*To Ophelia*] Read on this book;
45   That show of such an exercise may color
Your loneliness.—We are oft to blame in this,—
'Tis too much prov'd,—that with devotion's visage
And pious action we do sugar o'er
The devil himself.

KING: [*Aside*]   O, 'tis too true!
50   How smart a lash that speech doth give my conscience!
The harlot's cheek, beautied with plastering art,
Is not more ugly to the thing that helps it
Than is my deed to my most painted word:
O heavy burden!

55   POLONIUS: I hear him coming: let's withdraw, my lord.

(Exeunt King and Polonius.)

(Enter Hamlet.)

HAMLET: To be, or not to be,—that is the question:
Whether 'tis nobler in the mind to suffer
The slings and arrows of outrageous fortune,
Or to take arms against a sea of troubles,
60   And by opposing end them?—To die,—to sleep,—
No more; and by a sleep to say we end
The heart-ache and the thousand natural shocks
That flesh is heir to,—'tis a consummation
Devoutly to be wish'd. To die,—to sleep;—
65   To sleep! perchance to dream:—ay, there's the rub;
For in that sleep of death what dreams may come,
When we have shuffled off this mortal coil,
Must give us pause: there's the respect
That makes a calamity of so long life;
70   For who would bear the whips and scorns of time,
The oppressor's wrong, the proud man's contumely,
The pangs of déspis'd love, the law's delay,

The insolence of office, and the spurns
That patient merit of the unworthy takes,
75   When he himself might his quietus make
With a bare bodkin?[2] who would fardels[3] bear,
To grunt[4] and sweat under a weary life,
But that the dread of something after death,—
The undiscover'd country, from whose bourn[5]
80   No traveler returns,—puzzles the will,
And makes us rather bear those ills we have
Than to fly to others that we know not of?
Thus conscience does make cowards of us all;
And thus the native hue of resolution
85   Is sicklied o'er with the pale cast of thought;
And enterprises of great pith and moment,
With this regard, their currents turn awry,
And lose the name of action.—Soft you now!
The fair Ophelia.—Nymph, in thy orisons[6]
90   Be all my sins remember'd.
OPHELIA: Good my lord,
How does your honor for this many a day?
HAMLET: I humbly thank you; well, well, well.
OPHELIA: My lord, I have remembrances of yours,
That I have longed long to re-deliver;
95   I pray you, now receive them.
HAMLET: No, not I;
I never gave you aught.
OPHELIA: My honor'd lord, you know right well you did;
And with them, words of so sweet breath compos'd
As made the things more rich: their perfume lost,
100   Take these again; for to the noble mind
Rich gifts wax poor when givers prove unkind.

---

[2] Stiletto.

[3] Burdens.

[4] Groan.

[5] Boundary.

[6] Prayers.

There, my lord.

HAMLET: Ha, ha! are you honest?

OPHELIA: My lord?

105 HAMLET: Are you fair?

OPHELIA: What means your lordship?

HAMLET: That if you be honest and fair, your honesty should admit
no discourse to your beauty.

OPHELIA: Could beauty, my lord, have better commerce than with
110   honesty?

HAMLET: Ay, truly; for the power of beauty will sooner transform
honesty from what it is to a bawd than the force of honesty can
translate beauty into his likeness: this was sometime a paradox,
but now the time gives it proof. I did love you once.

115 OPHELIA: Indeed, my lord, you made me believe so.

HAMLET: You should not have believed me; for virtue cannot so
inoculate our old stock but we shall relish of it: I loved you not.

OPHELIA: I was the more deceived.

HAMLET: Get thee to a nunnery: why wouldst thou be a breeder of
120   sinners? I am myself indifferent[7] honest; but yet I could accuse me
of such things that it were better my mother had not borne me: I
am very proud, revengeful, ambitious; with more offences at my
beck than I have thoughts to put them in, imagination to give
them shape, or time to act them in. What should such fellows as I
125   do crawling between heaven and earth? We are arrant knaves, all;
believe none of us. Go thy ways to a nunnery. Where's your father?

OPHELIA: At home, my lord.

HAMLET: Let the doors be shut upon him, that he may play the fool
nowhere but in's own house. Farewell.

130 OPHELIA: O, help him, you sweet heavens!

HAMLET: If thou dost marry, I'll give thee this plague for thy
dowry,—be thou as chaste as ice, as pure as snow, thou shalt not
escape calumny. Get thee to a nunnery, go: farewell. Or, if thou
wilt needs marry, marry a fool; for wise men know well enough
135   what monsters you make of them. To a nunnery, go; and quickly
too. Farewell.

OPHELIA: O heavenly powers, restore him!

HAMLET: I have heard of your paintings too, well enough; God has

---

7 Tolerably.

140 given you one face and you make yourselves another: you jig, you
amble, and you lisp, and nickname God's creatures, and make
your wantonness your ignorance. Go to, I'll no more on't; it hath
made me mad. I say, we will have no more marriages: those that
are married already, all but one, shall live; the rest shall keep as
they are. To a nunnery, go. [*Exit.*]

145 OPHELIA: O, what a noble mind is here o'erthrown!
The courtier's, soldier's, scholar's eye, tongue, sword:
The expectancy and rose of the fair state,
The glass of fashion and the mould of form,
The observ'd of all observers,—quite, quite down!
150 And I, of ladies most deject and wretched
That suck'd the honey of his music vows,
Now see that noble and most sovereign reason,
Like sweet bells jangled, out of tune and harsh;
That unmatch'd form and feature of blown [8] youth
155 Blasted with ecstasy: O, woe is me,
To have seen what I have seen, see what I see!

(Re-enter King and Polonius.)

KING: Love! his affections do not that way tend;
Nor what he spake, though it lack'd form a little,
Was not like madness. There's something in his soul
160 O'er which his melancholy sits on brood;
And I do doubt [9] the hatch and the disclose
Will be some danger: which for to prevent,
I have in quick determination
Thus set it down:—he shall with speed to England
165 For the demand of our neglected tribute:
Haply, the seas and countries different,
With variable objects, shall expel
This something-settled matter in his heart;
Whereon his brains still beating puts him thus
170 From fashion of himself. What think you on't?
POLONIUS: It shall do well: but yet do I believe
The origin and commencement of his grief

---

[8] Full-blown.

[9] Fear.

Sprung from neglected love.—How now, Ophelia!
You need not tell us what Lord Hamlet said;
175   We heard it all.—My lord, do as you please;
But if you hold it fit, after the play,
Let his queen mother all alone entreat him
To show his grief: let her be round with him;
And I'll be plac'd, so please you, in the ear
180   Of all their conference. If she finds him not,[10]
To England send him; or confine him where
Your wisdom best shall think.
KING: It shall be so:
Madness in great ones must not unwatch'd go.

(Exeunt.)

SCENE II

A hall in the castle.

(Enter Hamlet and certain Players.)

HAMLET: Speak the speech, I pray you, as I pronounced it to you,
trippingly on the tongue: but if you mouth it, as many of your
players do, I had as lief the town-crier spoke my lines. Nor do not
saw the air too much with your hand, thus; but use all gently: for
5   in the very torrent, tempest, and, as I may say, the whirlwind of
passion, you must acquire and beget a temperance that may give it
smoothness. O, it offends me to the soul, to hear a robustious
periwigpated fellow tear a passion to tatters, to very rags, to split
the ears of the groundlings, who, for the most part, are capable of
10   nothing but inexplicable dumb shows and noise: I could have such
a fellow whipped for o'erdoing Termagant;[1] it out-herods
Herod:[2] pray you, avoid it.
1ST PLAYER: I warrant your honor.

---

[10]   Does not find him out.

[1]   A violent pagan deity, supposedly Mohammedan.

[2]   Outrants the ranting Herod, who figures in medieval drama.

HAMLET: Be not too tame neither, but let your own discretion be
15   your tutor; suit the action to the word, the word to the action;
         with this special observance, that you o'erstep not the modesty of
         nature: for anything so overdone is from the purpose of playing,
         whose end, both at the first and now, was and is, to hold, as
         'twere, the mirror up to nature; to show virtue her own feature,
20   scorn her own image, and the very age and body of the time his
         form and pressure. Now, this overdone or come tardy off, though
         it make the unskilful laugh, cannot but make the judicious grieve;
         the censure of the which one must, in your allowance, o'erweigh
         a whole theater of others. O, there be players that I have seen
25   play,—and heard others praise, and that highly,—not to speak it
         profanely, that, neither having the accent of Christians, nor the
         gait of Christian, pagan, nor man, have so strutted and bellowed
         that I have thought some of nature's journeymen had made men,
         and not made them well, they imitated humanity so abominably.
30 1ST PLAYER: I hope we have reformed that indifferently with us, sir.
    HAMLET: O, reform it altogether. And let those that play your clowns
         speak no more than is set down for them: for there be of them that
         will themselves laugh, to set on some quantity of barren spectators
         to laugh too; though, in the meantime, some necessary question of
35   the play be then to be considered: that's villainous, and shows a
         most pitiful ambition in the fool that uses it. Go, make you ready.

(Exeunt Players.)

(Enter Polonius, Rosencrantz, and Guildenstern.)

         How now, my lord! will the king hear this piece of work?
    POLONIUS: And the queen, too, and that presently.
    HAMLET: Bid the players make haste.

(Exit Polonius.)

40   Will you two help to hasten them?
    ROSENCRANTZ and GUILDENSTERN: We will, my lord. [*Exeunt.*]
    HAMLET: What, ho, Horatio!

(Enter Horatio.)

    HORATIO: Here, sweet lord, at your service.
    HAMLET: Horatio, thou art e'en as just a man
45   As e'er my conversation cop'd withal.

HORATIO: O, my dear lord,—
HAMLET: Nay, do not think I flatter;
    For what advancement may I hope from thee,
    That no revénue hast, but thy good spirits,
    To feed and clothe thee? Why should the poor be flatter'd?
50   No, let the candied tongue lick ábsurd pomp;
    And crook the pregnant hinges of the knee
    Where thrift may follow fawning. Dost thou hear?
    Since my dear soul was mistress of her choice,
    And could of men distinguish, her election
55   Hath seal'd thee for herself: for thou hast been
    As one, in suffering all, that suffers nothing;
    A man that Fortune's buffets and rewards
    Hast ta'en with equal thanks: and bless'd are those
    Whose blood and judgment are so well commingled
60   That they are not a pipe for Fortune's finger
    To sound what stop she please. Give me that man
    That is not passion's slave, and I will wear him
    In my heart's core, ay, in my heart of heart,
    As I do thee.—Something too much of this.—
65   There is a play to-night before the king;
    One scene of it comes near the circumstance
    Which I have told thee of my father's death:
    I pr'ythee, when thou see'st that act a-foot,
    Even with the very comment of thy soul
70   Observe mine uncle: if this his occulted guilt
    Do not itself unkennel in one speech,
    It is a damned ghost that we have seen;
    And my imaginations are as foul
    As Vulcan's stithy.[3] Give him heedful note:
75   For I mine eyes will rivet to his face;
    And, after, we will both our judgments join
    In censure of his seeming.
HORATIO: Well, my lord:
    If he steal aught the whilst this play is playing,
    And scape detecting, I will pay the theft.
80 HAMLET: They are coming to the play; I must be idle:[4]

---

[3]   Smithy.

[4]   Foolish.

Get you a place.

(Danish march. A flourish. Enter King, Queen, Polonius,
Ophelia, Rosencrantz, Guildenstern, and others.)

KING: How fares our cousin Hamlet?

HAMLET: Excellent, i'faith; of the chameleon's dish:[5] I eat the air,
promise-crammed: you cannot feed capons so.

85 KING: I have nothing with this answer, Hamlet; these words are not
mine.

HAMLET: No, nor mine now. [*To Polonius*] My lord, you played once
i'the university, you say?

POLONIUS: That did I, my lord, and was accounted a good actor.

90 HAMLET: And what did you enact?

POLONIUS: I did enact Julius Caesar: I was killed i' the Capitol;
Brutus killed me.

HAMLET: It was a brute part of him to kill so capital a calf there.—
Be the players ready.

95 ROSENCRANTZ: Ay, my lord; they stay upon your patience.

QUEEN: Come hither, my good Hamlet, sit by me.

HAMLET: No, good mother, here's metal more attractive.

POLONIUS: O, ho! do you mark that? [*To the King*]

HAMLET: Lady, shall I lie in your lap? [*Lying down at Ophelia's feet*]

100 OPHELIA: No, my lord.

HAMLET: I mean, my head upon your lap?

OPHELIA: Ay, my lord.

HAMLET: Do you think I meant country matters?

OPHELIA: I think nothing, my lord.

105 HAMLET: That's a fair thought to lie between maids' legs.

OPHELIA: What is, my lord?

HAMLET: Nothing.

OPHELIA: You are merry, my lord.

HAMLET: Who, I?

110 OPHELIA: Ay, my lord.

HAMLET: O, your only jig-maker. What should a man do but be
merry? for, look you, how cheerfully my mother looks, and my
father died within's two hours.

OPHELIA: Nay, 'tis twice two months, my lord.

---

[5] Chameleons were supposed to live on air.

115 HAMLET: So long? Nay, then, let the devil wear black, for I'll have a
suit of sables. O heavens! die two months ago, and not forgotten
yet? Then there's hope a great man's memory may outlive his life
half a year: but, by'r lady, he must build churches, then; or else
shall he suffer not thinking on, with the hobby-horse, whose
epitaph is,

120   *For, O, for, O, the hobby-horse is forgot.*

(Trumpets sound. The dumb show enters.)

*(Enter a King and a Queen, very lovingly; the Queen embracing him and he
her. She kneels, and makes show of protestation unto him. He takes her up, and
declines his head upon her neck: lays him down upon a bank of flowers: she,
seeing him asleep, leaves him. Anon comes in a fellow, takes off his crown,
kisses it, and pours poison in the King's ears, and exit. The Queen returns; finds
the King dead, and makes passionate action. The Poisoner, with some two
or three Mutes, comes in again, seeming to lament with her. The dead body
is carried away. The Poisoner woos the Queen with gifts: she seems loth
and unwilling awhile, but in the end accepts his love.)*

(Exeunt.)

OPHELIA: What means this, my lord?
HAMLET: Marry, this is miching mallecho;[6] it means mischief.
OPHELIA: Belike this show imports the argument of the play.

(Enter Prologue.)

HAMLET: We shall know by this fellow: the players cannot keep
counsel;
125   they'll tell all.
OPHELIA: Will he tell us what this show meant?
HAMLET: Ay, or any show that you'll show him: be not you ashamed
to show, he'll not shame to tell you what it means.
OPHELIA: You are naught, you are naught: I'll mark the play.
130 PROLOGUE: *For us, and for our tragedy,*
                            Here stooping to your clemency,
                            We beg your hearing patiently.
HAMLET: Is this a prologue, or the posy[7] of a ring?

---

6 A sneaking misdeed.

7 Motto or inscription.

OPHELIA: 'Tis brief, my lord.
135   HAMLET: As woman's love.

(Enter a King and a Queen.)

PROLOGUE KING: Full thirty times hath Phoebus' cart gone round
        Neptune's salt wash and Tellus' orbed ground,[8]
        And thirty dozen moons with borrow'd sheen
        About the world have times twelve thirties been,
140   Since love our hearts, and Hymen did our hands
        Unite commutual in most sacred bands.
PROLOGUE QUEEN: So many journeys may the sun and moon
        Make us again count o'er ere love be done!
        But, woe is me, you are so sick of late,
145   So far from cheer and from your former state
        That I distrust you.[9] Yet, though I distrust,
        Discomfort you, my lord, it nothing must:
        For women's fear and love holds quantity,[10]
        In neither aught, or in extremity.
150   Now, what my love is, proof hath made you know;
        And as my love is siz'd, my fear is so:
        Where love is great, the littlest doubts are fear;
        Where little fears grow great, great love grows there.
PROLOGUE KING: Faith, I must leave thee, love, and shortly too;
155   My operant powers their functions leave[11] to do:
        And thou shalt live in this fair world behind,
        Honor'd, belov'd; and haply one as kind
        For husband shalt thou,—
PROLOGUE QUEEN: O, confound the rest!
        Such love must needs be treason in my breast:
160   In second husband let me be accurst!
        None wed the second but who kill'd the first.
HAMLET: [*Aside*] Wormwood, wormwood.
PROLOGUE QUEEN: The instances that second marriage move
        Are base respects of thrift, but none of love:

---

8   The globe.

9   Worry about you.

10   Correspond in degree.

11   Cease.

165   A second time I kill my husband, dead,
     When second husband kisses me in bed.
   PROLOGUE KING: I do believe you think what now you speak;
     But what we do determine oft we break.
     Purpose is but the slave to memory;
170   Of violent birth, but poor validity:
     Which now, like fruit unripe, sticks on the tree;
     But fall unshaken when they mellow be.
     Most necessary 'tis that we forget
     To pay ourselves what to ourselves is debt:
175   What to ourselves in passion we propose,
     The passion ending, doth the purpose lose.
     The violence of either grief or joy
     Their own enactures with themselves destroy:
     Where joy most revels grief doth most lament;
180   Grief joys, joy grieves, on slender accident.
     This world is not for aye; nor 'tis not strange
     That even our loves should with our fortunes change;
     For 'tis a question left us yet to prove
     Whether love lead fortune or else fortune love.
185   The great man down, you mark his favorite flies;
     The poor advanc'd makes friends of enemies.
     And hitherto doth love on fortune tend:
     For who not needs shall never lack a friend;
     And who in want a hollow friend doth try,
190   Directly seasons him his enemy.
     But, orderly to end where I begun,—
     Our wills and fates do so contrary run
     That our devices still are overthrown;
     Our thoughts are ours, their ends none of our own:
195   So think thou wilt no second husband wed;
     But die thy thoughts when thy first lord is dead.
   PROLOGUE QUEEN: Nor earth to me give food, nor heaven light!
     Sport and repose lock from me day and night!
     To desperation turn my trust and hope!
200   An anchor's [12] cheer in prison be my scope!
     Each opposite, that blanks the face of joy,

---

12 Anchorite's, or hermit's.

Meet what I would have well, and it destroy!
Both here and hence, pursue me lasting strife,
If, once a widow, ever I be wife!
205 HAMLET: If she should break it now! [*To Ophelia*]
PROLOGUE KING: 'Tis deeply sworn. Sweet, leave me here awhile;
My spirits grow dull, and fain I would beguile
The tedious day with sleep. [*Sleeps*]
PROLOGUE QUEEN: Sleep rock thy brain,
And never come mischance between us twain! [*Exit.*]
210 HAMLET: Madam, how like you this play?
QUEEN: The lady doth protest too much, methinks.
HAMLET: O, but she'll keep her word.
KING: Have you heard the argument? Is there no offence in't?
HAMLET: No, no, they do but jest, poison in jest; no offence i' the
215   world.
KING: What do you call the play?
HAMLET: The Mouse-trap. Marry, how? Tropically.[13] This play is
the image of a murder done in Vienna: Gonzago is the duke's
name: his wife, Baptista: you shall see anon; 'tis a knavish piece of
220   work: but what o' that? your majesty, and we that have free souls,
it touches us not: let the galled jade wince, our withers are
unwrung.

(Enter Lucianus.)

This is one Lucianus, nephew to the king.
OPHELIA: You are a good chorus, my lord.
HAMLET: I could interpret between you and your love, if I could see
225   the puppets dallying.
OPHELIA: You are keen, my lord, you are keen.
HAMLET: It would cost you a groaning to take off my edge.
OPHELIA: Still better, and worse.
HAMLET: So you must take your husbands.—Begin, murderer; pox,
230   leave thy damnable faces and begin. Come:—*The croaking raven
doth bellow for revenge.*
LUCIANUS: Thoughts black, hands apt, drugs fit, and time agreeing;
Confederate season, else no creature seeing;

---

13 Figuratively, or metaphorically; by means of a "trope."

Thou mixture rank, of midnight weeds collected,
235 With Hecate's ban[14] thrice blasted, thrice infected,
Thy natural magic and dire property
On wholesome life usurp immediately.

(Pours the poison into the sleeper's ears.)

HAMLET: He poisons him i' the garden for's estate. His name's
Gonzago: the story is extant, and writ in choice Italian: you shall
240 see anon how the murderer gets the love of Gonzago's wife.
OPHELIA: The king rises.
HAMLET: What, frighted with false fire!
QUEEN: How fares my lord?
POLONIUS: Give o'er the play.
245 KING: Give me some light:—away!
ALL: Lights, lights, lights!

(Exeunt all but Hamlet and Horatio.)

HAMLET: Why, let the stricken deer go weep,
The hart ungalled play;
For some must watch, while some must sleep:
250 So runs the world away.—
Would not this, sir, and a forest of feathers,
If the rest of my fortunes turn Turk with me,
With two Provencial roses on my razed shoes,
Get me a fellowship in a cry[15] of players, sir?
255 HORATIO: Half a share.
HAMLET: A whole one, I.
For thou dost know, O Damon dear,
This realm dismantled was
Of Jove himself; and now reigns here
260 A very, very—pajock.[16]
HORATIO: You might have rhymed.
HAMLET: O good Horatio, I'll take the ghost's word for a thousand
pound. Didst perceive?

---

14 The spell of the goddess of witchcraft.

15 Company.

16 Peacock.

HORATIO: Very well, my lord.

265 HAMLET: Upon the talk of the poisoning,—

HORATIO: I did very well note him.

HAMLET: Ah, ha!—Come, some music! come, the recorders!—
For if the king like not the comedy,
Why, then, belike,—he likes it not, perdy. Come, some music!

(Re-enter Rosencrantz and Guildenstern.)

270 GUILDENSTERN: Good my lord, vouchsafe me a word with you.

HAMLET: Sir, a whole history.

GUILDENSTERN: The king, sir,—

HAMLET: Ay, sir, what of him?

GUILDENSTERN: Is, in his retirement, marvelous distempered.

275 HAMLET: With drink, sir?

GUILDENSTERN: No, my lord, rather with choler.

HAMLET: Your wisdom should show itself more richer to signify this
to his doctor; for, for me to put him to his purgation would
perhaps plunge him into far more choler.

280 GUILDENSTERN: Good my lord, put your discourse into some frame,
and start not so wildly from my affair.

HAMLET: I am tame, sir:—pronounce.

GUILDENSTERN: The queen, your mother, in most great affliction of
spirit, hath sent me to you.

285 HAMLET: You are welcome.

GUILDENSTERN: Nay, good my lord, this courtesy is not of the right
breed. If it shall please you to make me a wholesome answer, I
will do you mother's commandment: if not, your pardon and my
return shall be the end of my business.

290 HAMLET: Sir, I cannot.

GUILDENSTERN: What, my lord?

HAMLET: Make you a wholesome answer; my wit's diseas'd: but, sir,
such answer as I can make, you shall command; or, rather, as you
say, my mother: therefore no more, but to the matter: my mother,

295 you say,—

ROSENCRANTZ: Then thus she says: your behavior hath struck her
into amazement and admiration.

HAMLET: O wonderful son, that can so astonish a mother!—But is
there no sequel at the heels of this mother's admiration?

300 ROSENCRANTZ: She desires to speak with you in her closet[17] ere you
        go to bed.
    HAMLET: We shall obey, were she ten times our mother. Have you
        any further trade with us?
    ROSENCRANTZ: My lord, you once did love me.
305 HAMLET: So I do still, by these pickers and stealers.[18]
    ROSENCRANTZ: Good, my lord, what is your cause of distemper? you
        do, surely, bar the door upon your own liberty if you deny your
        griefs to your friend.
    HAMLET: Sir, I lack advancement.
310 ROSENCRANTZ: How can that be, when you have the voice of the
        king himself for your succession in Denmark?
    HAMLET: Ay, but *While the grass grows,*—the proverb is something
        musty.

(Re-enter the Players, with recorders.)

        O, the recorders:—let me see one.—To withdraw with you:—
315   why do you go about to recover the wind of me, as if you
        would drive me into a toil?
    GUILDENSTERN: O, my lord, if my duty be too bold, my love is too
        unmannerly.
    HAMLET: I do not well understand that. Will you play upon this pipe?
320 GUILDENSTERN: My lord, I cannot.
    HAMLET: I pray you.
    GUILDENSTERN: Believe me, I cannot.
    HAMLET: I do beseech you.
    GUILDENSTERN: I know no touch of it, my lord.
325 HAMLET: 'Tis as easy as lying: govern these ventages[19] with your
        finger and thumb, give it breath with your mouth, and it will
        discourse most eloquent music. Look you, these are the stops.
    GUILDENSTERN: But these cannot I command to any utterance of
        harmony; I have not the skill.
330 HAMLET: Why, look you now, how unworthy a thing you make of
        me! You would play upon me; you would seem to know my stops;

---

17   Boudoir.

18   Fingers.

19   Holes.

you would pluck out the heart of my mystery; you would sound
me from my lowest note to the top of my compass: and there is
much music, excellent voice, in this little organ; yet cannot you
335   make it speak. 'Sblood, do you think that I am easier to be played
on than a pipe? Call me what instrument you will, though you
can fret me you cannot play upon me.

(Enter Polonius.)

God bless you, sir!
POLONIUS: My lord, the queen would speak with you, and
340   presently.
HAMLET: Do you see yonder cloud that's almost in shape of a camel?
POLONIUS: By the mass, and 'tis like a camel indeed.
HAMLET: Methinks it is like a weasel.
POLONIUS: It is backed like a weasel.
345 HAMLET: Or like a whale?
POLONIUS: Very like a whale.
HAMLET: Then will I come to my mother by and by.—They fool me
to the top of my bent.—I will come by and by.
POLONIUS: I will say so.
350 HAMLET: By and by is easily said.

(Exit Polonius.)

Leave me, friends.

(Exeunt Rosencrantz, Guildenstern, Horatio, and Players.)

'Tis now the very witching time of night,
When churchyards yawn, and hell itself breathes out
Contagion to this world: now could I drink hot blood,
355   And do such bitter business as the day
Would quake to look on. Soft! now to my mother.—
O heart, lose not thy nature; let not ever
The soul of Nero[20] enter this firm bosom:
Let me be cruel, not unnatural:
360   I will speak daggers to her, but use none;
My tongue and soul in this be hypocrites,—

---

[20] Nero killed his mother, a crime of which Hamlet does not want to be guilty.

How in my words soever she be shent,
To give them seals never, my soul, consent! [*Exit.*]

S C E N E   I I I

A room in the castle.

(Enter King, Rosencrantz, and Guildenstern.)

KING: I like him not; nor stands it safe with us
To let his madness range. Therefore prepare you;
I your commission with forthwith despatch,
And he to England shall along with you:
5   The terms of our estate may not endure
Hazard so dangerous as doth hourly grow
Out of his lunacies.

GUILDENSTERN: We will ourselves provide:
Most holy and religious fear it is
To keep those many many bodies safe
10   That live and feed upon your majesty.

ROSENCRANTZ: The single and peculiar life is bound,
With all the strength and armor of the mind,
To keep itself from 'noyance; but much more
That spirit upon whose weal depend and rest
15   The lives of many. The cease of majesty
Dies not alone; but like a gulf doth draw
What's near it with it: it is a massy wheel,
Fix'd on the summit of the highest mount,
To whose huge spokes ten thousand lesser things
20   Are mortis'd and adjoin'd; which, when it falls,
Each small annexment, petty consequence,
Attends the boisterous ruin. Never alone
Did the king sigh, but with a general groan.

KING: Arm you, I pray you, to this speedy voyage;
25   For we will fetters put upon this fear,
Which now goes too free-footed.

ROSENCRANTZ and GUILDENSTERN: We will haste us.

(Exeunt Rosencrantz and Guildenstern.)

(Enter Polonius.)

POLONIUS: My lord, he's going to his mother's closet:

Behind the arras I'll convey myself
To hear the process; I'll warrant she'll tax him home:[1]
30   And, as you said, and wisely was it said,
'Tis meet that some more audience than a mother,
Since nature makes them partial, should o'erhear
The speech, of vantage. Fare you well, my liege:
I'll call upon you ere you go to bed,
35   And tell you what I know.
KING: Thanks, dear my lord.

(Exit Polonius.)

O, my offence is rank, it smells to heaven;
It hath the primal eldest curse upon't,—
A brother's murder!—Pray can I not,
Though inclination be as sharp as will:
40   My stronger guilt defeats my strong intent;
And, like a man to double business bound,
I stand in pause where I shall first begin,
And both neglect. What if this cursed hand
Were thicker than itself with brother's blood,—
45   Is there not rain enough in the sweet heavens
To wash it white as snow? Whereto serves mercy
But to confront the visage of offence?
And what's in prayer but this twofold force,—
To be forestalled ere we come to fall,
50   Or pardon'd being down? Then I'll look up;
My fault is past. But, O, what form of prayer
Can serve my turn? Forgive me my foul murder?—
That cannot be; since I am still possess'd
Of those effects for which I did the murder,—
55   My crown, mine own ambition, and my queen.
May one be pardon'd and retain the offence?[2]
In the corrupted currents of this world
Offence's gilded hand may shove by justice;
And oft 'tis seen the wicked prize itself
60   Buys out the law: but 'tis not so above;

---

[1]   Reprove him properly.

[2]   That is, the gains won by the offense.

There is no shuffling,—there the action lies
In his true nature; and we ourselves compell'd,
Even to the teeth and forehead of our faults,
To give in evidence. What then? what rests?[3]
65   Try what repentance can: what can it not?
Yet what can it when one can not repent?
O wretched state! O bosom black as death!
O limed[4] soul, that, struggling to be free,
Art more engag'd! Help, angels! make assay:
70   Bow, stubborn knees; and, heart, with strings of steel,
Be soft as sinews of the new-born babe!
All may be well. [*Retires and kneels*]

(Enter Hamlet.)

HAMLET: Now might I do it pat, now he is praying;
And now I'll do't—and so he goes to heaven;
75   And so am I reveng'd:—that would be scann'd:
A villain kills my father; and for that,
I, his sole son, do this same villain send
To heaven.
O, this is hire and salary, not revenge.
80   He took my father grossly, full of bread;
With all his crimes broad blown, as flush as May;
And how his audit stands who knows save heaven?
But in our circumstance and course of thought
'Tis heavy with him: and am I, then, reveng'd,
85   To take him in the purging of his soul,
When he is fit and season'd for his passage?
No.
Up, sword; and know thou a more horrid hent:[5]
When he is drunk, asleep, or in his rage;
90   Or in the incestuous pleasure of his bed;
At gaming, swearing; or about some act
That has no relish of salvation in't;—
Then trip him, that his heels may kick at heaven;

---

[3] Remains.

[4] Snared.

[5] Opportunity.

And that his soul may be as damn'd and black
95 As hell, whereto it goes. My mother stays:
This physic but prolongs thy sickly days. [*Exit.*]

(The King rises and advances.)

KING: My words fly up, my thoughts remain below:
Words without thoughts never to heaven go. [*Exit.*]

SCENE IV

Another room in the castle.

(Enter Queen and Polonius.)

POLONIUS: He will come straight. Look you lay home to him:
Tell him his pranks have been too broad to bear with,
And that your grace hath screen'd and stood between
Much heat and him. I'll silence me e'en here.
5 Pray you, be round with him.
HAMLET: [*Within*] Mother, mother, mother!
QUEEN: I'll warrant you:
Fear me not:—withdraw, I hear him coming.

(Polonius goes behind the arras.)

(Enter Hamlet.)

HAMLET: Now, mother, what's the matter?
QUEEN: Hamlet, thou hast thy father much offended.
10 HAMLET: Mother, you have my father much offended.
QUEEN: Come, come, you answer with an idle tongue.
HAMLET: Go, go, you question with a wicked tongue.
QUEEN: Why, how now, Hamlet!
HAMLET: What's the matter now?
QUEEN: Have you forgot me?
HAMLET: No, by the rood, not so:
15 You are the queen, your husband's brother's wife;
And,—would it were not so!—you are my mother.
QUEEN: Nay, then, I'll set those to you that can speak.
HAMLET: Come, come, and sit you down; you shall not budge;
You go not till I set you up a glass
20 Where you may see the inmost part of you.

QUEEN: What wilt thou do? thou wilt not murder me?—
    Help, help, ho!
POLONIUS: [*Behind*] What, ho! help, help, help!
HAMLET: How now! a rat?
    [*Draws.*]
    Dead, for a ducat, dead! [*Makes a pass through the arras*]
25   POLONIUS: [*Behind*] O, I am slain! [*Falls and dies.*]
QUEEN: O me, what hast thou done?
HAMLET: Nay, I know not:
    Is it the king? [*Draws forth Polonius*]
QUEEN: O, what a rash and bloody deed is this!
HAMLET: A bloody deed!—almost as bad, good mother,
30   As kill a king and marry with his brother.
QUEEN: As kill a king!
HAMLET: Ay, lady, 'twas my word.—
    Thou wretched, rash, intruding fool, farewell! [*To Polonius*]
    I took thee for thy better: take thy fortune;
    Thou find'st to be too busy is some danger.—
35   Leave wringing of your hands: peace; sit you down,
    And let me wring your heart: for so I shall,
    If it be made of penetrable stuff;
    If damned custom have not braz'd it so
    That it is proof and bulwark against sense.
40   QUEEN: What have I done, that thou dar'st wag thy tongue
    In noise so rude against me?
HAMLET: Such an act
    That blurs the grace and blush of modesty;
    Calls virtue hypocrite; takes off the rose
    From the fair forehead of an innocent love,
45   And sets a blister there; makes marriage-vows
    As false as dicers' oaths: O, such a deed
    As from the body of contraction plucks
    The very soul, and sweet religion makes
    A rhapsody of words: heaven's face doth glow;
50   Yea, this solidity and compound mass,
    With tristful[1] visage, as against the doom,
    Is thought-sick at the act.

---

[1] Gloomy.

QUEEN: Ah me, what act,
    That roars so loud, and thunders in the index?
  HAMLET: Look here upon this picture and on this,—
55   The counterfeit presentment of two brothers.
    See what grace was seated on this brow;
    Hyperion's curls; the front of Jove himself;
    An eye like Mars, to threaten and command;
    A station like the herald Mercury
60   New-lighted on a heaven-kissing hill;
    A combination and a form, indeed,
    Where every god did seem to set his seal,
    To give the world assurance of a man:
    This was your husband.—Look you now, what follows:
65   Here is your husband, like a mildew'd ear
    Blasting his wholesome brother. Have you eyes?
    Could you on this fair mountain leave to feed,
    And batten on this moor? Ha! have you eyes?
    You cannot call it love; for at your age
70   The hey-day in the blood is tame, it's humble,
    And waits upon the judgment: and what judgment
    Would step from this to this? Sense, sure, you have,
    Else could you not have motion: but sure that sense
    Is apoplex'd: for madness would not err;
75   Nor sense to ecstasy was ne'er so thrill'd
    But it reserv'd some quantity of choice
    To serve in such a difference. What devil was't
    That thus hath cozen'd you at hoodman-blind?[2]
    Eyes without feeling, feeling without sight,
80   Ears without hand or eyes, smelling sans all,
    Or but a sickly part of one true sense
    Could not so mope.
    O shame! where is thy blush! Rebellious hell,
    If thou canst mutine in a matron's bones,
85   To flaming youth let virtue be as wax,
    And melt in her own fire: proclaim no shame
    When the compulsive ardor gives the charge,
    Since frost itself as actively doth burn,

---

[2] Tricked you at blindman's buff.

And reason panders[3] will.

QUEEN: O Hamlet, speak no more:
90   Thou turn'st mine eyes into my very soul;
And there I see such black and grained spots
As will not leave their tinct.[4]

HAMLET: Nay, but to live
In the rank sweat of an enseamed bed,
Stew'd in corruption, honeying and making love
95   Over the nasty sty,—

QUEEN: O, speak to me no more;
These words like daggers enter in mine ears;
No more, sweet Hamlet.

HAMLET: A murderer and a villain;
A slave that is not twentieth part the tithe
Of your precedent lord; a vice of kings;[5]
100   A cutpurse of the empire and the rule,
That from a shelf the precious diadem stole,
And put it in his pocket!

QUEEN: No more.

HAMLET: A king of shreds and patches,—

(Enter Ghost.)

Save me, and hover o'er me with your wings,
105   You heavenly guards!—What would your gracious figure?

QUEEN: Alas, he's mad!

HAMLET: Do you not come your tardy son to chide,
That, laps'd in time and passion, lets go by
The important acting of your dread command?
110   O, say!

GHOST: Do not forget: this visitation
Is but to whet thy almost blunted purpose.
But, look, amazement on thy mother sits:
O, step between her and her fighting soul,—
115   Conceit in weakest bodies strongest works,—

---

3   Becomes subservient to.

4   As will not yield up their color.

5   A buffoon among kings. The "Vice" in morality plays.

Speak to her, Hamlet.

HAMLET: How is it with you, lady?

QUEEN: Alas, how is't with you,
That you do bend your eye on vacancy,
And with the incorporal air do hold discourse?
120   Forth at your eyes your spirits wildly peep;
And, as the sleeping soldiers in the alarm,
Your bedded hair, like life in excrements,[6]
Starts up and stands on end. O gentle son,
Upon the heat and flame of thy distemper
125   Sprinkle cool patience. Whereon do you look?

HAMLET: On him, on him! Look you, how pale he glares!
His form and cause conjoin'd, preaching to stones,
Would make them capable.—Do not look upon me;
Lest with this piteous action you convert
130   My stern effects: then what I have to do
Will want true color; tears perchance for blood.

QUEEN: To whom do you speak this?

HAMLET: Do you see nothing there?

QUEEN: Nothing at all; yet all that is I see.

HAMLET: Nor did you nothing hear?

135   QUEEN: No, nothing but ourselves.

HAMLET: Why, look you there! look, how it steals away!
My father, in his habit as he liv'd!
Look, where he goes, even now, out at the portal!

(Exit Ghost.)

QUEEN: This is the very coinage of your brain:
140   This bodiless creation ecstasy
Is very cunning in.

HAMLET: Ecstasy!
My pulse, as yours, doth temperately keep time.
And makes as healthful music: it is not madness
That I have utter'd: bring me to the test,
145   And I the matter will re-word; which madness
Would gambol from. Mother, for love of grace,
Lay not that flattering unction to your soul,

---

[6] In outgrowths or extremities.

That not your trespass, but my madness speaks:
It will but skin and film the ulcerous place,
150   Whilst rank corruption, mining all within,
Infects unseen. Confess yourself to Heaven;
Repent what's past; avoid what is to come;
And do not spread the compost on the weeds,
To make them ranker. Forgive me this my virtue;
155   For in the fatness[7] of these pursy times
Virtue itself of vice must pardon beg,
Yea, curb and woo for leave to do him good.
QUEEN: O Hamlet, thou hast cleft my heart in twain.
HAMLET: O, throw away the worser part of it,
160   And live the purer with the other half.
Good-night: but go not to mine uncle's bed;
Assume a virtue, if you have it not.
That monster custom, who all sense doth eat,
Of habits devil, is angel yet in this,—
165   That to the use of actions fair and good
He likewise gives a frock or livery
That aptly is put on. Refrain to-night;
And that shall lend a kind of easiness
To the next abstinence: the next more easy;
170   For use almost can change the stamp of nature,
And either curb the devil, or throw him out
With wondrous potency. Once more, good-night:
And when you are desirous to be bless'd,
I'll blessing beg of you.—For this same lord [*pointing to Polonius*]
175   I do repent: but Heaven hath pleas'd it so,
To punish me with this, and this with me,
That I must be their[8] scourge and minister.
I will bestow him, and will answer well
The death I gave him. So, again, good-night.—
180   I must be cruel only to be kind:
Thus bad begins and worse remains behind.—
One word more, good lady.
QUEEN: What shall I do?

---

7   Corruption.

8   Heaven's, or the heavens'.

HAMLET: Not this, by no means, that I bid you do:
Let the bloat king tempt you again to bed;
185 Pinch wanton on your cheek; call you his mouse;
And let him, for a pair of reechy kisses,
Or paddling in your neck with his damn'd fingers,
Make you to ravel all this matter out,
That I essentially am not in madness,
190 But mad in craft. 'Twere good you let him know;
For who that's but a queen, fair, sober, wise,
Would from a paddock,[9] from a bat, a gib,
Such dear concernings hide? who would do so?
No, in despite of sense and secrecy,
195 Unpeg the basket on the house's top,
Let the birds fly, and, like the famous ape,
To try conclusions, in the basket creep,
And break your own neck down.
QUEEN: Be thou assur'd, if words be made of breath
200 And breath of life, I have not life to breathe
What thou hast said to me.
HAMLET: I must to England; you know that?
QUEEN: Alack,
I had forgot: 'tis so concluded on.
HAMLET: There's letters seal'd: and my two school-fellows,—
205 Whom I will trust as I will adders fang'd,
They bear the mandate; they must sweep my way,
And marshal me to knavery. Let it work;
For 'tis the sport to have the engineer
Hoist with his own petard: and't shall go hard
210 But I will delve one yard below their mines,
And blow them at the moon: O, 'tis most sweet,
When in one line two crafts directly meet.—
This man shall set me packing:
I'll lug the guts into the neighbor room.—
215 Mother, good-night.—Indeed, this counsellor
Is now most still, most secret, and most grave,
Who was in life a foolish prating knave.
Come, sir, to draw toward an end with you:—

---

[9] Paddock: toad; gib: tomcat.

Good-night, mother.

(Exeunt severally; Hamlet dragging out Polonius.)

ACT IV SCENE I

A room in the castle.

(Enter King, Queen, Rosencrantz, and Guildenstern.)

KING: There's matter in these sighs, these prófound heaves:
        You must translate: 'tis fit we understand them.
        Where is your son?

QUEEN: Bestow this place on us a little while. [*To Rosencrantz and*
5   *Guildenstern, who go out*] Ah, my good lord, what have I seen
        to-night!

KING: What, Gertrude? How does Hamlet?

QUEEN: Mad as the sea and wind, when both contend
        Which is the mightier: in his lawless fit,
        Behind the arras hearing something stir,
10   He whips his rapier out, and cries, *A rat, a rat!*
        And, in this brainish apprehension,[1] kills
        The unseen good old man.

KING: O heavy deed!
        It had been so with us had we been there:
        His liberty is full of threats to all;
15   To you yourself, to us, to every one.
        Alas, how shall this bloody deed be answer'd?
        It will be laid to us, whose providence
        Should have kept short, restrain'd, and out of haunt
        This mad young man: but so much was our love,
20   We would not understand what was most fit;
        But, like the owner of a foul disease,
        To keep it from divulging, let it feed
        Even on the pith of life. Where is he gone?

QUEEN: To draw apart the body he hath kill'd:
25   O'er whom his very madness, like some ore

---

[1] Mad notion.

Among a mineral of metals base,
Shows itself pure; he weeps for what is done.
KING: O Gertrude, come away!
The sun no sooner shall the mountains touch
30 But we will ship him hence: and this vile deed
We must, with all our majesty and skill,
Both countenance and excuse.—Ho, Guildenstern!

(Enter Rosencrantz and Guildenstern.)

Friends both, go join you with some further aid:
Hamlet in madness hath Polonius slain,
35 And from his mother's closet hath he dragg'd him:
Go seek him out; speak fair, and bring the body
Into the chapel. I pray you, haste in this.

(Exeunt Rosencrantz and Guildenstern.)

Come, Gertrude, we'll call up our wisest friends;
And let them know both what we mean to do
40 And what's untimely done: so haply slander,—
Whose whisper o'er the world's diameter,
As level as the cannon to his blank,
Transports his poison'd shot,—may amiss our name,
And hit the woundless air.— O, come away!
45 My soul is full of discord and dismay.

(Exeunt.)

SCENE II

Another room in the castle.

(Enter Hamlet.)

HAMLET: Safely stowed.
ROSENCRANTZ and GUILDENSTERN: [*Within*] Hamlet! Lord
Hamlet!
HAMLET: What noise? who calls on Hamlet?
O, here they come.

(Enter Rosencrantz and Guildenstern.)

5   ROSENCRANTZ: What have you done, my lord, with the dead body?
     HAMLET: Compounded it with dust, whereto 'tis kin.
     ROSENCRANTZ: Tell us where 'tis, that we may take it thence,
        And bear it to the chapel.
     HAMLET: Do not believe it.
10 ROSENCRANTZ: Believe what?
     HAMLET: That I can keep your counsel, and not mine own. Besides,
        to be demanded of a sponge!—what replication should be made
        by the son of a king?
     ROSENCRANTZ: Take you me for a sponge, my lord?
15 HAMLET: Ay, sir; that soaks up the king's countenance, his rewards,
        his authorities. But such officers do the king best service in the
        end: he keeps them, like an ape, in the corner of his jaw; first
        mouthed, to be last swallowed: when he needs what you have
        gleaned, it is but squeezing you, and, sponge, you shall be dry
20   again.
     ROSENCRANTZ: I understand you not, my lord.
     HAMLET: I am glad of it: a knavish speech sleeps in a foolish ear.
     ROSENCRANTZ: My lord, you must tell us where the body is, and go
        with us to the king.
25 HAMLET: The body is with the king, but the king is not with the
        body. The king is a thing,—
     GUILDENSTERN: A thing, my lord!
     HAMLET: Of nothing: bring me to him.
        Hide fox, and all after.

(Exeunt.)

SCENE III

Another room in the castle.

(Enter King, attended.)

     KING: I have sent to seek him, and to find the body.
        How dangerous is it that this man goes loose!
        Yet must not we put the strong law on him:
        He's lov'd of the distracted multitude,
5   Who like not in their judgment, but their eyes;
        And where 'tis so, the offender's scourge is weigh'd,

But never the offence. To bear all smooth and even,
This sudden sending him away must seem
Deliberate pause: diseases desperate grown
10   By desperate appliance are reliev'd,
Or not at all.

(Enter Rosencrantz.)

How now! what hath befallen!
ROSENCRANTZ: Where the dead body is bestow'd, my lord,
We cannot get from him.
KING: But where is he?
15   ROSENCRANTZ: Without, my lord; guarded, to know your pleasure.
KING: Bring him before us.
ROSENCRANTZ: Ho, Guildenstern! bring in my lord.

(Enter Hamlet and Guildenstern.)

KING: Now, Hamlet, where's Polonius?
HAMLET: At supper.
20   KING: At supper! where?
HAMLET: Not where he eats, but where he is eaten: a certain
convocation of politic worms are e'en at him. Your worm is your
only emperor for diet: we fat all creatures else to fat us, and we fat
ourselves for maggots: your fat king and your lean beggar is but
25   variable service,—two dishes, but to one table: that's the end.
KING: Alas, alas!
HAMLET: A man may fish with the worm that hath eat of a king,
and eat of the fish that hath fed of that worm.
KING: What does thou mean by this?
30   HAMLET: Nothing but to show you how a king may go a progress
through the guts of a beggar.
KING: Where is Polonius?
HAMLET: In heaven; send thither to see: if your messenger find him
not there, seek him i' the other place yourself. But, indeed, if you
35   find him not within this month, you shall nose him as you go up
the stairs into the lobby.
KING: Go seek him there. [*To some Attendants*]
HAMLET: He will stay till ye come.

(Exeunt Attendants.)

KING: Hamlet, this deed, for thine especial safety,—

40   Which we do tender, as we dearly grieve
   For that which thou hast done,—must send thee hence
   With fiery quickness: therefore prepare thyself;
   The bark is ready, and the wind at help,
   The associates tend, and everything is bent
45   For England.
 HAMLET: For England!
 KING: Ay, Hamlet.
 HAMLET: Good.
 KING: So is it, if thou knew'st our purposes.
 HAMLET: I see a cherub that sees them.—But, come; for England!—
   Farewell, dear mother.
 KING: Thy loving father, Hamlet.
50 HAMLET: My mother: father and mother is man and wife; man and
   wife is one flesh; and so, my mother.—Come, for England! [*Exit.*]
 KING: Follow him at foot; tempt him with speed aboard;
   Delay it not; I'll have him hence to-night:
   Away! for everything is seal'd and done
55   That else leans on the affair, pray you, make haste.

   (Exeunt Rosencrantz and Guildenstern.)

   And, England, if my love thou hold'st at aught,—
   As my great power thereof may give thee sense,
   Since yet thy cicatrice looks raw and red
   After the Danish sword, and thy free awe
60   Pays homage to us,—thou mayst not coldly set
   Our sovereign process; which imports at full,
   By letters conjuring to that effect,
   The present death of Hamlet. Do it, England;
   For like the hectic in my blood he rages,
65   And thou must cure me: till I know 'tis done,
   Howe'er my haps, my joys will ne'er begin. [*Exit*]

SCENE IV

A plain in Denmark.

(Enter Fortinbras, and Forces marching.)

FORTINBRAS: Go, from me greet the Danish king:
   Tell him that, by his license, Fortinbras

Craves the conveyance of a promis'd march
Over his kingdom. You know the rendezvous,
5   If that his majesty would aught with us,
We shall express our duty in his eye,
And let him know so.
CAPTAIN: I will do't, my lord.
FORTINBRAS: Go softly on.

(Exeunt Fortinbras and Forces.)

(Enter Hamlet, Rosencrantz, Guildenstern, &c.)

HAMLET: Good sir, whose powers are these?
10   CAPTAIN: They are of Norway, sir.
HAMLET: How purpos'd, sir, I pray you?
CAPTAIN: Against some part of Poland.
HAMLET: Who commands them, sir?
CAPTAIN: The nephew to old Norway, Fortinbras.
15   HAMLET: Goes it against the main of Poland, sir,
Or for some frontier?
CAPTAIN: Truly to speak, and with no addition,
We go to gain a little patch of ground
That hath in it no profit but the name.
20   To pay five ducats, five, I would not farm it;
Nor will it yield to Norway or the Pole
A ranker[1] rate should it be sold in fee.
HAMLET: Why, then the Polack never will defend it.
CAPTAIN: Yes, it is already garrison'd.
25   HAMLET: Two thousand souls and twenty thousand ducats
Will not debate the question of this straw:
This is the imposthume[2] of much wealth and peace,
That inward breaks, and shows no cause without
Why the man dies.—I humbly thank you, sir.
30   CAPTAIN: God b' wi' you, sir. [*Exit.*]
ROSENCRANTZ: Will't please you go, my lord?
HAMLET: I'll be with you straight. Go a little before.

(Exeunt all but Hamlet.)

---

[1] Dearer.

[2] Ulcer.

How all occasions do inform against me,
And spur my dull revenge! What is a man,
35 If his chief good and market of his time
Be but to sleep and feed? a beast, no more.
Sure he that made us with such large discourse,[3]
Looking before and after, gave us not
That capability and godlike reason
40 To fust[4] in us unus'd. Now, whether it be
Bestial oblivion or some craven scruple
Of thinking too precisely on the event,—
A thought which, quarter'd, hath but one part wisdom
And ever three parts coward,—I do not know
45 Why yet I live to say, *This thing's to do;*
Sith[5] I have cause, and will, and strength, and means
To do't. Examples, gross as earth, exhort me:
Witness this army, of such mass and charge,
Led by a delicate and tender prince;
50 Whose spirit, with divine ambition puff'd,
Makes mouths at the invisible event;
Exposing what is mortal and unsure
To all that fortune, death, and danger dare,
Even for an egg-shell. Rightly to be great
55 Is not to stir without great argument,
But greatly to find quarrel in a straw
When honor's at the stake. How stand I, then,
That have a father kill'd, a mother stain'd,
Excitements of my reason and my blood,
60 And let all sleep? while, to my shame, I see
The imminent death of twenty thousand men,
That, for a fantasy and trick of fame,
Go to their graves like beds; fight for a plot
Whereon the numbers cannot try the cause,
65 Which is not tomb enough and continent[6]

---

[3] Reasoning faculty.

[4] Grow musty.

[5] Since.

[6] Container.

To hide the slain?— O, from this time forth,
My thoughts be bloody, or be nothing worth! [*Exit.*]

S C E N E   V

Elsinore. A room in the castle.

(Enter Queen and Horatio.)

QUEEN: I will not speak with her.
HORATIO: She is importunate; indeed, distract:
    Her mood will needs be pitied.
QUEEN: What would she have?
HORATIO: She speaks much of her father; says she hears
5   There's tricks i' the world; and hems, and beats her heart;
    Spurns enviously at straws; speaks things in doubt,
    That carry but half sense: her speech is nothing,
    Yet the unshapéd use of it doth move
    The hearers to collection; they aim at it,
10 And botch the words up fit to their own thoughts;
    Which, as her winks, and nods, and gestures yield them,
    Indeed would make one think there might be thought,
    Though nothing sure, yet much unhappily.
    'Twere good she were spoken with; for she may strew
15 Dangerous conjectures in ill-breeding minds.
QUEEN: Let her come in.

(Exit Horatio.)

To my sick soul, as sin's true nature is,
Each toy seems prologue to some great amiss:
So full of artless jealousy is guilt,
20 It spills itself in fearing to be spilt.

(Re-enter Horatio and Ophelia.)

OPHELIA: Where is the beauteous majesty of Denmark?
QUEEN: How now, Ophelia!
OPHELIA: [*Sings*]
                    How should I your true love know
                    From another one?
25   By his cockle hat and staff,

And his sandal shoon.

QUEEN: Alas, sweet lady, what imports this song?

OPHELIA: Say you? nay, pray you, mark.

(Sings)

He is dead and gone, lady,
He is dead and gone;
At his head a grass green turf,
At his heels a stone.

QUEEN: Nay, but, Ophelia,—

OPHELIA: Pray you, mark.

(Sings)

White his shroud as the mountain snow,

(Enter King.)

QUEEN: Alas, look here, my lord.

˙OPHELIA: [*Sings*]

Larded with sweet flowers;
Which bewept to the grave did go
With true-love showers.

KING: How do you, pretty lady?

OPHELIA: Well, God 'ild[1] you! They say the owl was a baker's
daughter.
Lord, we know what we are, but know not what we may be.
God be at your table!

KING: Conceit upon her father.

OPHELIA: Pray you, let's have no words of this; but when they ask
you what it means, say you this:

(Sings.)

To-morrow is Saint Valentine's day
All in the morning betime,
And I a maid at your window,
To be your Valentine.
Then up he rose, and donn'd his clothes,
And dupp'd the chamber-door;

---

[1] Yield you—that is, reward you.

Let in the maid, that out a maid
Never departed more.

KING: Pretty Ophelia!

55 OPHELIA: Indeed, la, without an oath, I'll make an end on't;

(Sings)

By Gis[2] and by Saint Charity,
Alack, and fie for shame!
Young men will do't, if they come to't;
By cock, they are to blame.
60 Quoth she, before you tumbled me,
You promis'd me to wed.
So would I ha' done, by yonder sun,
An thou hadst not come to my bed.

KING: How long hath she been thus?

65 OPHELIA: I hope all will be well. We must be patient: but I cannot
choose but weep, to think they should lay him i' the cold ground.
My brother shall know of it: and so I thank you; for your good
counsel.—Come, my coach!—Good-night, ladies; good-night,
sweet ladies; good-night, good-night. [*Exit.*]

70 KING: Follow her close; give her good watch, I pray you.

(Exit Horatio.)

O, this is the poison of deep grief; it springs
All from her father's death. O Gertrude, Gertrude,
When sorrows come, they come not single spies,
But in battalions! First, her father slain:
75 Next, your son gone; and he most violent author
Of his own just remove: the people muddied,
Thick and unwholesome in their thoughts and whispers
For good Polonius' death; and we have done but greenly
In hugger-mugger[3] to inter him: poor Ophelia
80 Divided from herself and her fair judgment,
Without the which we are pictures, or mere beasts:
Last, and as much containing as all these,
Her brother is in secret come from France;

---

2 A contraction for "by Jesus."

3 In great secrecy and haste.

Feeds on his wonder, keeps himself in clouds,
85   And wants not buzzers to infect his ear
With pestilent speeches of his father's death;
Wherein necessity, of matter beggar'd,
Will nothing stick our person to arraign
In ear and ear. O my dear Gertrude, this,
90   Like to a murdering piece,[4] in many places
Gives me superfluous death.

(A noise within.)

QUEEN: Alack, what noise is this?
KING: Where are my Switzers?[5] let them guard the door.

(Enter a Gentleman.)

What is the matter?
GENTLEMAN: Save yourself, my lord:
The ocean, overpeering of his list,
95   Eats not the flats with more impetuous haste
Than young Laertes, in a riotous head,
O'erbears your officers. The rabble call him lord;
And, as the world were now but to begin,
Antiquity forgot, custom not known,
100   The ratifiers and props of every word,
They cry, *Choose we, Laertes shall be king!*
Caps, hands, and tongues applaud it to the clouds,
Laertes shall be king, Laertes king!
QUEEN: How cheerfully on the false trail they cry!
105   O, this is counter, you false Danish dogs!
KING: The doors are broke.

(Noise within)

(Enter Laertes armed; Danes following.)

LAERTES: Where is this king?—Sirs, stand you all without.
DANES: No, let's come in.

---

[4] A cannon.

[5] Bodyguard of Swiss mercenaries.

LAERTES: I pray you, give me leave.

DANES: We will, we will. [*They retire without the door.*]

110   LAERTES: I thank you:—keep the door.—O thou vile king,
        Give me my father! .

QUEEN: Calmly, good Laertes.

LAERTES: That drop of blood that's calm proclaims me bastard;
        Cries cuckold to my father; brands the harlot
        Even here, between the chaste unsmirched brow

115   Of my true mother.

KING: What is the cause, Laertes,
        That thy rebellion looks so giant-like?—
        Let him go, Gertrude; do not fear our person:
        There's such divinity doth hedge a king,
        That treason can but peep to what it would,

120   Acts little of his will.—Tell me, Laertes,
        Why thou art thus incens'd.—Let him go, Gertrude:—
        Speak, man.

LAERTES: Where is my father?

KING: Dead.

QUEEN: But not by him.

KING: Let him demand his fill.

125   LAERTES: How came he dead? I'll not be juggled with:
        To hell, allegiance! vows, to the blackest devil!
        Conscience and grace, to the profoundest pit!
        I dare damnation:—to this point I stand,—
        That both the worlds I give to negligence,

130   Let come what comes; only I'll be reveng'd
        Most thoroughly for my father.

KING: Who shall stay you?

LAERTES: My will, not all the world:
        And for my means, I'll husband them so well,
        They shall go far with little.

KING: Good Laertes,

135   If you desire to know the certainty
        Of your dear father's death, is't writ in your revenge
        That, sweepstake, you will draw both friend and foe,
        Winner or loser?

LAERTES: None but his enemies.

KING: Will you know them, then?

140 LAERTES: To his good friends thus wide I'll ope my arms;
                  And, like the kind life-rendering pelican,[6]
                  Repast them with my blood.
       KING: Why, now you speak
                  Like a good child and a true gentleman.
                  That I am guiltless of your father's death,
145   And am most sensible in grief for it,
                  It shall as level to your judgment pierce
                  As day does to your eye.
       DANES: [*Within*]   Let her come in.
       LAERTES: How now! what noise is that?

(Re-enter Ophelia, fantastically dressed with straws and flowers.)

                  O heat, dry up my brains! tears seven times salt
150   Burn out the sense and virtue of mine eyes!—
                  By heaven, thy madness shall be paid by weight
                  Till our scale turn the beam. O rose of May!
                  Dear maid, kind sister, sweet Ophelia!—
                  O heavens! is't possible a young maid's wits
155   Should be as mortal as an old man's life!
                  Nature is fine in love; and where 'tis fine
                  It sends some precious instance of itself
                  After the thing it loves.
       OPHELIA: [*Sings*]
                         They bore him barefac'd on the bier;
160   Hey no nonny, nonny, hey nonny;
                         And on his grave rain'd many a tear,—
                              Fare you well, my dove!
       LAERTES: Hadst thou thy wits, and didst persuade revenge,
                  It could not move thus.
165 OPHELIA: You must sing, *Down-a-down, an you call him a-down-a.*
                  O,
                  how the wheel becomes it! It is the false steward, that stole his
                  master's daughter.
       LAERTES: This nothing's more than matter.
       OPHELIA: There's rosemary, that's for remembrance; pray, love,

---

6 The pelican mother was believed to draw blood from itself to feed its young.

170 remember: and there is pansies that's for thoughts.

LAERTES: A document in madness,—thoughts and remembrance fitted.

OPHELIA: There's fennel for you, and columbines:—there's rue for you; and here's some for me:—we may call it herb-grace o' Sundays:—

O, you must wear your rue with a difference.—There's a
175 daisy:—I would give you some violets, but they withered all when my father died:—they say, he made a good end,—

(Sings)

For bonny sweet Robin is all my joy,—

LAERTES: Thoughts and affliction, passion, hell itself, She turns to favor and to prettiness.

OPHELIA: [*Sings*]
180   And will he not come again?
        And will he not come again?
          No, no, he is dead,
          Go to thy death-bed,
        He never will come again.
185   His beard was as white as snow
        All flaxen was his poll:
          He is gone, he is gone,
          And we cast away moan:
        God ha' mercy on his soul!

190 And of all Christian souls, I pray God.—God b' wi' ye. [*Exit.*]

LAERTES: Do you see this, O God?

KING: Laertes, I must commune with your grief, Or you deny me right. Go but apart, Make choice of whom your wisest friends you will,
195 And they shall hear and judge 'twixt you and me: If by direct or by collateral hand They find us touch'd, we will our kingdom give, Our crown, our life, and all that we call ours, To you in satisfaction; but if not,
200 Be you content to lend your patience to us, And we shall jointly labor with your soul To give it due content.

LAERTES: Let this be so;

His means of death, his obscure burial,—
No trophy, sword, nor hatchment[7] o'er his bones
205   No noble rite nor formal ostentation,—
Cry to be heard, as 'twere from heaven to earth,
That I must call't in question.
KING: So you shall;
And where the offence is, let the great axe fall.
I pray you, go with me.

(Exeunt.)

SCENE VI

Another room in the castle.

(Enter Horatio and a Servant.)

HORATIO: What are they that would speak with me?
SERVANT: Sailors, sir: they say they have letters for you.
HORATIO: Let them come in.—

(Exit Servant.)

I do not know from what part of the world
5   I should be greeted, if not from Lord Hamlet.

(Enter Sailors.)

1ST SAILOR: God bless you, sir.
HORATIO: Let him bless thee too.
1ST SAILOR: He shall, sir, an't please him. There's a letter for you, sir;
it comes from the ambassador that was bound for England; if
10   your name be Horatio, as I am let to know it is.
HORATIO: [*Reads*] *Horatio, when thou shalt have overlooked this, give
these fellows some means to the king: they have letters for him. Ere we
were two days old at sea, a pirate of very warlike appointment gave us
chase. Finding ourselves too slow of sail, we put on a compelled valor;
15   and in the grapple I boarded them; on the instant they got clear of our
ship; so I alone became their prisoner. They have dealt with me like*

---

7   A tablet with coat of arms.

thieves of mercy: but they knew what they did; I am to do a good turn
for them. Let the king have the letters I have sent; and repair thou to
me with as much haste as thou wouldst fly death. I have words to speak
20 *in thine ear will make thee dumb; yet are they much too light for the*
bore of the matter. These good fellows will bring thee where I am.
Rosencrantz and Guildenstern hold their course for England: of them I
have much to tell thee. Farewell. He that thou knowest thine.

Hamlet

Come, I will give you way for these your letters;
25 And do't the speedier, that you may direct me
To him from whom you brought them.

(Exeunt.)

SCENE VII

Another room in the castle.

(Enter King and Laertes.)

KING: Now must your conscience my acquittance seal,
And you must put me in your heart for friend,
Sith you have heard, and with a knowing ear,
That he which hath your noble father slain
5 Pursu'd my life.
LAERTES: It well appears:—but tell me
Why you proceeded not against these feats,
So crimeful and so capital in nature.
As by your safety, wisdom, all things else,
You mainly were stirr'd up.
KING: O, for two special reasons;
10 Which may to you, perhaps, seem much unsinew'd,
But yet to me they are strong. The queen his mother
Lives almost by his looks; and for myself,—
My virtue or my plague, be it either which,—
She's so conjunctive to my life and soul,
15 That, as the star moves not but in his sphere,
I could not but by her. The other motive,
Why to a public count I might not go,
Is the great love the general gender bear him;

Who, dipping all his faults in their affection,
20 Would, like the spring that turneth wood to stone,
Convert his gyves to graces; so that my arrows,
Too slightly timber'd for so loud a wind,
Would have reverted to my bow again,
And not where I had aim'd them.
25 LAERTES: And so have I a noble father lost;
A sister driven into desperate terms,—
Whose worth, if praises may go back again,
Stood challenger on mount of all the age
For her perfections:—but my revenge will come.
30 KING: Break not your sleeps for that: you must not think
That we are made of stuff so flat and dull
That we can let our beard be shook with danger,
And think it pastime. You shortly shall hear more:
I lov'd your father, and we love ourself;
35 And that, I hope, will teach you to imagine,—

(Enter a Messenger.)

How now! what news?
MESSENGER: Letters, my lord, from Hamlet:
This to your majesty; this to the queen.
KING: From Hamlet! Who brought them?
MESSENGER: Sailors, my lord, they say; I saw them not:
40 They were given me by Claudio,—he receiv'd them
Of him that brought them.
KING: Laertes, you shall hear them.—Leave us.

(Exit Messenger.)

[*Reads*] *High and mighty,—You shall know I am set naked on your*
kingdom. To-morrow shall I beg leave to see your kingly eyes: when I
45 *shall, first asking your pardon thereunto, recount the occasions of my*
sudden and more strange return.   Hamlet
What should this mean? Are all the rest come back?
Or is it some abuse,[1] and no such thing?
LAERTES: Know you the hand?

---

[1] Ruse.

50 KING: 'Tis Hamlet's character:[2]—*Naked,*—
        And in a postscript here, he says, *alone.*
        Can you advise me?
    LAERTES: I am lost in it, my lord. But let him come;
        It warms the very sickness in my heart,
55   That I shall live, and tell him to his teeth,
        Thus diddest thou.
    KING: If it be so, Laertes,—
        As how should it be so? how otherwise?—
        Will you be rul'd by me?
    LAERTES: Ay, my lord:
        So you will not o'errule me to a peace.
60 KING: To thine own peace. If he be now return'd,—
        As checking at his voyage, and that he means
        No more to undertake it,—I will work him
        To an exploit, now ripe in my device,
        Under the which he shall not choose but fall:
65   And for his death no wind of blame shall breathe;
        But even his mother shall uncharge the practice
        And call it accident.
    LAERTES: My lord, I will be rul'd;
        The rather if you could devise it so
        That I might be the organ.
    KING: It falls right.
70   You have been talk'd of since your travel much,
        And that in Hamlet's hearing, for a quality
        Wherein they say you shine: your sum of parts
        Did not together pluck such envy from him
        As did that one; and that, in my regard,
75   Of the unworthiest siege.
    LAERTES: What part is that, my lord?
    KING: A very riband in the cap of youth,
        Yet needful too; for youth no less becomes
        The light and careless livery that it wears
        Than settled age his sables and his weeds,
80   Importing health and graveness.—Two months since,
        Here was a gentleman of Normandy,—

---

[2] Handwriting.

I've seen myself, and serv'd against, the French,
And they can well on horseback: but this gallant
Had witchcraft in't; he grew unto his seat;
85   And to such wondrous doing brought his horse,
As he had been incorps'd and demi-natur'd[3]
With the brave beast: so far he topp'd my thought,
That I, in forgery of shapes and tricks,[4]
Come short of what he did.

LAERTES: A Norman was't?
90 KING: A Norman.
LAERTES: Upon my life, Lamond.
KING: The very same.
LAERTES: I know him well: he is the brooch, indeed,
And gem of all the nation.

KING: He made confession of you;
95   And gave you such a masterly report
For art and exercise in your defence,
And for your rapier most especially,
That he cried out, 'twould be a sight indeed
If one could match you: the scrimers[5] of their nation,
100   He swore, had neither motion, guard, nor eye,
If you oppos'd them. Sir, this report of his
Did Hamlet so envenom with his envy,
That he could nothing do but wish and beg
Your sudden coming o'er, to play with him.
105   Now, out of this,—

LAERTES: What out of this, my lord?
KING: Laertes, was your father dear to you?
Or are you like the painting of a sorrow,
A face without a heart?

LAERTES: Why ask you this?
KING: Not that I think you did not love your father;
110   But that I know love is begun by time;
And that I see, in passages of proof,[6]

---

[3] Made as one body and formed into half man, half horse—or centaur.

[4] In imagining tricks of horsemanship.

[5] Fencers.

[6] The evidence of experience.

Time qualifies the spark and fire of it.
There lives within the very flame of love
A kind of wick or snuff that will abate it;
115 And nothing is at a like goodness still;
For goodness, growing to a pleurisy,[7]
Dies in his own too much: that we would do
We should do when we would; for this *would* changes,
And hath abatements and delays as many
120 As there are tongues, or hands, or accidents;
And then this *should* is like a spendthrift sigh
That hurts by easing. But to the quick o' the ulcer:
Hamlet comes back: what would you undertake
To show yourself your father's son in deed
125 More than in words?
LAERTES: To cut his throat i' the church.
KING: No place, indeed, should murder sanctuarize;
Revenge should have no bounds. But, good Laertes,
Will you do this, keep close within your chamber.
Hamlet return'd shall know you are come home:
130 We'll put on those shall praise your excellence,
And set a double varnish on the fame
The Frenchman gave you; bring you, in fine, together,
And wager on yours heads: he, being remiss,[8]
Most generous, and free from all contriving,
135 Will not peruse the foils; so that, with ease,
Or with a little shuffling, you may choose
A sword unbated, and, in a pass of practice,
Requite him for your father.
LAERTES: I will do't it:
And, for that purpose, I'll anoint my sword.
140 I bought an unction of a mountebank,
So mortal that but dip a knife in it,
Where it draws blood no cataplasm so rare,[9]
Collected from all simples that have virtue
Under the moon, can save the thing from death

---

[7] Plethora, an excess of blood.

[8] Unguarded and free from suspicion.

[9] No poultice, however remarkably efficacious.

145   That is but scratch'd withal: I'll touch my point
        With this contagion, that, if I gall him slightly,
        It may be death.
    King: Let's further think of this;
        Weigh what convenience both of time and means
        May fit us to our shape: if this should fail,
150   And that our drift look through our bad performance,
        'Twere better not assay'd: therefore this project
        Should have a back or second, that might hold
        If this should blast in proof. Soft! let me see:—
        We'll make a solemn wager on your cunnings,—
155   I ha't:
        When in your motion you are hot and dry,—
        As make your bouts more violent to that end,—
        And that he calls for drink, I'll have prepar'd him
        A chalice for the nonce; [10] whereon but sipping,
160   If he by chance escape your venom'd stuck
        Our purpose may hold there.

               (Enter Queen.)

                   How now, sweet queen!
    Queen: One woe doth tread upon another's heel,
        So fast they follow:—your sister's drown'd, Laertes.
    Laertes: Drown'd! O, where?
165 Queen: There is a willow grows aslant a brook,
        That shows his hoar leaves in the glassy stream;
        There with fantastic garlands did she come
        Of crowflowers, nettles, daisies, and long purples,
        That liberal shepherds give a grosser name,
170   But our cold maids do dead men's fingers call them.
        There, on the pendant boughs her coronet weeds
        Clambering to hang, an envious [11] sliver broke;
        When down her weedy trophies and herself
        Fell in the weeping brook. Her clothes spread wide;
175   And, mermaid-like, awhile they bore her up:
        Which time she chanted snatches of old tunes;

---

[10] Purpose.

[11] Malicious.

As one incapable of her own distress,
Or like a creature native and indu'd
Unto that element: but long it could not be
180 Till that her garments, heavy with their drink,
Pull'd the poor wretch from her melodious lay
To muddy death.

LAERTES: Alas, then, she is drown'd?

QUEEN: Drown'd, drown'd.

LAERTES: Too much of water hast thou, poor Ophelia,
185 And therefore I forbid my tears: but yet
It is our trick; nature her custom holds,
Let shame say what it will: when these are gone,
The woman will be out.[12]—Adieu, my lord:
I have a speech of fire, that fain would blaze,
190 But that this folly douts it.[13] [*Exit.*]

KING: Let's follow, Gertrude;
How much I had to do to calm his rage!
Now fear I this will give it start again;
Therefore let's follow.

(Exeunt.)

ACT V SCENE I

A churchyard.

(Enter two Clowns[1] with spades, &c.)

1ST CLOWN: Is she to be buried in Christian burial that wilfully
seeks her own salvation?

2ND CLOWN: I tell thee she is; and therefore make her grave straight:
the crowner[2] hath sat on her, and finds it Christian burial.

5 1ST CLOWN: How can that be, unless she drowned herself in her
own defence?

---

[12] That is, "I shall be ruthless."

[13] Drowns it.

[1] Rustic fellows.

[2] Coroner.

2ND CLOWN: Why, 'tis found so.

1ST CLOWN: It must be *se offendendo,*[3] it cannot be else. For here lies the point: if I drown myself wittingly, it argues an act: and an act hath three branches; it is to act, to do, and to perform: argal,[4] she drowned herself wittingly.

2ND CLOWN: Nay, but hear you, goodman delver,—

1ST CLOWN: Give me leave. Here lies the water; good: here stands the man; good: if the man go to this water and drown himself, it is, will he, nill he, he goes,—mark you that: but if the water come to him and drown him, he drowns not himself: argal, he that is not guilty of his own death shortens not his own life.

2ND CLOWN: But is this law?

1ST CLOWN: Ay, marry, is't; crowner's quest law.

2ND CLOWN: Will you ha' the truth on't? If this had not been a gentlewoman she should have been buried out of Christian burial.

1ST CLOWN: Why, there thou say'st: and the more pity that great folks should have countenance in this world to drown or hang themselves more than their even-Christian.[5]—Come, my spade. There is no ancient gentlemen but gardeners, ditchers, and grave-makers; they hold up Adam's profession.

2ND CLOWN: Was he a gentleman?

1ST CLOWN: He was the first that ever bore arms.

2ND CLOWN: Why, he had none.

1ST CLOWN: What, art a heathen? How dost thou understand the Scripture? The Scripture says, Adam digged: could he dig without arms? I'll put another question to thee: if thou answerest me not to the purpose, confess thyself,[6]—

2ND CLOWN: Go to.

1ST CLOWN: What is he that builds stronger than either the mason, the shipwright, or the carpenter?

2ND CLOWN: The gallows-maker; for that frame outlives a thousand tenants.

1ST CLOWN: I like thy wit well, in good faith: the gallows does well;

---

[3] In self-offense; he means *se defendendo,* in self-defense.

[4] He means *ergo,* therefore.

[5] Fellow Christian.

[6] Confess thyself an ass," perhaps.

40   but how does it well? it does well to those that do ill: now thou
dost ill to say the gallows is built stronger than the church: argal,
the gallows may do well to thee. To't again, come.

2ND CLOWN: Who builds stronger than a mason, a shipwright, or a
carpenter?

45   1ST CLOWN: Ay, tell me that, and unyoke.

2ND CLOWN: Marry, now I can tell.

1ST CLOWN: To't.

2ND CLOWN: Mass, I cannot tell.

(Enter Hamlet and Horatio, at a distance.)

1ST CLOWN: Cudgel thy brains no more about it, for your dull ass

50   will not mend his pace with beating; and when you are asked this
question next, say a grave-maker; the houses that he makes last
till doomsday. Go, get thee to Yaughan: fetch me a stoup of
liquor.

(Exit Second Clown.)

(Digs and sings)

In youth, when I did love, did love,
    Methought it was very sweet,

55   To contract, O, the time, for, ah, my behove,[7]
    O, methought there was nothing meet.

HAMLET: Has this fellow no feeling of his business, that he sings at
grave-making?

HORATIO: Custom hath made it in him a property of easiness.

60   HAMLET: 'Tis e'en so: the hand of little employment hath the
daintier sense.

1ST CLOWN: [*Sings*]
        But age, with his stealing steps,
          Hath claw'd me in his clutch,
        And hath shipp'd me intil the land,

65   As if I had never been such.

(Throws up a skull)

---

7 Behoof, or advantage.

HAMLET: That skull had a tongue in it, and could sing once: how
the knave joels[8] it to the ground, as if it were Cain's jawbone, that
did the first murder! This might be the pate of a politician, which
this ass now o'erreaches; one that would circumvent God, might
it not?

70 HORATIO: It might, my lord.

HAMLET: Or of a courtier; which could say, *Good-morrow, sweet lord!*
How dost thou, good lord? This might be my lord such-a-one, that
praised my lord such-a-one's horse, when he meant to beg it,—
might it not?

75 HORATIO: Ay, my lord.

HAMLET: Why, e'en so: and now my Lady Worm's; chapless,[9] and
knocked about the mazard[10] with a sexton's spade: here's fine
revolution, an we had the trick to see't. Did these bones cost no
more the breeding but to play at loggats[11] with 'em? Mine ache
80 to think on't.

1ST CLOWN: [*Sings*]

> A pick-axe and a spade, a spade,
> For and a shrouding sheet:
> O, a pit of clay for to be made
> For such a guest is meet.

(Throws up another)

85 HAMLET: There's another: why may not that be the skull of a lawyer?
Where be his quiddits[12] now, his quillets,[13] his cases, his tenures,
and his tricks? why does he suffer this rude knave now to knock
him about the sconce with a dirty shovel, and will not tell him of
his action of battery? Hum! This fellow might be in's time a great
90 buyer of land, with his statutes, his recognizances, his fines, his
double vouchers, his recoveries: is this the fine of his fines, and
the recovery of his recoveries, to have his fine pate full of fine

---

8 Throws.

9 Without a lower jaw.

10 Head.

11 A game in which small pieces of wood are hurled at a stake.

12 "Whatnesses"—that is, hair-splittings.

13 Quibbling distinctions.

dirt? will his vouchers vouch him no more of his purchases, and
double ones too, than the length and breadth of a pair of
95   indentures? The very conveyances of his lands will hardly lie in
this box; and must the inheritor himself have no more, ha?

HORATIO: Not a jot more, my lord.

HAMLET: Is not parchment made of sheep-skins?

HORATIO: Ay, my lord, and of calf-skins too.

100 HAMLET: They are sheep and calves which seek out assurance in
that. I will speak to this fellow.—Whose grave's this, sir?

1ST CLOWN: Mine, sir.—[*Sings*]
                O, a pit of clay for to be made
                For such a guest is meet.

105 HAMLET: I think it be thine indeed; for thou liest in't.

1ST CLOWN: You lie out on't, sir, and therefore it is not yours: for my
part, I do not lie in't, and yet it is mine.

HAMLET: Thou dost lie in't, to be in't, and say it is thine: 'tis for the
dead, not for the quick; therefore thou liest.

110 1ST CLOWN: 'Tis a quick lie, sir: 'twill away again from me to you.

HAMLET: What man dost thou dig it for?

1ST CLOWN: For no man, sir.

HAMLET: What woman, then?

1ST CLOWN: For none, neither.

115 HAMLET: Who is to be buried in't?

1ST CLOWN: One that was a woman, sir; but, rest her soul, she's
dead.

HAMLET: How absolute the knave is! we must speak by the card, or
equivocation will undo us. By the Lord, Horatio, these three
years I have taken note of it; the age is grown so picked[14] that the
120 toe of the peasant comes so near the heel of the courtier, he galls
his kibe.[15]—How long hast thou been a grave-maker?

1ST CLOWN: Of all the days i' the year, I came to't that day that our
last King Hamlet o'ercame Fortinbras.

HAMLET: How long is that since?

125 1ST CLOWN: Cannot you tell that? every fool can tell that: it was the
very day that young Hamlet was born,—he that is mad, and sent
into England.

---

[14] Refined or educated.

[15] Rubs and irritates the chilblain sore on the courtier's heel.

HAMLET: Ay, marry, why was he sent into England?

1ST CLOWN: Why, because he was mad: he shall recover his wits
130   there; or, if he do not, it's no great matter there.

HAMLET: Why?

1ST CLOWN: 'Twill not be seen in him there; there the men are as
      mad as he.

HAMLET: How came he mad?

135 1ST CLOWN: Very strangely, they say.

HAMLET: How strangely?

1ST CLOWN: Faith, e'en with losing his wits.

HAMLET: Upon what ground?

1ST CLOWN: Why, here in Denmark: I have been sexton here, man
140   and boy, thirty years.

HAMLET: How long will a man lie i' the earth ere he rot?

1ST CLOWN: Faith, if he be not rotten before he die,—as we have
      many pocky corses now-a-days, that will scarce hold the laying
      in,—he will last you some eight year or nine year: a tanner will
145   last you nine year.

HAMLET: Why he more than another?

1ST CLOWN: Why, sir, his hide is so tanned with his trade that he
      will keep out water a great while; and your water is a sore decayer
      of your whoreson dead body. Here's a skull now; this skull has
150   lain in the earth three-and-twenty years.

HAMLET: Whose was it?

1ST CLOWN: A whoreson mad fellow's it was: whose do you think
      it was?

HAMLET: Nay, I know not.

155 1ST CLOWN: A pestilence on him for a mad rogue! 'a poured a flagon
      of Rhenish on my head once. This same skull, sir, was Yorick's
      skull, the king's jester.

HAMLET: This?

1ST CLOWN: E'en that.

160 HAMLET: Let me see. [*Takes the skull*]—Alas, poor Yorick!—I knew
      him, Horatio; a fellow of infinite jest, of most excellent fancy: he
      hath borne me on his back a thousand times; and now, how
      abhorred in my imagination it is! my gorge rises at it. Here hung
      those lips that I have kissed I know not how oft. Where be your
165   gibes now? your gambols? your songs? your flashes of merriment,
      that were wont to set the table on a roar? Not one now, to mock
      your own grinning? quite chap-fallen? Now get you to my lady's

chamber, and tell her, let her paint an inch thick, to this favor [16]
she must come; make her laugh at that.—Pr'ythee, Horatio, tell

170 me one thing.

HORATIO: What's that, my lord?

HAMLET: Dost thou think Alexander looked o' this fashion i' the
earth?

HORATIO: E'en so.

HAMLET: And smelt so? pah! [*Throws down the skull*]

175 HORATIO: E'en so, my lord.

HAMLET: To what base uses we may return, Horatio! Why may not
imagination trace the noble dust of Alexander till he find it
stopping a bung-hole?

HORATIO: 'Twere to consider too curiously to consider so.

180 HAMLET: No, faith, not a jot; but to follow him thither with
modesty enough, and likelihood to lead it: as thus; Alexander
died, Alexander was buried, Alexander returneth into dust; the
dust is earth; of earth we make loam; and why of that loam
whereto he was converted might they not stop a beer-barrel?

185   Imperious Caesar, dead and turn'd to clay,
      Might stop a hole to keep the wind away:
      O, that that earth which kept the world in awe
        Should patch a wall to expel the winter's flaw!—
But soft! but soft! aside.—Here comes the king.

(Enter Priests, &c., in procession; the corpse of Ophelia, Laertes
and Mourners following; King, Queen, their Trains, &c.)

190 The queen, the courtiers: who is that they follow?
And with such maimed rites? This doth betoken
The corse they follow did with desperate hand
Fordo its own life: 'twas of some estate.
Couch we awhile and mark. [*Retiring with Horatio*]

195 LAERTES: What ceremony else?

HAMLET: That is Laertes,
A very noble youth: mark.

LAERTES: What ceremony else?

1ST PRIEST: Her obsequies have been as far enlarg'd
As we have warrantise: her death was doubtful,

---

[16] Face.

200 And, but that great command o'ersways the order,
 She should in ground unsanctified have lodg'd
 Till the last trumpet; for charitable prayers,
 Shards, flints, and pebbles, should be thrown on her,
 Yet here she is allowed her virgin rites,
205 Her maiden strewments, and the bringing home
 Of bell and burial.

LAERTES: Must there no more be done?

1ST PRIEST: No more be done:
 We should profane the service of the dead
 To sing a *requiem,* and such rest to her
210 As to peace-parted souls.

LAERTES: Lay her i' the earth;—
 And from her fair and unpolluted flesh
 May violets spring!—I tell thee, churlish priest,
 A ministering angel shall my sister be
 When thou liest howling.

HAMLET: What, the fair Ophelia!

215 QUEEN: Sweets to the sweet: farewell! [*Scattering flowers*]
 I hop'd thou shouldst have been my Hamlet's wife;
 I thought thy bride-bed to have deck'd, sweet maid,
 And not have strew'd thy grave.

LAERTES: O, treble woe
 Fall ten times treble on that cursed head
220 Whose wicked deed thy most ingenious sense
 Depriv'd thee of!—Hold off the earth awhile,
 Till I have caught her once more in mine arms:

(Leaps into the grave)

 Now pile your dust upon the quick and dead,
 Till of this flat a mountain you have made,
225 To o'er-top old Pelion [17] or the skyish head
 Of blue Olympus.

HAMLET: [*Advancing*] What is he whose grief
 Bears such an emphasis? whose phrase of sorrow
 Conjures the wandering stars, and makes them stand
230 Like wonder-wounded hearers? this is I, Hamlet the

---

[17] A mountain in Greece.

Dane. [*Leaps into the grave*]

LAERTES: The devil take thy soul! [*Grappling with him*]

HAMLET: Thou pray'st not well.

I pr'ythee, take thy fingers from my throat;
235   For, though I am not splenetive and rash,
Yet have I in me something dangerous,
Which let thy wiseness fear: away thy hand.

KING: Pluck them asunder.

QUEEN: Hamlet! Hamlet!

ALL: Gentlemen,—

HORATIO: Good my lord, be quiet.

(The Attendants part them, and they come out of the grave.)

240 HAMLET: Why, I will fight with him upon this theme
Until my eyelids will no longer wag.

QUEEN: O my son, what theme?

HAMLET: I lov'd Ophelia; forty thousand brothers
Could not, with all their quantity of love,
245   Make up my sum.—What wilt thou do for her?

KING: O, he is mad, Laertes.

QUEEN: For love of God, forbear him.

HAMLET: 'Swounds, show me what thou'lt do:
Woul't weep? woul't fight? woul't fast? woul't tear thyself?
250   Woul't drink up eisel?[18] eat a crocodile?
I'll do't.—Dost thou come here to whine?
To outface me with leaping in her grave?
Be buried quick[19] with her, and so will I:
And, if thou prate of mountains, let them throw
255   Millions of acres on us, till our ground,
Singeing his pate against the burning zone,[20]
Make Ossa[21] like a wart! Nay, an thou'lt mouth,
I'll rant as well as thou.

QUEEN: This is mere madness:

---

[18] Vinegar.

[19] Alive.

[20] The fiery zone of the celestial sphere.

[21] A high mountain in Greece.

And thus awhile the fit will work on him;
260　Anon, as patient as the female dove,
When that her golden couplets are disclos'd,[22]
His silence will sit drooping.
HAMLET:　　　　　　　　　　Hear you, sir;
What is the reason that you use me thus?
I lov'd you ever: but it is no matter;
265　Let Hercules himself do what he may,
The cat will mew, and dog will have his day. [*Exit.*]
KING:　I pray thee, good Horatio, wait upon him.—

(Exit Horatio.)

[*To Laertes*] Strengthen your patience in our last night's speech;
We'll put the matter to the present push.—
270　Good Gertrude, set some watch over your son.—
This grave shall have a living monument:
An hour of quiet shortly shall we see;
Till then, in patience our proceeding be.

(Exeunt.)

SCENE II

A hall in the castle.

(Enter Hamlet and Horatio.)

HAMLET:　So much for this, sir: now let me see the other;
You do remember all the circumstance?
HORATIO:　Remember it, my lord!
HAMLET:　Sir, in my heart there was a kind of fighting
5　That would not let me sleep: methought I lay
Worse than the mutines in the bilboes.[1] Rashly,
And prais'd be rashness for it,—let us know,
Our indiscretion sometimes serves us well,
When our deep plots do fail: and that should teach us

22　When the golden twins are hatched.

1　Mutineers in the iron stocks on board ship.

10   There's a divinity that shapes our ends,
        Rough-hew them how we will.
HORATIO: This is most certain.
HAMLET: Up from my cabin,
        My sea-gown scarf'd about me, in the dark
        Grop'd I to find out them: had my desire;
15   Finger'd their packet; and, in fine, withdrew
        To mine own room again: making so bold,
        My fears forgetting manners, to unseal
        Their grand commission; where I found, Horatio,
        O royal knavery! an exact command,—
20   Larded with many several sorts of reasons,
        Importing Denmark's health and England's too,
        With, ho! such bugs[2] and goblins in my life,—
        That, on the supervise, no leisure bated,
        No, not to stay the grinding of the axe,
25   My head should be struck off.
HORATIO: Is't possible?
HAMLET: Here's the commission: read it at more leisure.
        But wilt thou hear me how I did proceed?
HORATIO: I beseech you.
HAMLET: Being thus benetted round with villainies,—
30   Ere I could make a prologue to my brains,
        They had begun the play,—I sat me down;
        Devis'd a new commission; wrote it fair:
        I once did hold it, as our statists do,
        A baseness to write fair, and labor'd much
35   How to forget that learning; but, sir, now
        It did me yeoman's service. Wilt thou know
        The effect of what I wrote?
HORATIO: Ay, good my lord.
HAMLET: An earnest conjuration from the king,—
        As England was his faithful tributary;
40   As love between them like the palm might flourish;
        As peace should still her wheaten garland wear
        And stand a comma[3] 'tween their amities;

---

[2] Bugbears.

[3] Link.

And many such like as's of great charge,—
That, on the view and know of these contents,
45   Without debatement further, more or less,
He should the bearers put to sudden death,
Not shriving-time allow'd.

HORATIO: How was this seal'd?

HAMLET: Why, even in that was heaven ordinant.
I had my father's signet in my purse,
50   Which was the model of that Danish seal:
Folded the writ up in form of the other;
Subscrib'd it; gav't the impression; plac'd it safely,
The changeling never known. Now, the next day
Was our sea-fight; and what to this was sequent
55   Thou know'st already.

HORATIO: So Guildenstern and Rosencrantz go to't.

HAMLET: Why, man, they did make love to this employment;
They are not near my conscience; their defeat
Does by their own insinuation[4] grow:
60   'Tis dangerous when the baser nature[5] comes
Between the pass and fell[6] incensed points
Of mighty opposites.

HORATIO: Why, what a king is this!

HAMLET: Does it not, think'st thee, stand me now upon,[7]
He that hath kill'd my king and whor'd my mother;
65   Popp'd in between the election and my hopes;
Thrown out his angle for my proper life,
And with such cozenage,[8]—is't not perfect conscience
To quit him with this arm? and is't not to be damn'd,
To let this canker of our nature come
70   In further evil?

HORATIO: It must be shortly known to him from England
What is the issue of the business there.

---

4 By their own "sticking their noses" into the business.

5 Men of lower rank.

6 Fierce.

7 That is, "Don't you think it is my duty?"

8 Deceit.

HAMLET: It will be short: the interim is mine;
And a man's life's no more than to say One.
75 But I am very sorry, good Horatio,
That to Laertes I forgot myself;
For by the image of my cause I see
The portraiture of his: I'll court his favors:
But, sure, the bravery[9] of his grief did put me
Into a towering passion.
80 HORATIO: Peace; who comes here?

(Enter Osric.)

OSRIC: Your lordship is right welcome back to Denmark.
HAMLET: I humbly thank you, sir.—Dost know this water-fly?
HORATIO: No, my good lord.
HAMLET: Thy state is the more gracious; for 'tis a vice to know him.
85 He hath much land, and fertile: let a beast be lord of beasts, and
his crib shall stand at the king's mess: 'tis a chough;[10] but, as I say,
spacious in the possession of dirt.
OSRIC: Sweet lord, if your lordship were at leisure, I should impart a
thing to you from his majesty.
90 HAMLET: I will receive it with all diligence of spirit. Put your bonnet
to his right use; 'tis for the head.
OSRIC: I thank your lordship, 'tis very hot.
HAMLET: No, believe me, 'tis very cold; the wind is northerly.
OSRIC: It is indifferent cold, my lord, indeed.
95 HAMLET: Methinks it is very sultry and hot for my complexion.
OSRIC: Exceedingly, my lord; it is very sultry,—as't were,—I cannot
tell how.—But, my lord, his majesty bade me signify to you that
he has laid a great wager on your head. Sir, this is the matter,—
HAMLET: I beseech you, remember,—

(Hamlet moves him to put on his hat.)

100 OSRIC: Nay, in good faith; for mine ease, in good faith. Sir, here is
newly come to court Laertes; believe me, an absolute gentleman,
full of most excellent differences, of very soft society and great
showing: indeed, to speak feelingly of him, he is the card or

---

[9] Ostentation.

[10] He shall have his trough at the king's table: he is a chattering fool.

calendar of gentry, for you shall find in him the continent of what
105   part a gentleman would see.

Hamlet: Sir, his definement suffers no perdition in you;—though, I
know, to divide him inventorially would dizzy the arithmetic of
memory, and yet but yaw neither, in respect of his quick sail. But,
in the verity of extolment, I take him to be a soul of great article;
110   and his infusion of such dearth[11] and rareness as, to make true
diction of him, his semblable is his mirror; and who else would
trace him, his umbrage,[12] nothing more.

Osric: Your lordship speaks most infallibly of him.

Hamlet: The concernancy, sir? why do we wrap the gentleman in
115   our more rawer breath?

Osric: Sir?

Horatio: Is't not possible to understand in another tongue? You
will do't sir, really.

Hamlet: What imports the nomination[13] of this gentleman?
120 Osric: Of Laertes?

Horatio: His purse is empty already; all's golden words are spent.

Hamlet: Of him, sir.

Osric: I know, you are not ignorant,—

Hamlet: I would you did, sir; yet, in faith, if you did, it would not
125   much approve me.[14]—Well, sir.

Osric: You are not ignorant of what excellence Laertes is,—

Hamlet: I dare not confess that, lest I should compare with him in
excellence; but to know a man well were to know himself.

Osric: I mean, sir, for his weapon; but in the imputation laid on
130   him by them, in his meed he's unfellowed.[15]

Hamlet: What's his weapon?

Osric: Rapier and dagger.

Hamlet: That's two of his weapons: but, well.

Osric: The king, sir, hath wagered with him six Barbary horses:
135   against the which he has imponed,[16] as I take it, six French

---

[11] Rareness, or excellence.

[12] Shadow.

[13] Naming.

[14] If you, who are a fool, thought me not ignorant, that would not be particularly to my credit.

[15] In his worth he has no equal.

[16] Staked.

rapiers and poniards, with their assigns, as girdle, hangers, and so: three of the carriages, in faith, are very dear to fancy, very responsive to the hilts, most delicate carriages, and of very liberal conceit.

HAMLET: What call you the carriages?

140 HORATIO: I knew you must be edified by the margent ere you had done.[17]

OSRIC: The carriages, sir, are the hangers.

HAMLET: The phrase would be more german to the matter if we could carry cannon by our sides: I would it might be hangers till

145 then. But, on: six Barbary horses against six French swords, their assigns, and three liberal conceited carriages; that's the French bet against the Danish: why is this imponed, as you call it?

OSRIC: The king, sir, hath laid, that in a dozen passes between you and him he shall not exceed you three hits: he hath laid on twelve

150 for nine; and it would come to immediate trial if your lordship would vouchsafe the answer.

HAMLET: How if I answer no?

OSRIC: I mean, my lord, the opposition of your person in trial.[18]

HAMLET: Sir, I will walk here in the hall: if it please his majesty, it is

155 the breathing time of day with me: let the foils be brought, the gentleman willing, and the king hold his purpose, I will win for him if I can; if not, I will gain nothing but my shame and the odd hits.

OSRIC: Shall I re-deliver you[19] e'en so?

HAMLET: To this effect, sir; after what flourish your nature will.

160 OSRIC: I commend my duty to your lordship.

HAMLET: Yours, yours.

(Exit Osric.)

He does well to commend it himself; there are no tongues else for's turn.

HORATIO: This lapwing runs away with the shell on his head.[20]

---

17 Informed by a note in the margin of your instructions.

18 That is, the presence of your person as Laertes' opponent in the fencing contest.

19 Carry back your answer.

20 This precocious fellow is like a lapwing that starts running when it is barely out of the shell.

165 HAMLET: He did comply with his dug before he sucked it.[21] Thus
has he,—and many more of the same bevy, that I know the
drossy age dotes on,—only got the tune of the time, and outward
habit of encounter; a kind of yesty collection,[22] which carries
them through and through the most fanned and winnowed
opinions; and do but
170 blow them to their trial, the bubbles are out.

(Enter a Lord.)

LORD: My lord, his majesty commended him to you by young Osric,
who brings back to him that you attend him in the hall: he sends
to know if your pleasure hold to play with Laertes, or that you
will take longer time.
175 HAMLET: I am constant to my purposes; they follow the king's
pleasure: if his fitness speaks, mine is ready; now or whensoever,
provided I be so able as now.
LORD: The king and queen and all are coming down.
HAMLET: In happy time.
180 LORD: The queen desires you to use some gentle entertainment to
Laertes before you fall to play.
HAMLET: She well instructs me.

(Exit Lord.)

HORATIO: You will lose this wager, my lord.
HAMLET: I do not think so; since he went into France I have been in
185 continual practice: I shall win at the odds. But thou wouldst not
think how ill all's here about my heart: but it is no matter.
HORATIO: Nay, good my lord,—
HAMLET: It is but foolery; but it is such a kind of gain-giving[23] as
would perhaps trouble a woman.
190 HORATIO: If your mind dislike anything, obey it: I will forestall their
repair hither, and say you are not fit.
HAMLET: Not a whit, we defy augury: there's a special providence in
the fall of a sparrow. If it be now, 'tis not to come; if it be not to

---

[21] He paid compliments to his mother's breast before he sucked it.

[22] Yeasty or frothy affair.

[23] Misgiving.

195 come, it will be now; if it be not now, yet it will come: the
readiness is all. Since no man has aught of what he leaves, what
is't to leave betimes?[24]

(Enter King, Queen, Laertes, Lords, Osric, and Attendants with foils, &c.)

KING: Come, Hamlet, come, and take this hand from me.

(The King puts Laertes' hand into Hamlet's.)

HAMLET: Give me your pardon, sir: I have done you wrong:
But pardon't, as you are a gentleman.
200 This presence knows, and you must needs have heard,
How I am punish'd with sore distraction.
What I have done,
That might your nature, honor, and exception
Roughly awake, I here proclaim was madness.
205 Was't Hamlet wrong'd Laertes? Never Hamlet:
If Hamlet from himself be ta'en away,
And when he's not himself does wrong Laertes,
Then Hamlet does it not, Hamlet denies it.
Who does it, then? His madness: if't be so,
210 Hamlet is of the faction that is wrong'd;
His madness is poor Hamlet's enemy.
Sir, in this audience,
Let my disclaiming from a purpos'd evil
Free me so far in your most generous thoughts
215 That I have shot mine arrow o'er the house
And hurt my brother.
LAERTES: I am satisfied in nature,
Whose motive, in this case, should stir me most
To my revenge: but in my terms of honor
I stand aloof; and will no reconcilement
220 Till by some elder masters of known honor
I have a voice and precedent of peace
To keep my name ungor'd. But till that time
I do receive your offer'd love like love,
And will not wrong it.
HAMLET: I embrace it freely;

---

24 What does an early death matter?

225   And will this brother's wager frankly play.[25]—
        Give us the foils; come on.
  LAERTES: Come, one for me.
  HAMLET: I'll be your foil, Laertes; in mine ignorance
        Your skill shall, like a star in the darkest night,
        Stick fiery off indeed.
  LAERTES: You mock me, sir.
230 HAMLET: No, by this hand.
  KING: Give them the foils, young Osric.
        Cousin Hamlet,
        You know the wager?
  HAMLET: Very well, my lord;
        Your grace hath laid the odds o' the weaker side.
235 KING: I do not fear it; I have seen you both;
        But since he's better'd, we have therefore odds.
  LAERTES: This is too heavy, let me see another.
  HAMLET: This likes we well. These foils have all a length?

                    (They prepare to play.)

  OSRIC: Ay, my good lord.
240 KING: Set me the stoups of wine upon that table,—
        If Hamlet give the first or second hit,
        Or quit in answer of the third exchange,
        Let all the battlements their ordnance fire;
        The king shall drink to Hamlet's better breath;
245   And in the cup an union[26] shall he throw,
        Richer than that which four successive kings
        In Denmark's crown have worn. Give me the cups;
        And let the kettle[27] to the trumpet speak,
        The trumpet to the cannoneer without,
250   The cannons to the heavens, the heavens to earth,
        Now the king drinks to Hamlet.—Come, begin;—
        And you, the judges, bear a wary eye.
  HAMLET: Come on, sir.

---

[25] Fence with a heart free from resentment.

[26] A pearl.

[27] Kettledrum.

LAERTES: Come, my lord.

(They play.)

HAMLET: One.

LAERTES: No.

HAMLET: Judgment.

OSRIC: A hit, a very palpable hit.

LAERTES: Well;—again.

255   KING: Stay, give me a drink.—Hamlet, this pearl is thine;
Here's to thy health.—

(Trumpets sound, and cannon shot off within.)

Give him the cup.

HAMLET: I'll play this bout first; set it by awhile.—
Come.—Another hit; what say you?

(They play.)

260   LAERTES: A touch, a touch, I do confess.

KING: Our son shall win.

QUEEN: He's fat, and scant of breath.—
Here, Hamlet, take my napkin, rub thy brows:
The queen carouses to thy fortune, Hamlet.

HAMLET: Good madam!

KING: Gertrude, do not drink.

265   QUEEN: I will, my lord; I pray you, pardon me.

KING: [*Aside*] It is the poison'd cup; it is too late.

HAMLET: I dare not drink yet, madam; by and by.

QUEEN: Come, let me wipe thy face.

LAERTES: My lord, I'll hit him now.

KING: I do not think't.

270   LAERTES: [*Aside*] And yet 'tis almost 'gainst my conscience.

HAMLET: Come, for the third, Laertes: you but dally;
I pray you, pass with your best violence:
I am afeard you make a wanton of me.

LAERTES: Say you so? come on.

(They play.)

275   OSRIC: Nothing, neither way.

LAERTES: Have at you now!

(Laertes wounds Hamlet; then, in scuffling, they change rapiers, and Hamlet wounds Laertes.)

KING: Part them; they are incens'd.
HAMLET: Nay, come, again.

(The Queen falls.)

OSRIC: Look to the queen there, ho!
HORATIO: They bleed on both sides.—How is it, my lord?
OSRIC: How is't, Laertes?
280 LAERTES: Why, as a woodcock to my own springe, Osric;
      I am justly kill'd with mine own treachery.
HAMLET: How does the queen?
KING: She swoons to see them bleed.
QUEEN: No, no, the drink, the drink,— O my dear Hamlet,—
      The drink, the drink!—I am poison'd. [*Dies.*]
285 HAMLET: O villainy!—Ho! let the door be lock'd:
      Treachery! seek it out.

(Laertes falls.)

LAERTES: It is here, Hamlet: Hamlet, thou art slain;
      No medicine in the world can do thee good;
      In thee there is not half an hour of life;
290   The treacherous instrument is in thy hand,
      Unbated and envenom'd: the foul practice
      Hath turn'd itself on me; lo, here I lie,
      Never to rise again: thy mother's poison'd:
      I can no more:—the king, the king's to blame.
295 HAMLET: The point envenom'd too!—
      Then venom to thy work. [*Stabs the King.*]
OSRIC and LORDS: Treason! treason!
KING: O, yet defend me, friends; I am but hurt.
HAMLET: Here, thou incestuous, murderous, damned Dane,
300   Drink off this potion.—Is thy union here?
      Follow my mother.

(King dies.)

LAERTES: He is justly serv'd;
      It is a poison temper'd by himself.—
      Exchange forgiveness with me, noble Hamlet:

305　　Mine and my father's death come not upon thee,
　　　　Nor thine on me! [*Dies.*]
　　HAMLET:　Heaven make thee free of it! I follow thee.—
　　　　I am dead, Horatio.—Wretched queen, adieu!—
　　　　You that look pale and tremble at this chance,
310　　That art but mutes or audience to this act,
　　　　Had I but time,—as this fell sergeant, death,
　　　　Is strict in his arrest,—O, I could tell you,—
　　　　But let it be.—Horatio, I am dead;
　　　　Thou liv'st; report me and my cause aright
315　　To the unsatisfied.[28]
　　HORATIO:　Never believe it:
　　　　I am more an antique Roman than a Dane,—
　　　　Here's yet some liquor left.
　　HAMLET:　　　　　　　　As thou'rt a man,
　　　　Give me the cup; let go; by heaven, I'll have't.—
　　　　O good Horatio, what a wounded name,
320　　Things standing thus unknown, shall live behind me!
　　　　If thou didst ever hold me in thy heart,
　　　　Absent thee from felicity awhile,
　　　　And in this harsh world draw thy breath in pain,
　　　　To tell my story.—

　　　　　　(March afar off, and shot within.)

　　　　　　　　What warlike noise is this?
325　OSRIC:　Young Fortinbras, with conquest come from Poland,
　　　　To the ambassadors of England gives
　　　　This warlike volley.
　　HAMLET:　　　　　　　O, I die, Horatio;
　　　　The potent poison quite o'er-crows my spirit:
　　　　I cannot live to hear the news from England;
330　　But I do prophesy the election lights
　　　　On Fortinbras: he has my dying voice;
　　　　So tell him, with the occurrents, more and less,
　　　　Which have solicited.[29]—The rest is silence. [*Dies.*]
　　HORATIO:　Now cracks a noble heart.—Good-night, sweet prince,

---

[28]　The uninformed.

[29]　So tell him, together with the events, more or less, that have brought on this tragic affair.

335 And flights of angels sing thee to thy rest!
    Why does the drum come hither?

(March within. Enter Fortinbras, the English Ambassadors, and others.)

FORTINBRAS: Where is this sight?
HORATIO: What is it you would see?
    If aught of woe or wonder, cease your search.
FORTINBRAS: This quarry cries on havoc.[30]— O proud death,
340 What feast is toward in thine eternal cell,
    That thou so many princes at a shot
    So bloodily hast struck?
1ST AMBASSADOR: The sight is dismal;
    And our affairs from England come too late:
    The ears are senseless that should give us hearing,
345 To tell him his commandment is fulfill'd,
    That Rosencrantz and Guildenstern are dead:
    Where should we have our thanks?
HORATIO: Not from his mouth,
    Had it the ability of life to thank you:
    He never gave commandment for their death.
350 But since, so jump[31] upon this bloody question,
    You from the Polack wars, and you from England,
    Are here arriv'd, give order that these bodies
    High on a stage be placed to the view;
    And let me speak to the yet unknowing world
355 How these things came about: so shall you hear
    Of carnal, bloody, and unnatural acts;
    Of accidental judgments, casual slaughters;
    Of deaths put on by cunning and forc'd cause;
    And, in this upshot, purposes mistook
360 Fall'n on the inventors' heads: all this can I
    Truly deliver.
FORTINBRAS: Let us haste to hear it,
    And call the noblest to the audience.
    For me, with sorrow I embrace my fortune:

---

30 This collection of dead bodies cries out havoc.

31 Opportunely.

I have some rights of memory in this kingdom,[32]
365 Which now to claim my vantage doth invite me.
HORATIO: Of that I shall have also cause to speak,
And from his mouth whose voice will draw on more:
But let this same be presently perform'd,
Even while men's minds are wild: lest more mischance
370 On plots and errors happen.
FORTINBRAS: Let four captains
Bear Hamlet like a soldier to the stage;
For he was likely, had he been put on,[33]
To have prov'd most royally: and, for his passage,
The soldier's music and the rites of war
375 Speak loudly for him.—
Take up the bodies.—Such a sight as this
Becomes the field, but here shows much amiss.
Go, bid the soldiers shoot.

(A dead march)

(Exeunt, bearing off the dead bodies: after which a peal of ordnance is shot off.)

---

32 I have some unforgotten rights to this kingdom.

33 Tested by succession to the throne.

Discussion Questions

1. **The marriage of Gertrude and Claudius:** How is Hamlet affected by their marriage, which follows so closely on the death of his father? (Remember that in Hamlet's day such a marriage was considered incest.) Why does Claudius use his opening speech (1.2) to defend his actions? Is his "defense" necessary? Must a king explain his actions? At this point in the play, is the audience expected to accept Claudius's explanation? Is the audience expected to change its opinion later, after Hamlet meets with the Ghost?

2. **Hamlet's relationship with his parents—*before* the play begins:** What insights are provided in the play? What conclusions can be drawn? Consider his relationship with his parents *during* the play. What changes occur? What causes these changes? Does your attitude toward old Hamlet or Gertrude change as you learn more? If so, account for these changes.

3. **The Ghost:** Why does Shakespeare have the Ghost appear to others before he appears to Hamlet? What startling information does the Ghost reveal about his death? Could the Ghost be lying? What response does the Ghost expect from his son? More important, with regard to Gertrude, what restraint does the Ghost demand?

4. **Hamlet's delay in avenging his father's murder:** What factors hinder his taking prompt action? Is his delay justified? Could Hamlet have killed Claudius and gotten away with it? Does he have enough evidence to proceed? What does his restraint indicate about his integrity and mental control? Had Hamlet acted on impulse following the Ghost's revelation, would your opinion about him be different?

5. **Gertrude:** Was she in any way involved in the murder of King Hamlet? Is she aware of Claudius's guilt? (Be careful to base your responses on Shakespeare's play rather than on film versions or on what others have to say about the play.)

6. **Polonius:** Does Shakespeare intend for us to respect him? Why does Claudius retain him as a counselor? What is your reaction to Polonius in his role as Ophelia's protective father? How do you respond to his advice to Laertes? Explain why Claudius is alarmed after Hamlet kills Polonius. Is his alarm justified?

7. **Hamlet and Ophelia's relationship:** Do you believe their relationship *during* the play is different from the one they shared *before* the play? Is Hamlet's mistreatment of Ophelia justified? Is the deterioration of

Ophelia's state of mind credible as a reaction to Hamlet's behavior? Does she deserve better treatment? Are Laertes's cautions accurate? How do you react to Ophelia's being manipulated by Polonius and Claudius as they seek insights into Hamlet's behavior?

8. **Rosencrantz and Guildenstern:** Claudius has instructed Hamlet's "friends" to deliver Hamlet to his death. How do you react to their accepting the task and attempting to carry it out? Was Hamlet wrong to replace the letters and have Rosencrantz and Guildenstern killed? Is he any less culpable than is Claudius, whose plan failed?

9. **Hamlet's "madness":** Is Hamlet insane? Identify specific behavior which would justify your conclusion. How much of Hamlet's insanity is real? How much is feigned? Could one contend that Hamlet is overcome by emotion and therefore suffers from temporary insanity brought on by his having to cope with the circumstances related his father's death?

10. **The final scene:** Hamlet gains revenge, but he suffers a fatal wound in doing so. With the death of Prince Hamlet, then, is Claudius's treachery in murdering King Hamlet truly avenged? Must Gertrude die as well? Without incriminating himself, could Claudius have prevented Gertrude's drinking from the cup? Could Shakespeare have permitted Hamlet to survive? Who would have believed his story had he survived?

Research Topics

1. In "Reforming the Role," critic Mark Rose examines the double plot in *Hamlet,* noting that each member of Polonius's family "serves as a foil to some aspect of Hamlet's extraordinary cunning and discipline."[1] Investigate the roles played by Polonius, Ophelia, and Laertes. Agree or disagree with Rose's assertion.

2. As in *Macbeth,* the supernatural plays an important role in driving the action in *Hamlet. Macbeth* opens with a scene given entirely to the three Witches; *Hamlet* begins in similar fashion with the scene depending upon the appearance of the Ghost. Consider Shakespeare's use of supernatural elements in these two plays. What insights does the recurrence of these elements reveal about Shakespeare's stagecraft and his knowledge of his

---

[1] Rose's article is included on pages 182–94 of this Casebook.

audience? How might these scenes have been staged at the Globe Theatre?

3. In his Introduction to the Arden edition of *Hamlet*, Harold Jenkins provides interesting insights about the model for the *Murder of Gonzago*—Shakespeare's "play-within-the-play."[2] In October 1538, the Duke of Urbino, Francesco Maria I, was poisoned by a barber-surgeon who placed a lotion in his ears at the instigation of Luigi Gonzaga, a kinsman of the Duchess. "The combination of his name with the unusual method of killing," Jenkins contends, "leaves no doubt that we have here the prototype of the murder in *Hamlet*." Take this lead from Jenkins and investigate the circumstances surrounding the murder of the duke, whose portrait by Titian hangs in the Uffizi Gallery in Florence.

4. Hamlet and Laertes seek revenge, each in his own way. Hamlet carefully considers the action he undertakes—some contend to the point of delaying unnecessarily. Laertes, on the other hand, acts hastily and under the direction of Claudius. Analyze the course that each character pursues to achieve his goal. Closely study these situations and then create a defense for each method.

5. In his critical assessment of *Hamlet*, Samuel Johnson asserts that variety is the "particular excellence" that distinguishes it from Shakespeare's other plays, but Johnson also notes that Shakespeare is often criticized for having neglected "poetical justice"[3]—the ideal judgment that rewards virtue and punishes vice. The revenge that the Ghost demands is obtained at the price of his son's death. As a result, the "gratification" which should accompany the death of the usurping and murderous Claudius is diminished considerably. Provide your own analysis of this situation and respond by agreeing or disagreeing with the points raised by Johnson.

6. Many readers would likely agree with Samuel Johnson's opinion that Hamlet plays the part of the madman most convincingly in his rudeness to Ophelia—abuse which seems "useless and wanton cruelty."[4] With the assigned task of verifying that Hamlet occasionally displays symptoms of madness, examine the instances in which Hamlet mistreats Ophelia. (Note that Ophelia has unique opportunities for gaining insights into his

---

[2] Jenkins's insights are recorded at length on pages 145–55 of this Casebook.

[3] Johnson's comments about *Hamlet* are found in *Johnson on Shakespeare*, ed. Arthur Sherbo, vol. 8 (New Haven: Yale UP, 1968) 1010–1011.

[4] Johnson 1011.

character and offers a credible assessment: "O, what a noble mind is here o'erthrown!" [3.1.145]).

7. Can one help but feel sympathy for Ophelia? In a matter of hours, her relationship with Hamlet ends abruptly, her father is murdered by her former lover, and her brother (to whom she looks for guidance and support) leaves town. Such a series of events would challenge the resolve of even the most stouthearted, but Ophelia is especially vulnerable. Throughout the play, in fact, her weakness in character permits her to be manipulated by those whom she loves most—her father, her brother, and her lover. Examine the instances during which Polonius, Laertes, and Hamlet manipulate Ophelia to serve their own purposes, and then consider whether or not Ophelia's character furthers her suffering when the series of trying events occurs.

8. In "Man and Wife Is One Flesh,"[5] Janet Adelman claims that revenge is not the central issue in *Hamlet*. Instead, she contends that Hamlet's "fundamental task" is to save his mother. Examine the details of Adelman's position, especially those which relate to the "closet scene" (3.4). Her argument might weaken the conviction of those who are convinced this scene's chief purpose is to allow Hamlet to determine if Gertrude conspired with Claudius to murder Hamlet's father. Present your own detailed argument that Hamlet visits his mother so that she might be "purified" through her rejection of Claudius and all that he represents.

9. Shakespeare is often praised for his rich and colorful characters. Among the many outstanding characters in *Hamlet*, which do you consider most lifelike? Identify one of the characters whom you regard as surpassing the others in depth of development, and then compose a character analysis in which you express your opinion and elaborate on your reasons.

---

[5] A portion of Adelman's article is included on pages 194–99 of this Casebook.

Secondary Sources

The sources in this section have been selected for their general insights as well as their specific concerns regarding *Hamlet.* They may stimulate class discussions; they may help you generate ideas to be developed into an essay; or they may provide material to support a topic that you already have in mind. For further guidance in pursuing resources related to Shakespeare (his works in general and *Hamlet* in particular), consult the Bibliography that begins on page 245 of this Casebook. Remember to document any words or ideas that you borrow from these and any other sources. Consult the Appendix (pages 265–78) for an overview of Modern Language Association guidelines for documentation.

HAROLD JENKINS

SAXO

The first connected account of the hero whom later ages know as Hamlet is that of Saxo, called Grammaticus, in his *Historiae Danicae,* written at the end of the twelfth century and first published in 1514.[1]

Saxo tells how Amleth's father and uncle, Horwendil and Fengo,[2] ruled Jutland under Roric King of Denmark. The valiant deeds of Horwendil inspired the rivalry of the King of Norway,[3] whom he slew in single combat. He won the favour of Roric, whose daughter Gerutha became his wife and gave birth to their son Amleth. Fengo, jealous of his brother's success, killed him and, adding incest to murder, married Gerutha. The young Amleth, fearful for his own safety, took refuge in a pretence of imbecility, going about morose and covered in dirt. He took to shaping hooked sticks, their tips hardened in the fire, and said, when asked, that these were javelins to avenge his father. Such behavior aroused as much as quieted suspicion and led to attempts to trap him. In the belief that dissembling is defeated by concupiscence, a beautiful woman was appointed to waylay him; but he

---

* Note that many of these secondary sources do not use the parenthetical documentation style recommended by the Modern Language Association and explained in the Appendix (pages 265–78).

avoided this trap through the warnings of a foster-brother and the compliance of the woman, who had been a companion of his childhood. She agreed to deny that he had had her, so that when he told the truth it was taken as a sign of madness. But a skeptical friend of Fengo devised a second test whereby Amleth would be overheard in conversation with his mother, to whom he would speak without guile. The friend hid beneath the bedding in her chamber,[4] but Amleth in his mad antics (crowing, flapping his arms, and jumping up and down on the bedding) discovered him and killed him, cutting up his body and throwing it into a sewer, where it was devoured by pigs. He harangued his mother on her incestuous marriage with his father's murderer and, bringing her to repentance, confided in her the truth about his madness and his intention of revenge. His account of the eavesdropper's disappearance, again the truth disbelieved, seemed once more to confirm his madness while strengthening the suspicions of Fengo, who planned to do away with him. He despatched him to England with an escort of two retainers carrying a letter directing the King to put him to death; but Amleth changed the letter while his companions slept, substituting their deaths for his and requesting the King instead to give him his daughter in marriage; and all happened as he devised. Before leaving home Amleth had instructed his mother to put up woven hangings in the hall and in twelve months' time to celebrate his obsequies; and on the appointed day he returned in the middle of his funeral rites to the astonishment of the lords, whom he feasted till they were drunk. Then he brought down upon them the hangings which his mother had put up and secured them with the hooked sticks he had long before prepared. Next he set fire to the hall and proceeded to the chamber where Fengo was asleep. His own sword, because he kept wounding himself with it, had been nailed to his scabbard, and he now changed it for Fengo's, so that when his uncle awoke, to be told that vengeance was now come, it was he who was left with the sword that would not draw and was killed with his own weapon. Next day Amleth justified himself in an oration to the people, who acclaimed him as their king.

Amleth's further adventures do not concern Shakespeare. It is plausibly supposed that they may not always have concerned Amleth, and that two originally different heroes have here coalesced. Yet it contributes to our impression of Amleth that the continuation of his story repeats several of its motifs. He makes a second visit to England, where the King, to avenge Fengo's death, repeats Fengo's plan to have him killed by another ruler's hand. He is sent on an embassage to a fearsome Scottish queen, but by another substitution of letters while the bearer is asleep, death is once more changed to marriage and Amleth wins a second bride. By a characteristic trick, propping up yesterday's dead to look like today's army, he defeats the English king in battle and returns with his two wives to his own land. Roric is now dead and his successor regards Amleth as a usurper. In the ensuing war between them Amleth knows that his doom has come and dies a heroic death. His Scottish wife, notwithstanding a vow to be united with him in death, repeats the frailty of his mother and marries her husband's killer.

In this primitive and sometimes brutal story the essentials of Shakespeare's plot—fratricide, and incestuous marriage, feigned madness, and the ultimate achievement of a long-delayed revenge—are already present. And it is already the kind of potentially dramatic story in which "carnal, bloody, and unnatural acts" show "purposes mistook Fall'n on th'inventors' heads" (v.ii.386–390). The woman who waylays the hero, the man who spies on him in his mother's chamber, and the retainers who escort him to England to be killed already adumbrate the roles of Ophelia, Polonius, and Rosencrantz and Guildenstern. Less obviously the foster-brother, the one friend among foes, holds the germ of Horatio. Incidents in Shakespeare which have their origin in Saxo include the combat with King Fortinbras; and even in Shakespeare's very different catastrophe the hero gets back to Denmark in the middle of a funeral and achieves the crowning act of vengeance by way of an exchange of swords.

Likenesses do not stop at incidents. In Shakespeare's big set scene between Hamlet and his mother the very drift of the dialogue is anticipated in Saxo. With this passage from Elton's translation compare iii.iv.64–94:

> Most infamous of women! dost thou seek with such lying lamentations to hide thy most heavy guilt? Wantoning like a harlot, thou hast entered a wicked and abominable state of wedlock, embracing with incestuous bosom thy husband's slayer, and wheedling with filthy lures of blandishment him who had slain the father of thy son. This, forsooth, is the way that the mares couple with the vanquishers of their mates; for brute beasts are naturally incited to pair indiscriminately; and it would seem that thou, like them, hast clean forgot thy first husband.

Something of Saxo also remains in Hamlet's savage contempt for Polonius's corpse, as when he decides to "lug the guts" from the room (iii.iv.214) or expatiates on its being eaten (iv.iii.16–20). And other parts of the play reveal similar survivals: the filth that Amleth is smeared with in his pretended madness has left its traces on Hamlet's garb in the "foul'd" stockings (ii.i.79) which figure with the lover's more conventional dishabille; and Fengo's fear of his wife's displeasure becomes one of Claudius's reasons for not proceeding against Hamlet (iv.vii.9–16).

BELLEFOREST

All this is not to imply that Shakespeare ever read Saxo. Direct indebtedness is improbable, and arguments in favour of it appear to be without substance. What made the story available to the Elizabethans was its retelling in their own day by the Frenchman Belleforest as the third story of the fifth series of his popular *Histoires Tragiques*. Of the very complicated bibliography of the *Histoires Tragiques* it will be enough here to say that the seven volumes were published individually over the period 1559 to 1582, that each volume continued to be separately reprinted, and that the fifth, first appearing in 1570, had as many as eight editions before the end of the century.

Belleforest sticks fairly faithfully to the events of Saxo's story, the principal difference being that he tells it at twice the length. He drops some inconsequential incidents, notably those clever sayings of Amleth which belong to the oldest part of his legend and perhaps have lost their point, but more characteristically expands. He has little narrative invention but likes to make the most of the episodes he finds, sometimes with unfortunate results. For example, Saxo is able to say that Fengo slaughtered his brother and then gave out that he had done it to protect his brother's wife; but Belleforest makes the villain first fall upon his brother at a banquet and then pretend that he has killed him in the act of assaulting his wife. Elaborating the circumstance each time, he ends with a contradiction. Most of his elaboration, however, comes from his ubiquitous moralizing comment. Unlike Saxo, who, with an occasional terse observation on the ways of men, takes all in his stride, Belleforest is not always at ease with the story he is telling: he apologizes for what will seem barbarity to more polished and enlightened times; and although he can respond to the folk hero who comes out of degradation to triumph, Amleth's more fabulous achievements cause him some misgiving. Feats of clairvoyance at the English court elicit, instead of admiring wonder, an excursus on the dangers of divination and its association with the devil. The revenge itself gives less disquiet, though Belleforest is over-anxious to defend it as giving the wicked their true deserts. So Saxo's elemental story is now introduced by an "argument," decked out with classical and biblical parallels, as an instance of how murder is followed by God's vengeance; and Fengon's crimes are magnified by stressing not only fratricide and incest but tyranny and the oppression of his people. Amleth's address to the people after he has put his uncle to death places all its emphasis on the justice of his deed, which rights their wrongs as well as his. The primitive hero, whom Saxo praised for his combination of courage and cunning, now acquires an aura of chivalry in his pursuit of honour and glory. At his death Belleforest repeats Saxo's laments for one whose fortune was not equal to his gifts; but even so, remembering Amleth's two wives, he sees also the tragedy of a noble hero undone by his one weakness of susceptibility to women. Yet although the urge to improve every occasion leads the author into inconsistencies, what runs through Belleforest's narrative is the effort to view the tale of violence in a universal and edifying perspective; and one can hardly doubt that this was part of his appeal in the age of *A Mirror for Magistrates.* In fact Belleforest's prose comment did something to prepare for those high-flown philosophizing speeches which Nashe was to sneer at in the first dramatic *Hamlet.*

Belleforest himself did not neglect his opportunities for big set speeches. Those already existing in Saxo—Amleth's denunciation of his mother and his oration to the people—are done at much greater length; and the mother who only wails in Saxo has a long speech of her own to give still greater importance to the interview in her chamber. A passage from Belleforest, set against the one already cited from Saxo, will illustrate not only the characteristic difference between the two authors but how far this episode is developed in the narrative before it reaches the stage.

> What perfidy is this, O most infamous of all who have ever prostituted themselves to the will of an abominable whoremonger, that under the guise of a dissembling tear you should conceal the most wicked and detestable crime that man could ever imagine or commit? What trust can I have in you, who, like a lascivious wanton breaking out into every immodesty, run with outstretched arms after that villainous, treacherous tyrant who is the murderer of my father, and incestuously caress the robber of the lawful bed of your faithful spouse . . . ? Is it the part of a queen and daughter of a king to give way to the appetites of the brutes, and, like mares who couple with the vanquishers of their first mates, to submit to the will of the abominable king who has murdered a more valiant and virtuous man than himself and who, in massacring Horwendile, has extinguished the honour and glory of the Danes, who are of no account for strength, courage, or valour now that the lustre of knighthood has been brought to an end by the cruellest and most dastardly villain living upon earth? I will never acknowledge him my kinsman, and I cannot regard him as my uncle nor you as my beloved mother—the man who has shown no respect for the blood which ought to have united us more closely than any union with you, and the woman who could never, without dishonour and the suspicion of having consented to her husband's death, have agreed to a marriage with his cruel foe. Ah, Queen Geruth, it is the way of bitches to consort with several partners and to desire marriage and coupling

with various mates: it is nothing but licentiousness that has effaced from your mind the memory of the virtues and valiant achievements of the good king, your husband and my father . . .

(Cf. Gollancz, pp. 210–212.)

The comparison to beasts, taken directly from Saxo, is emphasized by repetition and the addition of bitches (*chiennes*) to mares. And Belleforest takes it still further, even at the cost of diminishing his hero, by making Amleth accuse his mother of leaving him to the mercy of a murderer when even the beasts—lions, tigers, ounces, leopards are enumerated—fight in defence of their young. It is Belleforest also who extends and heightens the antithesis between the brother-husbands which will be structural to Shakespeare's play. The charge, already in Saxo, that Amleth's mother has replaced the virtuous man by the bad man who has killed him is repeated no less than four times in the passage I have quoted. Moreover, this contrast between the two husbands is already made in Belleforest, as it is not in Saxo, from the moment the marriage takes place:

That wretched woman, who had had the honour to be the wife of one of the wisest and most valorous princes of the north, allowed herself to sink to such vileness as to break her faith to him; and what is worse, even to marry him who was the cruel murderer of her lawful husband.

(Cf. Gollancz, p. 188.)

Shakespeare of course likewise introduces the contrast from the start (even before the murder itself is known) with Hamlet's first soliloquy (I.ii.139–57; see also I.v.47–52).

Belleforest's persistent endeavour to heighten things contributes, along with a verbal copiousness, some new details to the story. The most sensational of these is the adultery of Amleth's mother. With nothing in Saxo to suggest this, Belleforest specifically says that before Fengon had murdered his brother he had incestuously seduced his brother's wife (*incestueusement soüillé la couche fraternelle, abusant de la femme . . .*), and again that he had already dishonoured her (*entretenoit execrablement*) during her husband's life. This is consistent with the aim of magnifying the villain's crimes, but the blackening of the wife undermines the excuses that Belleforest will presently give her in the interview with Amleth. Shakespeare omits the excuses, but takes over the extra dimension of her guilt[5] and accordingly of Hamlet's anguish.

Occasionally some circumstantial detail added by Belleforest gives the story a new direction, which may have far-reaching results. An instance occurs in his account of the combat with the Norwegian king. In Saxo there was simply a pact for the burial of the vanquished; but Belleforest adds that the loser should forfeit his ships' treasure. And once the idea of forfeiture takes root and—again with the help of Belleforest, who has the victor over-run the coast of Norway—is joined with the loss of lands, the way is open for Young Fortinbras and his enterprise to recover them. The episode of the woman employed to waylay Amleth supplies a more striking example. Saxo explains her co-operation with Amleth by the intimacy (*familiaritatem*) due to their common upbringing, but Belleforest, perhaps unwittingly going farther, says that she had loved him (*l'aymoit*) from childhood and adds that she would have been sorry not to enjoy the man whom she loved more than herself (*jouyr de celuy qu'elle aimoit plus que soymesme*). The lady's equivocal role as both temptress and lover is thus strengthened, and the first hint is given for that selfless devotion which is at the heart of Ophelia's tragedy. It is even possible that Belleforest helped to suggest the Ghost; for, as pointed out by Stabler, he twice refers to the shade (*ombre*) of the murdered man. When Amleth finally dispatches his uncle, he bids him report to his brother in the underworld that his son has avenged him, so that his shade may rest in peace (*son ombre s'appaise*). From a metaphorical shade to a visible speak-ing ghost is an immense imaginative leap and one for which Belleforest alone could provide no adequate springboard. But the errand to the under-world is of a kind to gratify the vengeful spirits of Seneca, whose vogue could facilitate the leap; and a tradition once established, a dramatist wish-ing to bring a ghost on to the stage might well find in Belleforest sugges-tions for its use. The Ghost in Shakespeare's *Hamlet*, unlike Belleforest's shade, is not mentioned at the end, but they have in common the need for vengeance from a son, who seeks to give the spirit rest (i.v.190); and it is es-pecially interesting that the other reference in Belleforest occurs just where in Shakespeare the Ghost makes a reappearance, during the son's interview with his mother. Amleth accuses her of failing to respect the manes of his father (*les ombres de Horwendille*), undeserving (*indigne*) of being treacher-ously murdered by his brother and shamefully betrayed by the wife he so well treated; and this of course is the burden of the Ghost's tale to Hamlet in an earlier scene in Shakespeare (i.v.42 ff.). Thus the functions of Shake-speare's Ghost—to tell of his murder and betrayal, to demand vengeance of his son, and to appear again in the Queen's chamber—whether or not they owe anything to Belleforest, may be said to be anticipated by him.

Verbal echoes of Belleforest in *Hamlet* are few; they could hardly be ex-pected to carry across the linguistic gap. Yet occasionally a word in Shake-speare, more often a turn of thought, may be traced back to a possible or probable origin in Belleforest. The interview between Amleth and his mother is again fruitful. He tells her not to be offended if he speaks to her severely; Shakespeare's Hamlet "Will speak daggers to her" (III.ii.387) and "must be cruel only to be kind" (III.iv.180). Geruthe laments how women's infidelities have bandaged their eyes (*bandé les yeux*); Hamlet accuses Gertrude of playing "hoodman-blind" (III.iv.77). Dissembling lamentations and incestuous embraces are already in Saxo, but Belleforest, with a dissembling tear (*un pleur dissimulé*) and the image of running with outstretched arms to incestuous caresses (*allez courant les bras tenduz . . . et caressez incestueusement le vouleur du lict legitime de vostre loyal espoux*), moves closer to the "unrighteous tears" and the speedy posting "to incestuous sheets" in Hamlet's first soliloquy (I.ii.154–7). Elsewhere Belleforest thinks of Amleth's supposed madness as a hindrance to his advancement (*un si grand defaut à son avancement*), Shakespeare's Hamlet complains "I lack advancement" (III.ii.331). Amleth presents himself to the people as the minister and executioner (*le ministre et executeur*) of just vengeance, Hamlet is made Heaven's "scourge and minister" (III.iv.177). Faced with the problem of miraculous knowledge, Belleforest speculates whether Amleth, instructed by the "malign spirit" which "abuses men," has become susceptible through his "melancholy" to diabolic revelations; and Hamlet, when he comes to question the honesty of the spirit he has seen, reminds himself that

> the *devil* hath power
> T'assume a pleasing shape, yea, and perhaps,
> Out of my weakness and my *melancholy*, . . .
> *Abuses* me to damn me. (II.ii.595–9)

Even the famous "To be or not to be" soliloquy appears to derive something from Belleforest. Vowing to his mother that he will avenge his father, Amleth asks, "What is the good of living when shame torments our conscience and cowardice holds us back from gallant enterprises? But the comparison with Shakespeare—

> Thus *conscience* does make cowards of us all . . .
> And *enterprises* of great pitch and moment
> . . . their currents turn awry (III.i.83–7)

—reveals a profound difference. Belleforest does not regard such failures as the common lot of men. The choice he offers Amleth is between two kinds of glory, either a glorious death or by the use of arms (*les armes au poing*) a glorious triumph over foes: the alternatives Hamlet debates, "to suffer" life's misfortunes or "to take arms" in a hopeless cause, afford no such simple heroics. Belleforest, following Saxo, likens Amleth to Hercules: the comparison persists in Shakespeare, but those who were like are now unlike (1.ii.152–3). The mind of Hamlet, confronting the enigma of man's life, is not in Belleforest at all.

THE MURDER OF GONZAGO

It is often assumed that the introduction of the Ghost into the story involved the change in the method of the murder. In Saxo Hamlet's father was butchered (*trucidatus*), with bloodshed (*manu cruenta*), and Belleforest adds explicitly that he was set on at a banquet. The murder done in secret was an innovation. But although a secret murder might require a ghost to reveal it, the converse does not follow. We may accept the usual complaint that the secret murder deprives Hamlet of his traditional motive for pretending madness; but this weakness, if it is one, can easily be exaggerated— indeed Shakespeare seems to capitalize it by linking the pretended madness with a genuine emotional disturbance—and the corresponding advantages are great. There are consequences for the murderer's character as well as for the revenger's task, and a revenge that cannot be openly declared invites a subtler intrigue. The King's moves to penetrate Hamlet's madness are matched with Hamlet's to establish the King's guilt. The device of imaging the crime in a play requires, if it is to be unmistakable both by the perpetrator and by us, a murder of a singular kind; and a model for this was found, whether by Shakespeare or his predecessor, in an actual occurrence in Italy.

Francesco Maria I della Rovere, Duke of Urbino, died in October 1538. There were rumours of poison, and the barber-surgeon who had attended him confessed under torture that, at the instigation of Luigi Gonzaga, a kinsman of the Duchess, he had poisoned him by a lotion in his ears. The affair remains mysterious, for although the barber was put to death, Gonzaga's guilt was never proved; but the combination of his name with the unusual method of killing leaves no doubt that we have here the prototype of the murder in *Hamlet*. The statement that "the story is extant, and written in very choice Italian" (III.ii.256–7) may have been true to fact, but no printed source has been traced. The name of the alleged murderer has been switched to his victim, but Luigi may have suggested Lucianus; and though the Duchess was called not Baptista but Leonora, an earlier Duke of Urbino had married Battista Sforza. For dramatic reasons the murderer is made the "nephew," and the better to mirror Claudius and Gertrude the Duke and Duchess become a King and Queen. When Hamlet nevertheless says "Gonzago is the Duke's name" (III.ii.233–4), this is presumably a relic of the source. As a relic unlikely to survive rehandling it points rather to

Shakespeare than his predecessor as the innovator in the matter of the poisoning; and the freedom with adopted names is quite in Shakespeare's manner. The dead Duke was a famous soldier, a portrait of him in armour by Titian is in the Uffizi Gallery in Florence, and Bullough conjectures that the dramatist may have been familiar with an engraving of it, perhaps in the hypothetical source. The idea that this bearded figure "in complete steel" with hand on truncheon and a helmet behind him with its "beaver up" may have suggested some details for the description of King Hamlet is not intrinsically implausible.

NOTES

[1] *Danorum Regum heroumque Historiae,* Paris, 1514; variously referred to as *Historiae Danicae* from the running title and less correctly *Historia Danica* from the prologue and preface. Saxo's Latin was translated by Oliver Elton (*The First Nine Books of the Danish History of Saxo Grammaticus,* 1894). The relevant portion of it, from Books 3 and 4, is most conveniently given with the English face to face in Gollancz, *The Sources of Hamlet,* 1926. Both are also printed in the margins of Dover Wilson's Cranach *Hamlet* (1930). The English only is most easily accessible in Bullough's *Narrative and Dramatic Sources of Shakespeare,* vol. vii. See also below, p. 90n. A new translation of Saxo by Peter Fisher, but not noticeably better for our purposes, has recently appeared (1979), and a companion volume of commentary is promised.

[2] So in Saxo; Englished by Elton as Feng; Fengon in Belleforest.

[3] Coller(us) in Saxo, Collere in Belleforest, becomes in Elton Koll.

[4] In the straw, according to the translators and the ordinary meaning of *stramentum;* but the word can mean a coverlet, so that Belleforest is probably right to render it by *loudier* (quilt), and the primitiveness of Amleth's world is a degree less than has been made out.

[5] The adultery of the Queen in *Hamlet* is sometimes disputed, but when Hamlet accuses his mother of being false to her marriage-vows (iii.iv.44–5) and his uncle of having whored her (v.ii.64), the matter is more than implicit.

JOHN BLIGH

The Women in the Hamlet Story

In the prose narratives upon which Shakespeare is directly or indirectly dependent, a pagan prince Hamlet ravishes a girl in a dark wood, then takes two wives, the first an English princess, and the second a Scottish queen named Hermetrude. In Shakespeare we find this lusty young Prince transformed into a melancholy, misogynistic bachelor, who over-reacts to his mother's remarriage,[1] discards Ophelia with extreme brutality, and regards women in general as breeders of sinners. This paper will indicate how the metamorphosis came about: it resulted from the imposition of a tragic pattern upon a story which was not originally tragic.

As is well known, the Hamlet story was told and retold in various forms before it was used by Shakespeare.[2] For the sake of brevity, its history can be divided into three phases: first, we have the prose narratives of Saxo Grammaticus (c. 1200) and of Francois de Belleforest (1576);[3] secondly, we do not possess but know of an early Elizabethan play called *Hamlet*, written (before 1589) almost certainly by Thomas Kyd, author of *The Spanish Tragedy;* and thirdly, we possess Shakespeare's masterpiece (1601). In this paper, I propose to examine, first, the structure of the story as it is in Saxo and Belleforest, with special attention to the role of women in Hamlet's life; it will be shown that, at this stage, the Hamlet story falls into two parts, the first half a success story, the second half a tragedy. Then I shall show how Kyd and Shakespeare have taken the first half (only), and, in transforming it into a tragedy, have refashioned the roles of the women, and turned Hamlet into a misogynist. There are many aspects of Shakespeare's Hamlet which cannot be satisfactorily explained except genetically, that is to say, by describing the genesis or growth of the story.[4]

First, then, the story as told by Saxo and Belleforest. (The major steps in the storyline are here numbered, to facilitate comparisons; the numbers are not in the two sources.)

1. Rorik (or Roderick), king of Denmark, appoints the brothers Horwendil and Feng (=Hamlet Sr. and Claudius) joint governors of Jutland.[5] Horwendil distinguishes himself by killing Koll (=Fortinbras Sr.), King of Norway, in single combat. As his reward, Rorik gives him his daughter Gerutha (=Gertrude) for his wife.

2. Feng, jealous of his brother's military glory and of his royal marriage, kills Horwendil, marries Gerutha, and becomes sole Duke of Jutland.[6] The murder is committed in public. Feng justifies himself by saying that he killed his brother in defense of Gerutha, whom Horwendil was on the point of slaying.

3. Amleth, the son of Horwendil and Gerutha, fears that Feng will take his life, to forestall any attempt he might make to avenge his father's death. He feigns lassitude and madness, so that Feng will despise him and suppose him free from all ambition.

4. However, some members of Feng's court suspect that Amleth's lassitude is a pose. They therefore devise two tests. First, it is arranged that an

attractive young girl, whom Amleth has known since childhood, will meet him in a wood; if he ravishes her, it will be plain that his lassitude is feigned. However, a friend tells Amleth that he is being tempted. So what does he do? He takes her to a *very* dark part of the wood, ravishes her, and gets her to promise to say that he did nothing of the sort. When they return, she says that he did nothing, and he says that he did ravish her, while lying on the ceiling (which was true, because he had provided himself with a piece of ceiling to lie on); and the whole thing passed off as a joke.—The young temptress (whom Shakespeare transforms into the chaste Ophelia) has now served her purpose and drops right out of the story. The encounter in the dark wood is purely episodic, except that it casts some light on the character of Amleth.

5. For the second test, it is arranged that Feng is absent from his castle. Gerutha calls Amleth to an interview, and the (unnamed) courtier who proposed this test is hidden in her closet, under rushes in Saxo, behind an arras in Belleforest. It is hoped that if Amleth is feigning, in privacy with his mother, he will put aside his pretence and speak frankly. But Amleth suspects that it is a trap; in Belleforest he cleverly uses his feigned madness to discover the eavesdropper; he comes in crying "Cock-a-doodle-do" and flapping his arms like a cock's wings. He flaps against the arras, feels the eavesdropper, cries out, "A rat!" and stabs him. Then he cuts the eavesdropper into pieces and throws them into a sewer. (The eavesdropper in this incident is not the father of the temptress in the last.)

6. After disposing of the body, Amleth returns to his mother and severely rebukes her for incestuously marrying the murderer of his father. How, he asks, does she endure such a foul embrace? (Belleforest's version of this rebuke is longer and more impassioned than Saxo's.) Gerutha is moved to repentance. Like the temptress in the previous incident, she promises not to tell Feng that her son's madness is feigned. In Belleforest's version, she is delighted to know that her son is not mad; she later becomes his accomplice in his plans to kill Feng.

7. When Feng returns, he questions Amleth about the eavesdropper (who of course cannot be found), but again Amleth is clever enough to pass off the incident with a funny remark: "He fell into the sewer and was eaten by hogs."

8. Feng, convinced that Amleth is dangerous, but not wishing to offend Gerutha by killing him, sends Amleth to England with two (unnamed)

courtiers as escort. Before leaving, Amleth asks Gerutha to have the court celebrate his funeral on the same day of the following year, and to hang a large curtain or awning over the great hall.

9. The two courtiers carry a letter from Feng requiring the English king to kill Amleth. But during the journey, Amleth discovers the letter and writes instead that the king of England is to kill the two courtiers and give his daughter in marriage to Amleth.

10. The king of England does as the letter requires of him. Amleth marries the English princess. For the time being he leaves her in England. Towards the end of the year, he returns to Denmark.

11. On the anniversary of his departure for England, Amleth enters the court of Feng dressed as a madman. As was prearranged, the court is, this very day, celebrating his funeral. The appearance of this mad fellow at his own funeral causes general merriment. Amleth joins in and gets the lords all drunk. Then he pulls down the awning, pegs it to the ground, and sets fire to it. Having dealt with the lords in this way, he can now go to Feng's sleeping chamber, where he kills him with his own sword.

12. Amleth then makes a long speech justifying his action, and ascends the throne of his father amid general rejoicing.

This ends the first half of the Amleth story. It is a story of revenge, but it is certainly not a tragedy. Amleth, through his own ingenuity and on his own initiative, with a little help from his friends, outwits and kills his father's murderer, succeeds to his father's throne, and gets an English princess for his wife into the bargain. The second half of the story comprises the chain of events leading to Amleth's downfall.

13. Amleth goes to England to fetch his wife. When the English king hears that Amleth has killed Feng, he is in a fix; he has sworn a compact with Feng that either will kill the murderer of the other. To fulfil his oath, he sends Amleth on an errand which he believes will lead him to death: Amleth is to go as his proxy to woo a Scottish princess, Hermetrude, who judges no man worthy to be her husband and kills off anyone who presents himself as a suitor. However, things turn out contrary to the English king's expectation. When this Amazon and Amleth meet, they fall in love. Hermetrude persuades Amleth that he deserves a much nobler wife than the English princess and offers herself. Amleth agrees and takes Hermetrude as his second wife. This naturally causes trouble

with the English king; but after some fighting, our valiant hero gets away to Denmark with two wives.

14. On the way back, Amleth receives the bad news that there has been a *coup d'état* in his absence. His uncle Wiglere, brother of Gerutha, who has succeeded Roderick, has seized Amleth's kingdom, "saying that neither Horwendil nor any of his held it but by permission." By means of rich presents, Amleth induces Wiglere to withdraw from his territories. But after a while, Hermetrude secretly negotiates with Wiglere to return: she "had secret intelligence with him, and promised him marriage, so that he would take her out of the hands of him that held her" (viz. Amleth).[7]

15. Meanwhile, Hermetrude protests to Amleth that her love for him is so great that she will follow him anywhere and even die with him. Accordingly, she accompanies him to the battle in which he confronts Wiglere. But no sooner is he killed in battle, than she yields herself to Wiglere, who gives orders that their marriage be celebrated forthwith.

In this second half of the story, Amleth's tragic mistake or *hamartia* is to fall in love with an ambitious and deceitful woman, who, to attain a still more noble marriage, engineers his overthrow. As Belleforest puts it:

> The thing that spoiled this virtuous prince was the overgreat trust and confidence he had in his wife Hermetrude, and the vehement love that he bare unto her, not once repenting the wrong in that case done to his lawful spouse.[8]

Aesthetically, the original ending of the story is all the more satisfying because, through this mistake or fault, Amleth dies as a result of a crime similar to the one which destroyed his own father: as Feng murdered Horwendil for the sake of a noble marriage, so Hermetrude engineers the death of Amleth for a nobler marriage.

Let us now look at the role of the women in this version of the story, beginning with Gerutha. Her conduct fills Amleth with disgust, but the precise cause of this disgust is not her overhaste in marrying Feng; it is her willingness to lie in the arms of the man who murdered her husband. It is not so much the unchastity but rather the treachery of these embraces that moves Amleth's loathing. He hates the thought that Gerutha is caressing in bed the man whom he wants to kill in vengeance. But although Gerutha's conduct is revolting to Amleth, it does not affect his relationship with women in general. He remains a lusty young bachelor, willing to ravish a pretty girl in a wood and make a joke of it, and clever enough to win himself a royal wife by forging a letter.

After her second marriage Gerutha continues to love Amleth. His seeming madness causes her acute anguish, especially as she fears that his madness is divine punishment for her sins:

> She was sore grieved to see her only child made a mere mockery, every man reproaching her with his folly . . . which was no small prick to her conscience, esteeming that the gods sent her that punishment for joining incestuously in marriage with the tyrannous murderer of her husband.[9]

Therefore, at the end of her interview with Amleth, although she has been stung by his severe rebukes, her joy is greater than her remorse:

> She forgot all disdain and wrath, which thereby she might have had (hearing herself so sharply chidden and reproved), for the joy she then conceived, to behold the gallant spirit of her son.[10]

When he leaves for England the first time, he can trust her to help him with his plans for revenge; and when he leaves the second time to fetch his bride, he apparently entrusts the kingdom to her keeping.

The second woman in the story is the temptress. She is a coquettish young woman of the court, willing to have intercourse for fun, and to pass it off with a lie or a joke. There is nothing tragic about her; she has no strong hold on Amleth's affections, nor he on hers. She belongs to a humorous escapade of his youth (in which, be it noted, he behaves with just that lasciviousness against which Laertes warns Ophelia in *Hamlet*, I, iii[11]).

Thirdly, there is the English princess. She is a beautiful girl, whom Amleth marries partly for love, but partly too from ambition—since he has not seen her at the time when he forges the letter asking for her hand. She too acquires no very firm hold on his affections, since he is so easily amenable to the persuasions of Hermetrude. And fourthly, there is Hermetrude, who admits to being less beautiful than the English princess, but is able to win Amleth's favour by appealing to his ambition. Later, she herself becomes ambitious for a still higher match (since Wiglere is Amleth's overlord); and she brings about Amleth's downfall.

The theme of woman's infidelity is prominent in the Saxo-Belleforest story (as it remains in Shakespeare's play). Amleth is disgusted with his mother's infidelity to Horwendil; and Hermetrude is as unfaithful to Amleth as Gerutha was to Horwendil. But the story itself (as contrasted with Belleforest's comments on it[12]) is not anti-feminist. Frailty is not confined to women. Amleth is unfaithful to his English wife when he marries a second wife and prefers her; it is poetic justice that he should be betrayed by Hermetrude.

Although the Amleth story is presented by Belleforest as an *histoire tragique,* only the second half of it can be called tragic. The first half is a revenge story, but nothing in it is likely to evoke the tragic emotions of pity and fear. Sometimes it is amusing, and often it is exciting. We marvel at Amleth's ingenuity; we do not regret Feng's downfall—the villain gets what was coming to him. It is the second half of the story which is tragic: there we see an ingenious, attractive, daring, humorous, courageous young prince overreaching himself through greed and ambition, and coming to an untimely end. Though he has one beautiful wife already, he allows himself the indulgence of a second; and she, under professions of extremest fidelity, betrays him to his death. The irony of the Amleth story is that in the second half the hero falls through a fault similar to the one which he punishes in the first half.

As the text of Kyd's *Hamlet* has unfortunately perished, it is impossible to describe in detail what changes he made in the story. One thing is certain, however: in his version of the story, Claudius killed Hamlet Sr. secretly, and the murder was revealed to Hamlet by his father's ghost. This is clearly implied in the pamphlet by Lodge (1596) describing how the ghost cried "like an oyster-wife, 'Hamlet, revenge!'"[13]

It is tempting to conjecture that Kyd also introduced the players and the Mouse Trap play. He uses the device of an inner play in *The Spanish Tragedy;* and, being fond of parallel scenes, he may have wished to show not only Claudius testing Hamlet's madness, but also Hamlet testing Claudius's left in some uncertainty as to whether Claudius is really guilty. Therefore the introduction of the ghost at the beginning of the play may well be a consequence of the decision to introduce the inner play: the ghost tells Hamlet of Claudius's guilt, but Hamlet decides to doubt its veracity until he has tested Claudius with the Mouse Trap play.[14] Similarly, in *The Spanish Tragedy* Hieronymo first learns that Lorenzo is the murderer from Belimperia's letter, but he decides to doubt its veracity until he has further evidence (which he receives in Pedringano's letter). However, as we do not possess Kyd's text, conjectures such as these are unsafe. It is better to compare Shakespeare's story with the Saxo-Belleforest story, and to observe the differences without trying to decide which are due to Kyd and which to Shakespeare.

What Kyd and Shakespeare did was to impose a tragic pattern on the first half of Belleforest's story. They take the narrative up to the point where Hamlet kills the usurper, but make Hamlet himself die in the act of taking revenge. In this revised version, the cause of his fall can no longer be the infidelity of his wife (for he does not reach England or Scotland, and remains unmarried); instead his fall has to come about through the machinations of the usurper Claudius. The simplest solution to the problem of how to close the story at the end of its first half would have been to make Hamlet and Claudius stab and kill each other simultaneously; but either Kyd or Shakespeare decided that other changes were needed to make the story tragic, quite apart from Hamlet's death; and these further changes suggested a different way of closing the story.

There are two episodes in the Belleforest story which could easily be developed in the direction of tragedy: the gay young temptress could be made to find herself pregnant, disgraced and abandoned, and could be made to take her own life from grief and shame; and the eavesdropper might have a son or daughter or preferably both, who would grieve over their father's death. Either Kyd or Shakespeare had the idea of making the temptress the daughter of the eavesdropper and of giving him a son, who would then have a double motive for wanting to kill Hamlet, namely, desire to avenge both his sister and his father. The next step was to make this young man enter into alliance with Claudius to compass Hamlet's death.

Further, if Hamlet was to be a tragic figure not in the last act alone but throughout the play, he could not be presented as a merry young pagan who jokes about lying with a girl on the ceiling. To make him into a tragic figure it was necessary to show him from the beginning as mourning deeply over the death of his father and as feeling profound disgust for his mother's yielding of her body to the murderer. Kyd and/or Shakespeare make these two subjects of meditation bite so deeply into Hamlet's soul that he loses all delight in life and conceives a horror of women in general. Such being his frame of mind, the temptress is sent, not to test the genuineness of his lethargy, but to uncover the cause of his melancholy. He is so embittered that he rejects her harshly and cruelly.

Let us next consider how this reshaping of the story by Kyd and Shakespeare affected the functions and roles of the women characters.

The chief function of Gertrude in the workings of the revised story is to provoke in Hamlet an intense, almost pathological aversion, which destroys his delight in life and shatters his esteem for all women, including Ophelia. Whether or not he is over the borderline of sanity, he is sadly changed—as we are able to see through the eyes of Ophelia: "O what a noble mind is here o'erthrown . . ." (III, i, 153–164). The tragic transformation of the basically cheerful and lusty young Amleth into the brooding, black-suited, melancholic, misogynistic Hamlet is brought about by increasing the effect of Gertrude's sins upon Hamlet. In Shakespeare's play, the intensification of his aversion has been pushed so far that he presents us with a serious psychological problem, which some critics have sought to resolve by attributing to him a powerful Odeipus complex.[15]

Partly as a result of his extreme aversion to her sins, Hamlet places little or not trust in his mother, and does not make her his ally or ask her aid in overthrowing Claudius. But this reduction of Gertrude's role is chiefly the result of the substitution of a new dénouement to the revenge story. In the closet scene, nothing is said of Gertrude's gladness at discovering that Hamlet is not mad.[16] All the emphasis is on her repentance, brought about by Hamlet's severe admonitions. Indeed, the closet scene (III, iv), designed by Polonius to be a testing scene, becomes a repentance scene and forms a pair with the scene of Claudius's attempted repentance (III, iii). There is a didactic, moralizing element in these scenes (as also in I, iii) which is carried over into the play from the prose sources.[17]

In the revised version of the story the role of Ophelia is greatly enlarged. It seems not unlikely that in Kyd she was represented as a girl who, on some earlier occasion (before the beginning of the play), had slept with Hamlet. (In *The Spanish Tragedy*, Belimperia has slept with Don Andrea and is willing to sleep with Horatio.) But Shakespeare, who often makes his heroines more chaste than they were in his sources,[18] presents Ophelia as a pure maiden, with only the slightest suggestion that she may at some time have slept with Hamlet. The gentleman who secures her an interview with Gertrude in IV, v is plainly anxious to avoid saying what he thinks while at the same time giving some hint of the indelicacy of the matter: ". . . would make one think, there might be thought, though nothing sure, yet much unhappily."

In Shakespeare, Ophelia still retains something of the original function of the young temptress in the older story. When Polonius talks of "loosing" his daughter to Hamlet, he expects that some unseemly conduct will ensue from the encounter. (Dover Wilson informed the learned world in 1935 that he had heard farmers in the north of England using the verb "to loose" when discussing the breeding of horses and cattle.[19]) Hamlet seems to guess that he is being tested, and proceeds to treat Ophelia with extreme cruelty, pouring upon her all his aversion to women in general. Why Shakespeare has made him so cruel may perhaps be explained by this hypothesis: that Kyd made Hamlet drive Ophelia to suicide by sleeping with her and then rejecting her; and Shakespeare, wishing to present her as a chaste maiden, has to make Hamlet drive her to suicide by the very cruelty of his rejection.

By making Ophelia the daughter of Polonius, Kyd and/or Shakespeare have greatly intensified the tragedy of her lot. To the burden of her grief over her cruel rejection is added the anguish of her father's death at the hands of the prince who once loved her. These accumulating griefs drive her out of her mind, and she takes her own life. We are made to feel the full pathos of her fate through its effect upon Gertrude (IV, vii, 163–183) and upon Laertes (IV, v, 154–163 and V, i, 248–256).[20] If a tragic figure is one whose fate evokes in the audience the emotions of pity and fear, Ophelia is more tragic than Hamlet.

Almeth's English wife has no place in Shakespeare's play. But one incident which occurs during his visit to the English court has a parallel in *Hamlet*. After feasting with the English king, Amleth is overheard telling his companions that the king has the eyes of a slave; the king is informed, makes enquiries, and finds that he was born as a result of his mother's adultery with a slave.[21] Could this perhaps have suggested the scene where Hamlet stares hard into the eyes of Ophelia? At least it can be said that in the earlier story Hamlet is a man capable of reading a person's character in his eyes.

Amleth's Scottish wife, Hermetrude, lives on in Shakespeare, in a curious place: she survives in the queen who does protest too much in the inner play. *The Murder of Gonzago,* besides resembling the murder of Hamlet Sr., bears quite a strong resemblance to the downfall of Hamlet himself, as it is described in Belleforest; indeed the picture of the over-protesting queen matches Hermetrude's treatment of Amleth more closely than it matches Gertrude's treatment of Hamlet Sr.

To conclude, then: Kyd and Shakespeare have altered and reduced Gertrude's role, and have enlarged Ophelia's, to fit them into a tragic story and to make them both into tragic figures. Gertrude is deprived of her share in the overthrow of Claudius, but she wins our sympathy and compassion by her penitence in the closet scene. Ophelia is turned into a chaste and innocent girl, upon whom Hamlet vents his misogyny. The tragedy of Gertrude and of Ophelia is an extension of the tragedy of Hamlet: in overreacting to his mother's sins, he is sadly and wastefully ruined; he is possessed by a spirit of intense bitterness which, when vented upon Gertrude and Ophelia, causes them extreme anguish. All this suffering taken together works upon the imagination of the reader or spectator of the play and through his imagination evokes the tragic response. Anyone who can recall in his own past a time when he was estranged from a person or persons whom he loved, feeling that he could not behave otherwise because more sinned against than sinning, and hating himself for maintaining the estrangement while unable to break it—such a person knows how *Hamlet* works as a tragedy. In trying to understand how a tragedy is meant to function, we must not fasten our attention upon the tragic hero alone, in isolation. In *Hamlet* we must feel the tragic quality of Hamlet's estrangement from his mother and from Ophelia whom he loved. Shakespeare was guided, not by Aristotle, but by his own genius, and also, no doubt, by personal experiences of his own, about which we know nothing, though we may guess.

NOTES:

[1] Cf. Ernest Jones, "Hamlet Diagnosed" (from *Hamlet and Oedipus,* 1949) reprinted in F. Kermode, *Four Centuries of Shakespearian Criticism* (New York, 1965), pp. 437–451.

[2] Cf. M. A. Taylor, *A New Look at the Old Sources of Hamlet* (The Hague, 1968).

[3] The texts, with English translations, are given in Israel Gollancz, *The Sources of Hamlet* (London, 1926). I have not delayed to indicate all the divergences between Saxo and Belleforest.

[4] Cf. Charlton M. Lewis, *The Genesis of Hamlet* (New York, 1907).

[5] In Saxo and Belleforest, Horwendil and Feng are dukes rather than kings—a point which is of importance at a later stage of the story (under no. 14).

[6] In Belleforest (Gollancz, p. 187), but not in Saxo (p. 101), Feng has "incestuously abused" Gerutha before he murders Horwendil. Cf. Baldwin Maxwell, "Hamlet's Mother," *ShakQ* 15 (1964) 235–246.

[7] Both quotations are from Belleforest, in Gollancz, p. 301.

[8] Gollancz, p. 303.

[9] Gollancz, p. 209.

[10] Gollancz, p. 219.

[11] The description of Ophelia given by Rebecca West in "The Nature of Will," *The Court and the Castle* (Yale U.P., 1957), reprinted in C. Sacks and E. Whann (eds.), *Hamlet Enter Critic* (New York, 1960), p. 256, is more appropriate to the original temptress: "The truth is that Ophelia was a disreputable young woman; not scandalously so, but still disreputable."

[12] Cf. Gollancz, p. 307.

[13] Cf. Lewis, *The Genesis of Hamlet,* pp. 37 and 71.

[14] A. P. Stabler, "King Hamlet's Ghost in Belleforest," *PMLA* 77 (1962) 18–20, points out that although the ghost of Horwendil does not appear to Amleth in Belleforest, there are two references to this ghost—the first in Amleth's rebuke to his mother (p. 212), the second in his words to Feng as he kills him (p. 257). In a later article, Stabler points out that in Belleforest (p. 237) Amleth is said to have been instructed in the devilish and misleading art of magic, through which "the evil spirit used to inform Amleth of things past." See A. P. Stabler, "Melancholy, Ambition, and Revenge in Belleforest's Hamlet," *PMLA* 81 (1966) 207–213. Kyd may have taken his cue from these passages in Belleforest.

¹⁵ Cf. Ernest Jones, cited above, no. 1; and K. R. Eissler, *Discourse on Hamlet and HAMLET* (New York, 1971), p. 420.

¹⁶ In Shakespeare's closet scene, Hamlet sometimes behaves as if he *is* mad (when the ghost appears); and yet—a relic of the source—he makes Gertrude promise not to tell Claudius that he is really sane.

¹⁷ The moralizing purpose is even plainer in the repentance scene in John Marston, *The Malcontent*, IV, v.

¹⁸ For example, in Ser Giovanni's *Il Pecorone*, the source of the plot of *The Merchant of Venice*, the test set by the lady of Belmonts was not a choice of three caskets. The suitor had to sleep with the lady; if he could "enjoy" her, she was his; if not, he lost everything he had. See J. R. Brown (ed.), *The Merchant of Venice* (Arden Shakespeare, London, 1955), p. 142. In Gascoigne's *Supposes*, which is the source of the Bianca plot in *The Taming of the Shrew*, Polynesta (who corresponds to Bianca) is pregnant throughout the play. The plot of *Twelfth Night*, again, is much more chaste than its probable source, Barnabe Rich's *Of Apolonius and Silla*. See H. Baker's Signet edition of *Twelfth Night* (New York, 1965), pp. 143–165. The twin brother makes "Olivia" pregnant; she claims "Viola" as her husband; "Viola" bares her breasts to show that she is not responsible for the pregnancy.

¹⁹ Cf. *What Happens in Hamlet* (Cambridge, 1935), reprinted in *Hamlet Enter Critic*, p. 269.

²⁰ Not, however, through its effect on Hamlet.

²¹ Cf. Gollancz, p. 121. There is a similar incident in *Othello*, IV, ii, 25.

ZHANG SIYANG

Hamlet's Melancholy

Hamlet has suffered the utmost afflictions, the most miserable fate in life. His honorable father was murdered, his mother stained, his inherited throne usurped, his beloved alienated—such miseries as few people could endure. But Hamlet does not yield. From personal misfortunes he has learned of the adversity of life precipitated by an irrational society: "The time is out of joint" (1.5.196),¹ the world "a goodly [prison]" (2.2.245).

To "set it right" (1.5.197) he must wage a life-or-death war against reactionary forces. Linking the hero's personal misfortune with the destiny of humankind is, intellectually, the play's claim on immortality. Yet because of the limitations of historical conditions and circumstances, Hamlet's eventual

---

* Originally published in Chinese in *Wenke zhiyou* [companion to the *Humanities*] no. 2 (1983): 19–22. Translated and edited by Mason Y. H. Wang.

triumph is only a moralistic, not a real victory in life. He perishes with his enemies; his person, family, love, career are all destroyed. Even the rule of the kingdom falls into a stranger's hands.

The character of Hamlet has been the primary problem in studies of the play. What kind of man is he? Cowardly weak-minded or dauntlessly determined? Indecisive or stubbornly resolute? A mere babbler or man of action? Fanciful or pragmatic? Hungry for power or an unswerving fighter for justice? A pessimistic misanthrope or optimistic go-getter? Faced with these questions, we may add still more, about his melancholy and depression, his love or lack of love for Ophelia, and the reasons for his procrastinations.

Hamlet's ideology and sustaining interest are both congregated in the prince; the playwright's intent also finds its expression through him. His first appearance on stage is as a melancholy soul, woebegone, silent, depressed, and deeply reflective. Surely he must once have been an open-minded, agile, and witty man, for his humorous side frequently manifests itself, even in moments of utmost suffering. But man changes with the changes in his environment. Returning from the University of Wittenberg, Hamlet cannot but feel saddened with righteous anger at a marriage any humanist would consider not only heartless and unjust, without moral principle, a violation of holy matrimony, but also an act of shameless, destructive incest. Moreover, the man Gertrude marries is loutish, ugly of soul, and offensive in appearance. Educated in the university's humanistic tradition, idealizing everything, endowed with new ways of thinking and, as a consequence, new moral principles, Hamlet has to be affected emotionally and intellectually when he confronts the disparity between his environment and his vision of life. This disparity causes an aversion to and, consequently, a skepticism about humanity, life, and the world. Hamlet can find no other outlet than letting his suffering and melancholy gnaw at his heart.

Melancholy is therefore the mark of his character. Indeed, stripped of melancholy, Hamlet would not be Hamlet. Marx once observed, "And the Empire with the victories of the Empire reminds one of the adaptation of Shakespeare's *Hamlet* which not only lacks the melancholy of the Prince of Denmark but also the Prince himself."[2] Elsewhere he called this kind of melancholy a "Hamletlike expression."[3] Hamlet's melancholy, though, is not merely an exhibition of his personal despair; it involves a compassion for humanity and deep concern for his kingdom and its people; and it is inseparable from the procrastination and despondency precipitated by his search for a course of action. Nor can melancholy leave Hamlet, since he cannot transcend "this harsh world" (5.2.353) until the very moment before his death.

Not inborn with him, this melancholy is fostered by the realities of his environment, by the deep wounds inflicted upon him by life's indifferent whips, and by the burden gnawing at his heart. Aware of the tremendous responsibilities imposed upon him, he is in an isolated position, prevented from resorting to outside help, incapacitated in confronting his arch-enemy. A witness to the suffering people, corroding bureaucracy, and deteriorating morality, he cannot help but fall into a state of burning anxiety. If Hamlet were an ordinary man, he could be blind to what he saw, turn a deaf ear to what he heard, and simply await his position on the throne. But Hamlet is not this sort of man. He despises such a way of life: "If [man's] chief good and market of his time / Be but to sleep and feed?" (4.4.34–35). Possessed with a vision of perfection for humankind, Hamlet nevertheless cannot find a way toward its realization. He is thus inevitably baffled by an intense conflict between reality and vision.

Closely associated with his melancholy are his world-weariness, feeling of loss, his sense of life's impermanence and futility, the notion of this world as being like a dream. Less significant than his melancholy, such sentiments are occasioned by chance encounters with unexpected situations, and may be regarded as the outpourings of a warrior's sufferings, his sense of negation stirred up by special circumstances. Hamlet's feelings are like those expressed by the poet in Sonnet 66: "Tired with all these, for restful death I cry." No matter how strong-willed or courageous Hamlet is, he is powerless to resist such onslaughts, and this causes his fiery, revolutionary spirit to sink into a state of melancholic contemplation and puzzling vacillation. In accord with the law of human conduct, it is quite natural for a man like Hamlet to appear psychologically contradictory, unpredictably changeable in his emotions, and self-destructive in his desires. All these chance encounters, these unexpected situations, however, do not diminish the hero's ideological struggle. Instead, he has been constantly undergoing self-criticism to overcome these negations and transform them into positive pursuits.

Beclouded in melancholy, Hamlet is still not dumbfounded, idling with nothing to do, sucking melancholy for its own sake. Quite the contrary, his mind under stress has quickened and is activated even more than usual. He cannot help questioning the evils of the world, as they embrace body and soul, phenomenon and essence, individuals, families, society, nations, humankind. Moral standards, human relationships, exemplary human behavior, love, life and death, ideals, heaven and hell, time and eternity—such are the issues that swarm in his mind; the whole universe seems to have squeezed itself into his head. Hamlet's strength does not reside in being able to solve the world's problems but in his recognition that in an irrational society the good, the noble-minded, become victimized by the power of evil. This awakening has pushed his melancholy to an ultimate point. "The time is out of joint. O cursed spite, / That ever I was born to set it right" (1.5.196–97—Hamlet's exclamation, as pointed out by many critics, is the crux to the evolvement of the play's plot as well as the development of his character. Earlier, Hamlet was merely in a melancholy frame of mind— depressed, sorrowful, suspicious. But when the Ghost reveals to Hamlet the cause of his death, and demands that his son "revenge his foul and most un-natural murder" (1.5.25) through a private vengeance, Hamlet extends the evil of his father's death to the whole of society, moving from personal to public grievance. His determination to bring fairness, justice, even happiness to all humanity is indeed a tremendous task, and Hamlet is fully aware of its difficulty and complexity. He is also aware of his limited personal strength. When he can find no way to carry out the undertaking, he only intensifies his melancholy.

Hamlet's repeated delays in carrying out his revenge have been attributed by some critics to his inborn cowardice or weakness in character, his regression to empty daydreaming. Such claims, I believe, are unfounded, nor are they in conformity with Hamlet's character. We need to be concerned not just with what Hamlet ought to do but with his environment, one that prohibits him from action. It is true that Hamlet is at times indulgent in his fantasizing, is highly sensitive, and lacks resolution; but he is certainly not an idle man. At the critical moment, facing the choice between right and wrong, he engages in struggles. Let us remember how he bitterly castigates the wicked; how with a sharp tongue he taunts the Queen; how relentlessly he pushes his former school acquaintances to the corners; the arrogance he daringly exhibits toward Claudius, whose crime Hamlet had bravely enacted on the stage; and how courageously Hamlet proves himself in the fencing match with Laertes. All these show that Hamlet is not by nature a weakling. He is quite brave and resolute, capable of transforming words into action.

If there is a flaw in Hamlet's character, it is in the abundance of his heart. Only a man with such innate goodness could become so intensely melancholy. Such a man could not imagine that the harsh realities he faces would turn out to be even worse; nor could he suspect that his fencing match with Laertes would be a trap for his destruction. Claudius takes advantage of this noble quality of Hamlet, as he reminds Laertes that Hamlet has a heart "most generous, and free from all contriving" (4.7.134). Oftentimes a man of such goodness cannot appraise adequately what a wicked man would do, and in this regard Hamlet's kind heart lacks imagination. Hamlet's very decency strengthens the wicked and, in turn, inflicts a fatal blow on himself. Shakespeare through Adam in *As You Like It* has said, "to some kind of men / Their graces serve them but as enemies" (2.3.10–11). Hamlet's character has such tragic contradictions.

What we see in Hamlet cannot be easily stated. He undergoes changes of a most complex and contradictory nature: he is at once gentle and brash, loving and full of hate, selfish and magnanimous, rational and emotional, prattling and eager for action, cold-heartedly cruel and full of warm feelings, indecisive and resolute, dispirited and full of energy, at times scrupulous and then reckless, reserved and impulsive, sometimes mad and at other times clear-headed, depressed and hateful of life and yet unwilling to die; scholar and soldier, prince and commoner, childishly naive and highly sophisticated. These characteristics seem to intermingle in a most complicated way, constantly changing, coming to the surface in fashions seemingly incomprehensible, eluding our grasp. Tolstoy, who was madly against Shakespeare's art, has noted that "one moment [Hamlet] is awestruck at his father's ghost, another moment he begins to chafe at it, calling it "old mole"; one moment he loves Ophelia, another moment he teases her, and so forth. There is no possibility of finding any explanation whatever of Hamlet's actions or words, and therefore no possibility of attributing any character to him."[4] The fact, however, is that the contradictions in Hamlet's character must be regarded as the labyrinth he himself establishes in his search for truth, indeed are a microcosm of human history. From time immemorial, how often have human ideals of happiness been truly realized? How many fluctuations and repetitions must history go through before one step can be advanced? And how heavy and slow our step is! Hamlet's character embodies the very principles of Shakespeare's theater: to "hold . . . the mirror up to nature" (3.2.22); to show "the very age and body of the time his form and pressure" (3.2.23–24); to be "the abstract and brief chronicles of the time" (2.2.520).

Hamlet *is* a mystery. A man's character is so complex, so hidden, so difficult to grasp. This is true of any man in real life. Everyone is a mystery. A man is a world. And Hamlet's complexities are those of his world. Because of the limitations of historical realities, he has not been able to explore and find the revolutionary truth and way. At the time of his death, Denmark is still a "harsh world." This is the greatest tragedy in Hamlet's life, one necessitated by historical determinism.

Related to Hamlet by their former love, Ophelia naturally has a deep and thorough understanding of him. Her words of immeasurable sorrow and pity may supplement my own thoughts:

> O, what a noble mind is here o'erthrown!
> The courtier's, soldier's, scholar's, eye, tongue, sword,
> Th' expectancy and rose of the fair state,
> The glass of fashion and the mould of form,
> Th' observ'd of all observers, quite, quite down
> . . . .
> Now see that noble and most sovereign reason
> Like sweet bells jangled out of tune and harsh,
> That unmatch'd form and feature of blown youth
> Blasted with ecstasy.
>
> (3.1.152–56, 159–62)

Had Hamlet been a man in real life, how would we mourn his destruction? How the world, past and present, would mourn him! Alas, what a pity!

Notes

1 All citations from *Hamlet* are from the New Arden edition, edited by Harold Jenkins (London: Methuen, 1982).

2 Karl Marx and Frederick Engels, *Collected Works* (New York: International, 1980), 14: 297.

3 Ibid., 17: 116.

4 Leo Tolstoy, "Shakespeare and the Drama," in *Shakespeare in Europe,* ed. Oswald LeWinter (Cleveland: World, 1963), p 259.

Mark Rose

Reforming the Role

Classical and Elizabethan tragedy represent polar opposites in dramatic structure, the one tightly focused with few characters and a sharply defined action, the other loose and sprawling with many characters, multiple locales,

---

* From *Homer to Brecht: The European Epic and Dramatic Traditions,* edited by Michael Seidel and Edward Mendelson. © 1977 by Yale University. Yale University Press, 1977. Originally entitled "Hamlet."

and complex plots which may span years of narrative time. And yet all tragedies tend to share certain central concerns. Sophocles' Oedipus fled Corinth to prevent the oracle's prophecy from coming true, but in the process of trying to escape his fate he only succeeded in fulfilling it. Sophocles' play is concerned, we might say, with the degree to which our lives are not in our own control. The words of the player king in *Hamlet* are apposite:

> Our wills and fates do so contrary run
> That our devices still are overthrown;
> Our thoughts are ours, their ends none of our own.
>
> (3.2.217–219)

Hamlet, too, is concerned with the limits imposed upon mortal will, with the various restrictions that flesh is heir to; and it is upon this central tragic theme that I wish to dwell, suggesting how Shakespeare employs a characteristically Renaissance self-consciousness to transmute a popular Elizabethan dramatic form, the revenge play, into a tragedy the equal of Sophocles'.

Early in the play Polonius speaks to Ophelia of the "tether" with which Hamlet walks. The image is a useful one to keep in mind, for it suggests both that the prince does have a degree of freedom and that ultimately he is bound. Laertes cautions Ophelia in a similar manner and develops more explicitly the limits on Hamlet's freedom. The prince's "will is not his own," Laertes says,

> For he himself is subject to his birth,
> He may not, as unvalued persons do,
> Carve for himself; for on his choice depends
> The safety and the health of this whole state.
>
> (1.3.18–21)

What Laertes means is simply that Hamlet as heir apparent may not be free to marry Ophelia, but he says much more than he realizes. Hamlet is indeed subject to his birth, bound by being the dead king's son, and upon his "carving"—his rapier and dagger-work—the safety and health of Denmark do literally depend. Possibly Shakespeare has in mind the imagery of *Julius Caesar* and Brutus's pledge to be a sacrificer rather than a butcher, to carve Caesar as a dish fit for the gods, for, like Brutus, Hamlet is concerned with the manner of his carving. But the word is also Shakespeare's term for sculptor, and perhaps he is thinking of Hamlet as this kind of carver, an artist attempting to shape his revenge and his life according to his own standards. Yet here, too, Hamlet's will is not his own: there is, he discovers, "a divinity that shapes our ends, / Rough-hew them how we will" (5.2.10–11).

From the first scene in which the prince appears, Shakespeare wishes us to perceive clearly that Hamlet is tethered. He contrasts the king's permission to Laertes to return to France with his polite refusal of Hamlet's request to return to Wittenberg. Denmark is in fact a prison for Hamlet, a kind of detention center in which the wary usurper can keep an eye on his disgruntled stepson. Claudius acclaims Hamlet's yielding as "gentle and unforced" and announces that he will celebrate it by firing his cannon to the heavens, but what he has done in fact is to cut ruthlessly the avenue of escape that the prince had sought from a court and a world he now loathes. One other, more desperate avenue still seems open, and as soon as the stage is cleared the prince considers the possibility of this course, suicide, only to remind himself that against this stands another sort of "canon," one fixed by God. Hamlet is tied to Elsinore, bound by his birth; on either side the road of escape is guarded and all that remains to him is his disgust for the world and the feeble wish that somehow his flesh will of itself melt into a puddle.

Hamlet's real prison is of course more a matter of mental than physical space. "Oh God," he exclaims to Rosencrantz and Guildenstern, "I could be bounded in a nutshell and count myself a king of infinite space, were it not that I have bad dreams" (2.2.258–60). The erstwhile friends suppose Hamlet means he is ambitious for the crown, but the bad dream the prince is thinking of, the insubstantial "shadow" as he calls it, is evidently the ghost and its nightmarish revelation. If Claudius has tied him to Elsinore it is of little consequence compared to the way the ghost has bound him to vengeance. Hamlet's master turns out to be even a more formidable figure than the king. Ironically, Laertes' and Polonius's remarks upon what they conceive to be the limits placed upon Hamlet's freedom immediately precede the scene in which the prince at last encounters the ghost and discovers what it means to be subject to one's birth. "Speak," Hamlet says to the ghost, "I am bound to hear," and the ghost in his reply picks up the significant word *bound* and throws it back at the prince: "So art thou to revenge, when thou shalt hear" (1.5.6–7). Hamlet cannot shuffle off his father's spirit any more than he can the mortal coil. The ghost's command is "Remember me," and after his departure Shakespeare dramatizes how from this charge there is no escape. Hamlet rushes about the stage seeking a place to swear his companions to secrecy, but wherever he makes his stand the ghost is there directly—"Hic et ubique," the prince says—its voice crying from the cellarage: "Swear!"

The ghost binds Hamlet to vengeance, but there is another and more subtle way in which the spirit of his father haunts the prince. It is one of the radical ironies of the tragedy that the same nightmarish figure who takes from Hamlet his freedom should also embody the ideal of man noble in reason and infinite in faculties—the ideal of man, in other words, as free. The ghost of King Hamlet, stalking his son dressed in the same armor he wore in heroic combat with Fortinbras of Norway, becomes a peripatetic emblem of human dignity and worth, a memento of the time before the "falling-off" when Hamlet's serpent-uncle had not yet crept into the garden, infesting it with things rank and gross in nature. It is no accident that Hamlet bears the same name as his father: the king represents everything to which the prince aspires. Hamlet, too, has his single-combats, his duels both metaphorical and literal, but the world in which he must strive is not his father's. The memory of those two primal, valiant kings, face to face in a royal combat ratified by law and heraldry, haunts the tragedy, looming behind each pass of the "incensed points" of the modern "mighty opposites," Hamlet and Claudius, and looming also behind the final combat, Hamlet's and Laertes' poisoned play, swaddled in a show of chivalry as "yeasty" as the eloquence of Osric, the waterfly who presides as master of the lists.

Subject to his birth, tethered by Claudius, and bound by the ghost, Hamlet is obsessed with the idea of freedom, with the dignity that resides in being master of oneself. One must not be "passion's slave," a "pipe for Fortune's finger / To sound what stop she please" (3.2.72–74)—nor for that matter a pipe for men to play. The first three acts are largely concerned with the attempts of Claudius and Hamlet to play upon each other, the king principally through Rosencrantz and Guildenstern, Hamlet through "the Mousetrap." It is Hamlet who succeeds, plucking at last the heart of Claudius's mystery, pressing the king to the point where he loses his self-control and rises in a passion, calling for light. "Dids't perceive?" Hamlet asks, and Horatio replies: "I did very well note him" (3.2.293, 296). I should like to see a musical pun in Horatio's word *note*, but perhaps it is farfetched. At any rate, Hamlet's immediate response is to call for music, for the recorders to be brought, as if he thinks to reenact symbolically his triumph over the king. What follows is the "recorder scene" in which Rosencrantz and Guildenstern once again fail with Hamlet precisely where he has succeeded with the king:

> Why, look you now, how unworthy a thing you make of me! You would play upon me; you would seem to know my stops; you would pluck out the heart of my mystery; you would sound me from my lowest note to the top of my compass; and there is much music, excellent voice, in this little organ, yet cannot you make it speak. 'Sblood, do you think I am easier to be played on than a pipe? Call me what instrument you will, though you can fret me, you cannot play upon me.
>
> (3.2.371–80)

Immediately after speaking this, Hamlet returns to Polonius, who has just entered, and leads the old courtier through the game of cloud shapes, making him see the cloud first as a camel, then as a weasel, and finally as a whale. Though Claudius and his instruments cannot play upon him, Hamlet is contemptuously demonstrating that he can make any of them sound what tune he pleases.

Hamlet's disdain for anyone who will allow himself to be made an instrument perhaps suggests his bitter suspicion that he, too, is a kind of pipe. One of the most interesting of the bonds imposed upon Hamlet is presented in theatrical terms. Putting it baldly and exaggerating somewhat for the sake of clarity, one might say that Hamlet discovers that life is a poor play, that he finds himself compelled to play a part in a drama that offends his sense of his own worth. Hamlet is made to sound a tune that is not his own, the whirling and passionate music of the conventional revenger, a stock character familiar to the Elizabethans under a host of names, including Thomas Kyd's Hieronomo, his Hamlet, and Shakespeare's own Titus Andronicus. The role of revenger is thrust upon Hamlet by the ghost, and once again it is profoundly ironic that the figure who represents the dignity of man should be the agent for casting his son in a limited, hackneyed, and debasing role. That Hamlet should be constrained to play a role at all is a restriction of his freedom, but that it should be this particular, vulgar role is especially degrading.

Lest I should seem to be refashioning Shakespeare in the modern image of Pirandello, let me recall at this point that he is a remarkably self-conscious playwright, one who delights in such reflexive devices as the play within the play, the character who is either consciously or unconsciously an actor, or the great set speech on that favorite theme of how all the world is a stage. Of all Shakespeare's plays, perhaps the most reflexive, the most dramatically self-conscious, is *Hamlet*. This is possibly due in part to the circumstance not unprecedented but still rather special that Shakespeare is here reworking a well-known, even perhaps notorious, earlier play, a circumstance which permits him to play off his own tragedy and his own protagonist against his audience's knowledge of Kyd's *Hamlet*. In any case, the self-consciousness of Shakespeare's *Hamlet* is evident. Here the play within the play is not merely a crucial element in the plot but a central figure in the theme. Here Shakespeare actually introduces a troop of professional actors to discuss their art and give us examples of their skill onstage. Here even a figure like Polonius has had some experience on the boards, acting Julius Caesar to a university audience, and nearly every character in the play from the ghost to the king is at some time or other seen metaphorically as an actor. So pervasive is the play's concern with theater that, as many critics have noted, simple terms like *show, act, play,* and *perform* seem drawn toward their specifically theatrical meaning even when they appear in neutral contexts.

If *Hamlet* is Shakespeare's most self-conscious play, the prince is surely his most self-conscious character. An actor of considerable ability himself, he is also a professed student of the drama, a scholar and critic, and a writer able on short notice to produce a speech to be inserted in a play. The prince is familiar with the stock characters of the Elizabethan stage—he lists a string of them when he hears that the players have arrived—and he is familiar, too, with at least two Elizabethan revenge plays (not counting *The Murder of Gonzago*), for at various times he burlesques both *The True Tragedy of Richard III,* that curious mixture of revenge play and chronicle history, and *The Spanish Tragedy.* Moreover, Hamlet habitually conceives of his life as a play, a drama in which he is sometimes actor and sometimes actor and playwright together. We recall immediately that in the third soliloquy ("O, what a rogue and peasant slave am I!") he speaks of having the "motive and the cue for passion" (2.2.571). Only slightly less familiar is his description of how on the voyage to England he devised the plot of sending Rosencrantz and Guildenstern to their deaths with a forged commission:

> Being thus benetted round with villains,
> Or I could make a prologue to my brains,
> They had begun the play. I sat me down,
> Devised a new commission, wrote it fair.
>
> (5.2.29–32)

And we remember that in the final scene the dying Hamlet addresses the court—and probably the actual spectators in the Globe as well—as you "that are but mutes or audience to this act" (5.2.336).

Hamlet's first reaction to the ghost is to leap enthusiastically into the familiar role. "Haste me" to know the truth, he cries, that I may "sweep to my revenge" (1.5.29–31). And a few lines later he launches into his vow of vengeance, the furious second soliloquy ("O all you host of heaven!") in which he calls upon heaven, earth, and hell, addresses his heart and his sinews, and pledges to wipe from his brain everything except the commandment of the ghost. It is a tissue of rhetoric passionate and hyperbolical in the true Senecan tradition, a piece of ranting of which Kyd's Hieronomo would be proud. Hamlet's self-consciousness as a revenger is suggested by the speech he requests when the players arrive, the story of Pyrrhus's bloody vengeance for his father's death. What he sees in this story is an image of his own father's fall in the crash of father Priam and, in the grief of Hecuba, the "mobled queen," an image of how Queen Gertrude ought to have behaved after her husband's death. But he also sees in Pyrrhus a horrible reflection of his own role, and, significantly, it is the prince himself who enacts the first dozen lines describing the dismal heraldry of the avenger.

Art for Hamlet is the mirror of nature, designed to provoke self-examination. Very reasonably, then, his interview with the players prompts him in the third soliloquy to consider his own motive and cue for passion, to examine how well he has performed as a revenger. Excepting his stormy vow of vengeance, Hamlet has so far controlled himself rather strictly in his duel with Claudius; he has not, by and large, indulged in much cleaving of the general ear with horrid speech in the normal manner of a revenger, and his contempt for such a manner is implicit in his description of what the common player would do with his cue: amaze the very faculties of eyes and ears and drown the stage with tears. Hamlet's aristocratic taste is for a more subtle species of drama, for plays like the one from which the story of Pyrrhus comes, which he praises to the players for being written with as much "modesty"—by which he means restraint—as cunning. Yet now, with the stock role he is to play brought home to him by the actors, Hamlet falls into the trap of judging himself by the very standards he has rejected and is disturbed by his own silence. Theatrically self-conscious as he is, Hamlet is naturally preoccupied by the relationship between playing and genuine feeling. He touches upon this in his first scene when he speaks to Gertrude of his outward "shapes of grief":

> These indeed seem,
> For they are actions that a man might play,
> But I have that within which passes show;
> These but the trappings and the suits of woe.
>
> (1.3.83–86)

How is one to distinguish mere shape—in theatrical parlance the word means costume or role as well as form—from the real thing? Or conversely, if the usual shape is lacking, how can one be sure of the substance? After the interview with the players, it is the latter problem which concerns Hamlet, for now he wonders whether his refusal to play the revenger in the usual shape, his reluctance to drown the stage with tears, means simply that he is unpregnant of his cause. As if to prove to himself that this is not so, he winds himself up again to the ranting rhetoric of the revenger, challenging some invisible observer to call him coward, pluck his beard, tweak his nose, and finally hurling at Claudius a passion stream of epithets:

> Bloody, bawdy villain!
> Remorseless, treacherous, lecherous, kindless villain!
> O vengeance!
>
> (2.2.591–93)

By this time, at any rate, the role playing is conscious, and a moment later the aristocrat in Hamlet triumphs and he curses himself for a whore, a drab. To rant is cheap and vulgar; moreover, what is presently required is not the player's whorish art but action. And so, with superb irony in his choice of means, Hamlet decides to take his own kind of action:

> I'll have these players
> Play something like the murder of my father
> Before mine uncle.
>
> (2.2.606–08)

Hamlet's difficulty is aesthetic. His problem is one of form and content, of suiting the action to the word, the word to the action—that is, of finding a satisfactory shape for his revenge. Inevitably he is drawn to the preexisting pattern of the familiar revenge plays: life imitates art. Inevitably, too, his sensibility rebels, refusing to permit him to debase himself into a ranting simpleton. I find no evidence that the idea of revenge, of taking life, is itself abhorrent to Hamlet—he is not after all a modern exponent of nonviolence—rather it is the usual style of the revenger that he disdains. He objects to passionate rhetoric because to him it typifies bestial unreason. The conventional revenger, the Hieronomo or the Titus Andronicus, responds mechanically to circumstances, beating his breast in grief and crying wildly for revenge. Such a man is Fortune's pipe, the puppet of his circumstances, and the prisoner of his own passion. When Hamlet praises the man who is not "passion's slave," he is not merely repeating a humanist commonplace; he is commenting on an immediate problem, asserting a profound objection to the role in which he has been cast. At stake, then, for Hamlet is an aesthetic principle, but it is a moral principle as well: the issue is human dignity. In a play in which the earsplitting rhetoric becomes the symbol of the protagonist's burden, it is suitable that "silence" is the final word from his lips as he dies. "The rest," he says, referring to all that must be left unspoken but also to the repose of death, "is silence."

The nature of Hamlet's objection to his role is elaborated in his address to the players—a speech too frequently overlooked in interpretations of this play—which Shakespeare has included because it permits the prince to comment indirectly on his most vital concern, how one ought to play the part of a revenger. Hamlet's demand is for elegance and restraint—in a word, for dignity in playing. Lines are to be spoken "trippingly on the tongue"—that is, with grace—rather than clumsily "mouthed" in the fashion of a town crier. Nor should the player permit himself gross gestures, as sawing the air with his hand; rather he must "use all gently," and even in the very torrent, tempest, and whirlwind of passion—the moment of extremity when the temptation to strut and bellow is greatest—must "acquire and beget a temperance that may give it smoothness" (3.2.7–8). The actor who tears a passion to tatters may win the applause of the groundlings who are only amused by noise, but he is worse than Termagant or Herod, those proverbially noisy stock characters of the old mystery plays which Hamlet disdains as ignorant and vulgar drama. It is interesting that Hamlet mentions Herod and the mythical infidel god Termagant: he means to suggest that undisciplined acting is not merely poor art, an offense against the "modesty of Nature," but an offense to all that a Christian gentleman, a humanist like himself, stands for. "O, there be players," he says a few lines later,

> that I have seen play . . . that neither having th' accent of Christians, nor the gait of Christian, pagan, nor man, have so strutted and bellowed that I have thought some of Nature's journeymen had made men, and not made them well, they imitated humanity so abominably.
>
> (3.2.30–37)

To rage and rant is to make oneself into a monster. The crux of the issue is this: like his father—"'A was a man, take him for all in all" (1.3.187)—Hamlet intends to be a man.

The player answers Hamlet's indictment of vulgar acting by assuring him that his company has improved its style: "I hope we have reformed that indifferently with us, sir." This complacency irritates Hamlet. "O, reform it altogether" (3.2.39–40), he snaps in reply. Hamlet's concern is intense and personal precisely because his own life has taken the shape of a vulgar play, a crude and commonplace tragedy of revenge. The prince's resolve—tantalizingly like Shakespeare's, working over what must have seemed to him the crude and commonplace material of Kyd's *Hamlet*—is to "reform it altogether." Since he cannot escape the role, Hamlet intends at least to be a revenger in a style that offends neither the modesty of nature nor his sense of human dignity. He intends to exercise discipline. I do not mean to suggest that Hamlet, like the singing gravedigger, has no feeling for his work. On the contrary, much of the drama lies in Hamlet's war with himself, his struggle to reduce his whirlwind passion to smoothness.

Hamlet and *Lear* are the only two of Shakespeare's tragedies with double plots. The Gloucester plot in *Lear* provides a relatively simple moral exemplum of one who stumbled when he saw and lost his eyes in consequence. This is a commonplace species of Elizabethan moral fable designed to set off the more complex and ambiguous story of the king. The story of Polonius's family works analogously in *Hamlet*. Each member of the family is a fairly ordinary person who serves as a foil to some aspect of Hamlet's extraordinary cunning and discipline. Polonius imagines himself a regular Machiavel, an expert at using indirections to find directions out, but compared to Hamlet he is what the prince calls him, a great baby. Ophelia, unable to control her grief, lapses into madness and a muddy death, reminding us that it is one of Hamlet's achievements that he does not go mad but only plays at insanity to disguise his true strength. And Laertes, of course, goes mad in a different fashion and becomes the model of the kind of revenger that Hamlet so disdains.

Hamlet knows he is playing a role, but Laertes is blissfully unselfconscious about his part. The prince boasts to his mother that his pulse "doth temperately keep time" (3.4.141), but Laertes' brag is of his stereotyped rage: "That drop of blood that's calm proclaims me bastard" (4.5.117). Laertes—to adapt Nashe's famous allusion to Kyd's old *Hamlet*—if you entreat him fair in a frosty morning, will shamelessly afford you handfuls of tragical speeches, ranting in the best manner of English Seneca:

> To hell allegiance, vows to the blackest devil,
> Conscience and grace to the profoundest pit!
> I dare damnation. To this point I stand,
> That both the worlds I give to negligence,
> Let come what comes, only I'll be revenged
> Most thoroughly for my father.
>
> (4.5.131–136)

What comes is not quite the revenge Laertes expects, for the situation is not so simple as he supposes; rather he finds himself on account of his unthinking passion as an easy instrument for Claudius to play, becoming, in his own word, the king's "organ." The advice that Polonius gave Laertes might have stood the young man in good stead if he had followed it: "Give thy thoughts no tongue, / Nor any unproportioned thought his act (1.3.59–60). Ironically, Polonius's words perfectly describe not Laertes' but Hamlet's approach to revenge. From the very first Hamlet has understood the practical as well as the aesthetic importance of controlling his rage. "But break my heart, for I must hold my tongue" (1.2.159), he says at the end of the first soliloquy, and it is interesting in the light of the play's general association of lack of discipline with noise, with rant, that even here control is connected with silence.

Shakespeare contrives to have his two revengers, the typical Laertes and the extraordinary Hamlet, meet at Ophelia's grave, where the prince finds Laertes true to form tearing a passion to tatters, bellowing to be buried alive with his sister. Hamlet steps forward and the technical rhetorical terms he uses, *emphasis* and *phrase,* together with the theatrical simile of making the stars stand like "wonder-wounded hearers," like an audience, reveal his critical attitude, his professional interest in the quality of Laertes' performance:

> What is he whose grief
> Bears such an emphasis, whose phrase of sorrow
> Conjures the wand'ring stars, and makes them stand
> Like wonder-wounded hearers?
>
> (5.1.256–59)

According to the probably authentic stage direction of the first quarto, Hamlet at this point leaps into the grave alongside Laertes, suiting outrageous word to outrageous action by challenging the young man to a contest of noise, of rant. What will Laertes do to prove his love for Ophelia, weep, tear himself, drink vinegar, eat a crocodile? Hamlet will match him. Does Laertes mean to whine, to prate of being buried under a mountain higher than Pelion? Why, then Hamlet will say he'll be buried too, and let the imaginary mountain be so high that it touches the sphere of fire and makes Ossa by comparison a wart. "Nay, an thou'lt mouth," the prince says, using the same word with which he had earlier described the manner of vulgar actors, "I'll rant as well as thou" (5.1.285–86).

Hamlet is mocking Laertes' style, but the bitterness of his mockery, the nastiness of it, derives from his own sincere grief for Ophelia. In a world of overblown rhetoric, of grotesque elephantine shows, how can a man of taste and discernment be understood? Moreover, since the usual sound and fury so often signify nothing, how will a man of genuine feeling be believed? This burlesque of Laertes is Hamlet's last act of bitter rebellion against the vulgarity of his world and the role he has been constrained to play in it. Moreover, it is a reversion to his earlier and fiercer mood, the proud, contemptuous spirit of the prince before the sea voyage; for, as most critics observe, the prince who returns from sea is a changed man, resigned, detached, perhaps "tragically illuminated." Having refused to kill the king when the time was every way propitious—that is, when he found Claudius kneeling in empty not genuine prayer—and then, having chosen his own moment to act only to find that instead of the king he has murdered Polonius, Hamlet seems to have allowed his sinews to relax. He has let himself be thrust aboard ship, let himself in effect be cast onto the sea of fortune that is so common an image in Shakespeare and the Elizabethan poets, an image recalling that "sea of troubles" against which he had earlier taken arms. When the opportunity to escape the king's trap arises, Hamlet seizes it, leaping aboard the pirate ship, but what he is doing now is reacting to circumstances rather than trying to dominate them wholly. The prince returns to Denmark at once sad and amused, but, except for the single flash of "towering passion" at Ophelia's grave, relatively impassive. He has ceased to insist that he must be above being played upon by any power.

And yet, before Hamlet consents to the duel with Laertes, about which he has justified misgivings, he plays a scene with that impossible fop, Osric, the emblem of the empty courtesy of Claudius's court. Just as Hamlet earlier led Polonius through the game of cloud shapes, so now he toys with Osric, leading him to proclaim first that the weather is warm, then that it is cold, and finally warm again. At the penultimate moment, Hamlet is demonstrating that if he wished he might still play upon the king and his instruments like so many pipes. Hamlet's mocking Osric, like the scene with Laertes in the grave, recalls the early proud manner of the prince; nevertheless, Hamlet no longer seems to be in rebellion: rather than bitter contempt he displays amusement that at the end he should be forced to share the stage with a waterfly. The prince's motto is no longer "heart, lose not thy nature," but "let be." He has ceased to struggle for absolute freedom in his role, ceased to insist that he alone must be the artist who, in all senses of the term, shapes his life. He understands now that, in Laertes' words, he cannot carve for himself. One can at best be a collaborator in one's life, for there is always another artist to be taken into account, "a divinity that shapes our ends, / Rough-hew them how we will."

The Hamlet who speaks of special providence in the fall of a sparrow is not perhaps so exciting a figure as the earlier Hamlet heroically refusing to be manipulated. There is something almost superhuman in the discipline, consciousness, and cunning of the earlier Hamlet: certainly he makes superhuman demands upon himself, insisting that he be in action like an angel, in apprehension like a god. But Hamlet has discovered that, finally, he is subject to his birth, that he is neither angel nor god, and, in an ironically different sense, it can now be said of him what he said of his father, "'A was a man, take him for all." King Hamlet fought his single combat in an unfallen world of law and heraldry; his son must seek to emulate him in a corrupt world of empty chivalry and poisoned foils; and yet, in its way, Hamlet's duel with Laertes is as heroic as his father's with Fortinbras, and in his own manner Hamlet proves himself worthy of the name of soldier.

"Bear Hamlet like a soldier to the stage (5.2.397) is the command of Fortinbras which concludes the play, a command which not only ratifies Hamlet's heroism by using the term *soldier,* but in its theatrical allusion reminds us that much of his achievement has been in the skill with which he has played his inauspicious role. If all the world is a stage and all the men and women merely players, then the reckoning of quality must be by professional standards. By these standards Hamlet has proven himself a very great actor indeed, for he has taken a vulgar role and reformed it so that it no longer offends the modesty of nature or the dignity of man. Even a man on a tether, to pick up Polonius's image again, has a certain degree of freedom. One may be cast in a vulgar role and still win distinction in the manner the role is played. Or one may be tied to the story line of a crude melodrama and still produce a *Hamlet.*

ADELMAN

Man and Wife Is One Flesh:
Hamlet and the Confrontation with the Material Body

The first mother to reappear in Shakespeare's plays is adulterous, I think, because maternal origin is in itself felt as equivalent to adulterating betrayal of the male, both father and son; *Hamlet* initiates the period of Shakespeare's greatest tragedies because it in effect rewrites the story of Cain and Abel as the story of Adam and Eve, relocating masculine identity in the presence of the adulterating female. This rewriting accounts, I think, for Gertrude's odd position in the play, especially for its failure to specify the degree to which she is complicit in the murder. Less powerful as an independent character than as the site for fantasies larger than she is, she is preeminently mother as other, the intimate unknown figure around whom these fantasies swirl. She is kept ambiguously innocent as a character, but in the deep fantasy that structures the play's imagery, she plays out the role of the missing Eve: her body is the garden in which her husband dies, her sexuality the poisonous weeds that kill him, and poison the world—and the self—for her son. This is the psychological fantasy registered by the simultaneity of funeral and marriage: the reappearance of the mother in *Hamlet* is tantamount to the death of the idealized father because her presence signals his absence, and hence the absence of the son's defense against her rank mixture, her capacity to annihilate or contaminate; as in Marcellus's purifying fantasy, what the idealized father ultimately protects against is the dangerous female powers of the night. The boy-child masters his fear of these powers partly through identification with his father, the paternal presence who has initially helped him to achieve separation from his mother; but if his father fails him—if the father himself seems subject to her—then that protective identification fails. This is exactly the psychological situation at the beginning of *Hamlet*, where Hamlet's father has become unavailable to him, not only through the fact of his death but through the complex vulnerability that his death demonstrates. This father cannot protect his son; and his disappearance in effect throws Hamlet into the domain of the engulfing mother, awakening all the fears incident to the primary mother-child bond. Here as in Shakespeare's later plays, the loss of the father turns out in fact to mean the psychic domination of the mother: in the end, it is the specter of his mother, not his uncle-father, who paralyzes his will. The Queen, the Queen's to blame.

This shift of agency and of danger from male to female seems to me characteristic of the fantasy-structure of *Hamlet* and of Shakespeare's imagination in the plays that follow. The ghost's initial injunction sets as the prime business of the play the killing of Claudius; he specifically asks Hamlet to leave his mother alone, beset only by the thorns of conscience (1.5.85–87). But if Gertrude rather than Claudius is to blame, then Hamlet's fundamental task shifts; simple revenge is no longer the issue. Despite his ostensible agenda of revenge, the main psychological task that Hamlet seems to set himself is not to avenge his father's death but to remake his mother: to remake her in the image of the Virgin Mother who could guarantee his father's purity, and his own, repairing the boundaries of his selfhood. Throughout the play, the covert drama of reformation vies for priority with the overt drama of revenge, in fact displacing it both from what we see of Hamlet's consciousness and from center stage of the play: when Hamlet accuses himself of lack of purpose (3.4.107–110), of failing to remember his father's business of revenge (4.4.40), he may in part be right. Even as an avenger, Hamlet seems motivated more by his mother than by his father: when he describes Claudius to Horatio as "he that hath kill'd my king and whor'd my mother" (5.2.64), the second phrase clearly carries more intimate emotional weight than the first. And he manages to achieve his revenge only when he can avenge his mother's death, not his father's: just where we might expect some version of "rest, perturbed spirit" to link his killing of Claudius with his father's initial injunction, we get "Is thy union here? / Follow my mother" (5.2.331–332).

This shift—from avenging the father to saving the mother—accounts in part for certain peculiarities about this play as a revenge play: why, for example, the murderer is given so little attention in the device ostensibly designed to catch his conscience, why the confrontation of Hamlet with Gertrude in the closet scene seems much more central, much more vivid, than any confrontation between Hamlet and Claudius. Once we look at "The Murder of Gonzago" for what it is, rather than for what Hamlet tells us it is, it becomes clear that the playlet is in fact designed to catch the conscience of the queen: its challenge is always to her loving posture, its accusation "A second time I kill my husband dead / When second husband kisses me in bed." The confrontation with Gertrude (3.4) follows so naturally from this attempt to catch her conscience that Hamlet's unexpected meeting with Claudius (3.3) feels to us like an interruption of a more fundamental purpose. Indeed, Shakespeare stages 3.3 very much as an interruption: Hamlet comes upon Claudius praying as he is on his way to his mother's closet, worrying about the extent to which he can repudiate the Nero in himself; and we come upon Claudius unexpectedly in the same way. That is: the moment that should be the apex of the revenge plot—the potential confrontation alone of the avenger and his prey—becomes for the audience and for the avenger himself a lapse, an interlude that must be gotten over before the real business can be attended to. It is no wonder that Hamlet cannot kill Claudius here: to do so would be to make of the interlude a permanent interruption of his more fundamental purpose. Not even Hamlet could reasonably expect to manage his mother's moral reclamation immediately after he has killed her husband.

Nor would that avenging death regain the mother whom Hamlet needs: once his mother has been revealed as the fallen and possessed garden, she can be purified only by being separated from her sexuality. This separation is in fact Hamlet's effort throughout 3.4. In that confrontation, Hamlet first insists that Gertrude acknowledge the difference between Claudius and Old Hamlet, the difference her adultery and remarriage had undermined. But after the initial display of portraits, Hamlet attempts to induce in her revulsion not at her choice of the wrong man but at her sexuality itself, the rebellious hell that mutinies in her matron's bones (3.4.82–83), the "rank corruption, mining all within" (3.4.150). Here, as in the play within the play, Hamlet recreates obsessively, voyeuristically, the acts that have corrupted the royal bed, even when he has to subject his logic and syntax to considerable strain to do so:

QUEEN:　　　　　What shall I do?

HAM.:　　Not this, by no means, that I bid you do:
　　　　　Let the bloat King tempt you again to bed
　　　　　Pinch wanton on your cheek, call you his mouse,
　　　　　And let him, for a pair of reechy kisses,
　　　　　Or paddling in your neck with his damn'd fingers,
　　　　　Make you to ravel all this matter out
　　　　　That I essentially am not in madness,
　　　　　But mad in craft.

(3.4.182–190)

There has to be an easier way of asking your mother not to reveal that your madness is an act. "Not this, by no means, that I bid you do": Hamlet cannot stop imagining, even commanding, the sexual act that he wants to undo. Moreover, the bloated body of this particular king is not particular to him: it is the sexualized male body, its act any sexual act. The royal bed of Denmark is always already corrupted, already a couch for luxury, as Hamlet's own presence testifies. "Go not to my uncle's bed" (3.4.161), Hamlet tells his mother; but his disgust at the incestuous liaison rationalizes a prior disgust at all sexual concourse, as his attempt to end the specifically incestuous union rationalizes an attempt to remake his mother pure by divorcing her from her sexuality.

Act 3 scene 4 records Hamlet's attempt to achieve this divorce, to recover the fantasied presence of the asexual mother of childhood, the mother who can restore the sense of sanctity to the world her sexuality has spoiled: his first and last word in the scene is "mother" (3.4.7; 3.4.219). And in his own mind at least, Hamlet does seem to achieve this recovery. He begins the scene by wishing that Gertrude were not his mother ("would it were not so, you are my mother" [3.4.15]); but toward the end, he is able to imagine her as the mother from whom he would beg—and receive—blessing:

　　　　　Once more, good night,
　　And when you are desirous to be blest,
　　I'll blessing beg of you.

(3.4.172–174)

This mother can bless Hamlet only insofar as she herself asks to be blessed by him, signaling her conversion from husband to son and inverting the relation of parent and child; Hamlet is very much in charge even as he imagines asking for maternal blessing. Nonetheless, coming near the end of

Hamlet's long scene of rage and disgust, these lines seem to me extraordinarily moving in their evocation of desire for the maternal presence that can restore the sense of the world and the self as blessed. And the blessedness they image is specifically in the relation of world and self: as mother and son mirror each other, each blessing each, Shakespeare images the reopening of the zone of trust that had been foreclosed by the annihilating mother. For the first time, Hamlet imagines something coming to him from outside himself that will neither invade nor contaminate him: the recovery of benign maternal presence for a moment repairs the damage of the fall in him, making safe the boundary-permeability that had been a source of terror. Toward the end of the scene, all those night-terrors are gone: Hamlet's repeated variations on the conventional phrase "good night" mark his progression from rage at his mother's sexuality to repossession of the good mother he had lost. He begins with "Good night. But go not to my uncle's bed. . . . Refrain tonight" (3.4.161, 167), attempting to separate her from her horrific night-body; but by the end—through his own version of Marcellus's purifying fantasy—he has succeeded in imagining both her and the night wholesome. If he begins by wishing Gertrude were not his mother, he ends with the poignant repeated leave-taking of a child who does not want to let go of the mother who now keeps him safe: "Once more, good night . . . So again, good night. . . . Mother, good night indeed. . . . Good night, mother" (3.4.172, 179, 215, 219).

In the end, we do not know whether or not Gertrude herself has been morally reclaimed; it is the mark of the play's investment in Hamlet's fantasies that, even here, we are not allowed to see her as a separate person. To the extent that she looks into the heart that Hamlet has "cleft in twain" (3.4.158) and finds the "black and grained spots" (3.4.90) that he sees there, she seems to accept his version of her soiled inner body; in any case, her response allows him to think of his initial Nero-like aggression—speaking daggers though using none (3.2.387)—as moral reclamation. But as usual in this play, she remains relatively opaque, more a screen for Hamlet's fantasies about her than a fully developed character in her own right: whatever individuality she might have had is sacrificed to her status as mother. Nonetheless, though we might wonder just what his evidence is, Hamlet at least believes that she has returned to him as the mother he can call "good lady" (3.4.182). And after 3.4, her remaining actions are ambiguous enough to nourish his fantasy: though there are no obvious signs of separation from Claudius in her exchanges with him, in her last moments she seems to become a wonderfully homey presence for her son, newly available to him as the loving and protective mother of childhood, worrying about his condition, wiping his face as he fights, even perhaps intentionally drinking the poison intended for him.

In the end, whatever her motivation, he seems securely possessed of her as an internal good mother; and this possession gives him a new calm about his place in the world and especially about death, that domain of maternal dread. Trusting her, he can begin to trust in himself and in his own capacity for action; and he can begin to rebuild the masculine identity spoiled by her contamination. For his secure internal possession of her idealized image permits the return of his father to him, and in the form that he had always wanted: turning his mother away from Claudius, Hamlet wins her not only for himself but also for his father—for his father conceived as Hyperion, the bodiless godlike figure he had invoked at the beginning of the play. If her sexuality had spoiled this father, her purification brings him back; after 3.4, the guilty father and his ghost disappear, replaced by the distant heavenly father into whom he has been transformed, the one now acting through the sign of the other: "Why, even in that was heaven ordinant. / I had my father's signet in my purse" (5.2.48–49). Unexpectedly finding this sign of the father on his own person, Hamlet in effect registers his repossession of the idealized father within; and, like a good son, Hamlet can finally merge himself with this father, making His will his own.

ELLEN J. O'BRIEN

Revision by Excision: Rewriting Gertrude

From 1755 until 1900 (and not infrequently from 1900 to World War II) actors playing Gertrude found in their scripts a significantly different role than those in either the First Folio or Second Quarto texts. That Gertrude's role was both radically and nearly consistently cut throughout the era will scarcely be startling news to anyone acquainted with the performance practices of the nineteenth century. But the consequences of such cutting may be. Close comparison of Gertrude's role as it appears in the Folio and Second Quarto texts with the role as it emerges from the standard nineteenth-century version reveals the potential for subtle but powerful revision inherent—though often nearly invisible—in cutting.

To grasp the significance of this, we must understand that the Shakespearian actor grounds decisions about the role in the patterns of thought, speech, and action inherent in the text. Cuts, or conversely, added lines and stage directions, can create patterns at odds with those of the original texts.

Many actors, when asked to play a cut role, will attempt to act the implications of the full version, to play the role as it was written rather than as it was cut. Yet since the editions of *Hamlet* most commonly used as nineteenth-century promptbooks regularly omitted lines, added stage directions, and, on occasion, revised lines, the actors had no choice but to respond to a very different set of performance signals. In Gertrude's case, these editions destroyed many of the verbal patterns of the role and eviscerated patterns of visual imagery established by the Folio and Second Quarto texts. The result was a very different Gertrude.

Before we can see the impact of the nineteenth-century cuts, we must examine the patterning of the original texts. As Steven Urkowitz has demonstrated, the First Quarto, Second Quarto, and Folio texts each give Gertrude a different textual pattern. Nevertheless, while the First Quarto is too distinctive to be treated with the others, the Folio and Second Quarto texts do share a subtle but consistent complex of textual patterns in Gertrude's language and the stage directions affecting her. Most striking is the marked shift in these patterns which occurs around the closet scene—suggesting that Gertrude's encounter with Hamlet in that scene has some lasting effect and that the role is therefore dynamic rather than static. The verbal patterns are too complex to be explored within the limits of this paper, but the simpler patterns of visual imagery created by stage directions explicit and implicit in the text offer a manageable example.

For Gertrude almost nothing beyond entrances and exits is made explicit in the stage directions of the Folio or Second Quarto texts. Nevertheless, these do create an intriguing visual pattern which, up to the closet scene, establishes an association between Claudius and Gertrude and then, in succeeding scenes, seriously undercuts that association. Before the closet scene, Gertrude always enters with Claudius; in that scene she enters with Polonius, here strongly associated with the King through their collusion in arranging this encounter between Hamlet and his mother. However, her first entrance after the closet scene (4.5) is made with Horatio and a gentleman (in the Folio, Horatio only): a telling switch. While the gentleman may be regarded as neutral, Horatio is clearly aligned with Hamlet, visually associating Gertrude with Hamlet as Polonius associates her with Claudius in the closet scene. Indeed, this may be the reason for Horatio's somewhat odd inclusion in the scene. Although neither the Folio nor the Second Quarto offers any equivalent to the First Quarto scene which establishes a specific alliance between Gertrude, Horatio, and Hamlet, the visual image here carries forward at least some of its suggestion. In 4.7 Gertrude enters alone to announce Ophelia's death, and while her first line may be a response to Claudius (particularly if he speaks the Folio's 'How sweet Queen?' rather than the Second Quarto's impersonal 'but stay, what noise?') the rest of her speeches are almost certainly directed to Laertes, not Claudius. After the closet scene, Gertrude enters with Claudius only in 5.1 and 5.2—for the funeral and the fencing match—both large court entrances on formal occasions which would almost automatically assign her a place with the King. When given any choice in the matter, she seems to remain separate from him.

Exits are more ambiguous, but suggest a parallel pattern. In every exit before the end of the play-within-the-play, Claudius either leaves with Gertrude or makes verbal provision for her exit. Here, however, he issues only a general 'Away' (3.2.257) not specifically addressed to Gertrude. The context and Gertrude's 'How fares my lord?' (3.2.255) certainly suggest that she exits in his wake, yet he, for the first time, does nothing to determine this. This loosening of corporate identity on the King's part functions as an ironic anticipation of Gertrude's behaviour following the closet scene. Her exits in those scenes fall into two patterns. In 4.1 and 4.7, Claudius not only asks Gertrude to come with him but does so twice, repeating 'come' or 'let's follow' within a few lines. Repetition of this kind occurs nowhere in Claudius' exit lines to other characters, though a similar double command to Gertrude does occur in 4.5 when he tells her twice to release Laertes. It seems clear that Gertrude does not let go of Laertes on the first command, and the double exit lines in 4.1 and 4.7 suggest a parallel response. Gertrude may well hesitate to follow her husband at first command after the revelations of the closet scene.

Gertrude's remaining exits, in 4.5 and 5.1, are not made specific: both the Folio and the Second Quarto simply indicate mass exits ('Exeunt') at the end of the scene. Since no other provision is made for the Queen, this might logically be expected to include her, yet such an exit works in opposition to the substance of these scenes as well as the pattern of her other exits. At the time of the exit in 4.5, Claudius is completely focused on the rebellious Laertes, having said nothing to or about Gertrude since telling her to let Laertes speak his piece before Ophelia's entrance. Moreover, if Claudius' exit line—'I pray you go with me' (4.5.217)—were to include Gertrude as well as Laertes, the Queen would almost become one of the conspirators in the plot against her son, particularly since the line is immediately preceded by a veiled threat to Hamlet: ". . . where th'offence is, let the great axe fall" (4.5.216). Given what Claudius is about to discuss with Laertes, he could hardly want Gertrude to go with them. In performance, Gertrude frequently follows Ophelia out earlier in the scene, leaving the conspirators to exit together—as they will re-enter in 4.7. Indeed, in the nineteenth century, Gertrude's early exit was so regular a practice that it was printed in many of the standard editions, and it is not unusual today. The absence from both the Folio and the Second Quarto of stage directions for Gertrude at several points where stage business is clearly implied (including her exit before the nunnery scene) makes it tempting to believe that such an exit was intended but not recorded. The First Quarto almost requires it: while no separate exit is indicated for the Queen (only 'exeunt om.' at the end of the scene), the stage direction which follows immediately, 'Enter Horatio and the Queene' (H2v line 4, 5) suggests strongly that she has exited before Laertes and Claudius. With only a few exceptions, Shakespeare's characters do not exit at the end of one scene and immediately re-enter in the first lines of the next. Yet even if Gertrude remains on stage until the end, the dialogue invites visual emphasis on the association of the two men. Gertrude might simply be left behind, forgotten—or deliberately excluded—in the heat of the exchange between Laertes and the King. Whenever her exit occurs, the textual patterning suggests an image associating Claudius and Laertes while isolating Gertrude from them.

The closing lines of the funeral scene suggest a similar effect, for Claudius is once again focused on a volatile Laertes, turning to Gertrude only to say 'Good Gertrude set some watch over your son' (5.1.293)—a line which may well prompt her exit before Claudius delivers the final lines of the scene to Laertes. Here, too, a final image of the two conspirators is likely.

What emerges from the original stage directions, then, is a visual pattern which not only undercuts the initial visual association of Claudius and Gertrude after the closet scene, but simultaneously focuses our eyes on the developing bond between Claudius and Laertes. In addition, the later scenes establish a parallel association between Gertrude and Hamlet. This is initiated by the closet scene's pact of secrecy between mother and son and is extended visually by Gertrude's entrance with Horatio, a visual link to Hamlet, at the opening of 4.5. But it is most powerfully embodied in the implicit stage imagery of the moments preceding Gertrude's death. The proffering of her napkin all but requires proximity to Hamlet, and her subsequent offer to wipe his face strongly suggests intimacy as well as proximity. This visual association is corroborated by the focus of Gertrude's dialogue. Her first words in the scene, although prompted by Claudius' "Our son shall win," hardly seem addressed to the King, for they focus entirely on Hamlet: "He's fat and scant of breath . . ." (5.2.239; 240). The only other words she addresses to Claudius are a flat rejection of his order not to drink: "I will, my lord, I pray you pardon me" (5.2.244). Her remaining lines are directed exclusively to Hamlet. At the same moment that Gertrude and Hamlet are drawn into visual association, the private exchange between Claudius and Laertes necessitates at least a momentary visual association of the two conspirators.

LAERTES: My lord, I'll hit him now.
CLAUDIUS: I do not think't.

(5.2.248–249)

Thus, the demands of the dialogue call for a stage picture which pairs Gertrude with Hamlet and Claudius with Laertes, echoing and reinforcing the pattern of exits and entrances in Acts 4 and 5.

This pattern has frequently been obscured by the tradition of a Gertrude who dotes on Claudius, yet the patterning of Gertrude's language suggest no such obsession. To begin with, we have the striking fact that Gertrude never speaks Claudius' name; before the play-within-the-play she never addresses him even by title and refers to him only once (as 'Denmark' 1.2.69), although others speak of the King frequently. He, on the other hand, refers to the Queen often and uses her name thirteen times, four times with the epithet "dear," "sweet" or "good" attached to it. Moreover, up to this point she never speaks to Claudius without first being spoken to by him. The King doesn't seem to be much on Gertrude's mind. In striking contrast, Hamlet's name occurs in Gertrude's speech fifteen times, twelve in direct address, and four with precisely those epithets Claudius attaches to her name: "dear," "sweet" and "good." The intensity of attachment Claudius manifests for her is thus paralleled not in her language to or about Claudius but in what she says to and about her son. Indeed, prior to the closet scene she says nothing that isn't at least indirectly related to Hamlet, taking no part in Claudius' discussion of other matters—not even their marriage. In light of all of this, the tradition of a Gertrude who dotes on Claudius seems very much at odds with her textual patterning. Instead, she appears preoccupied from the first with Hamlet. It is Claudius who finds Gertrude "so conjunctive to [his] life and soul / That, as the star moves not but in his sphere, [he] could not but by her" (4.7.14–16)—not vice versa. The preoccupations of her language suggest that, if pushed to a choice, Gertrude is more disposed to ally herself with Hamlet than with Claudius.

The patterning of her entrances and exits suggests that, after the closet scene, she has, consciously or unconsciously, made that choice. The association between Gertrude and Claudius established prior to that scene is broken in the succeeding scenes as Gertrude is paired with Hamlet and

Claudius with Laertes. (As I noted earlier, Gertrude's verbal patterns also shift at this point in the play, underscoring the strength of the shift and pinpointing its location.) While I would not argue that Gertrude is now actively in league with Hamlet, as she is in the First Quarto, the visual patterning of the play moves her toward him and away from Claudius.

Yet nineteenth-century texts and performances suggested no such thing. Apparently insignificant alterations actually created radical revisions in the visual patterns of the play: maintaining the pre-closet scene association of Gertrude and Claudius to the final scene, while eliminating the post-closet scene association of Claudius and Laertes. Far more damaging—indeed, fatal—is the fact that the standard cuts of the nineteenth century completely obliterated the association of Hamlet and Gertrude by paring away so much of the defining context for the entrance/exit pattern that neither actor nor audience could be expected to discern their underlying significance. Thus, for nearly two hundred years, actors playing Gertrude worked from a text which implied a very different character— a woman ultimately unaffected by her closet scene encounter with Hamlet.

This is not to say that nineteenth-century performance practice disregarded the implications of visual association. We have already seen that Gertrude's awkward presence at the end of 4.5 was frequently dealt with by making explicit her potential early exit with Ophelia. There, the adjustment reinforced the patterning of the role. But all too frequently, awareness of visual implications led to alterations which obscured that patterning by making the association of Gertrude and Claudius a constant in the play. At the end of the funeral scene, nineteenth-century productions apparently sensed the implications of Gertrude's presence with the conspirators, though they responded with less unanimity to this than to the similar problem in 4.5. Only the Oxberry edition printed an exit for Gertrude before Claudius' ambiguous closing couplet: "An hour of quiet shortly shall we see; / Till then, in patience our proceeding be" (5.1.295–296). The printed stage directions of other standard editions either explicitly or implicitly kept the King and Queen together in the closing moments of the scene. Yet in performance, there seems to have been discomfort with combining this image and these lines. A number of promptbooks write in the Oxberry's early exit, and one 1864 promptbook keeps Gertrude onstage but has her walk to the right of Ophelia's grave while the King and Laertes remain to the left as the curtain falls. But more often the promptbooks cut the couplet, closing the scene on the King's "This grave shall have a living monument" and eliminating the closing image of the two conspirators. Similarly, in 4.1, 4.5, and 4.7, Claudius' repeated exit lines to Gertrude, with their implication of hesitation, were nearly always cut, thus reinforcing the impression of stability in the Gertrude/Claudius visual association.

Perhaps the most devastating cut occurred in the closet scene itself, eliminating both Hamlet's appeal to the Queen not to reveal that his madness is feigned and her vow to do so. Here we have the most direct manifestation of an association between Gertrude and her son, yet with overwhelming consistency, the acting editions and promptbooks of the day cut the final twenty-eight lines of the Folio text (along with the Second Quarto's additional nine lines), ending the scene with Hamlet's couplet: "I must be cruel only to be kind: / Thus bad begins, and worse remains behind" (3.4.162–163). Indeed, the cut seems to be almost universal: of the 182 nineteenth-century promptbooks collated in *Shakespeare as Spoken*, all but six cut this entire block. The first appearance of the block cut seems to be in the Woodfall edition of 1767 after which it became almost immediately universal. But editors and performers had begun chiselling away at the scene much earlier. Gertrude's vow itself (3.4.181–183) disappeared in the 1755 Witford edition, perhaps under Garrick's influence. After 1755 the vow appears only in reprints of the 1743 Knapton edition (1756, 1758, 1759, 1760) and the Hitch edition of 1759. Even the 1763 Hawes edition, which largely follows Knapton, cuts the vow. It does not reappear until the late nineteenth century—and even then in a mere handful of texts, only one of which appears to be a promptbook. For all practical purposes, Gertrude is not heard promising to keep Hamlet's secret from 1755 to 1900. Moreover, since nearly all the standard acting editions did not even print the excised lines, many actors probably never knew such a vow existed, creating a serious distortion in the textual patterns from which they might work.

In many cases, this led to stage business which not only ignored but specifically reversed the pattern of association between Hamlet and Gertrude initiated by the closet scene. In a mid-century promptbook, Hamlet's final "good night" led to the following business:

> Queen goes to door, clasps her hand in grief, turns to throw herself upon Hamlet's neck. He shrinks from her. She sighs heavily and exits overwhelmed with grief.
> (Folger: *Hamlet* 29)

Although I have yet to find stage directions of this kind actually printed in nineteenth-century editions, the number of times that similar business is written into contemporaneous promptbooks suggests a powerful tradition. For Kemble, Forrest, Booth and their imitators, the image was elaborated to include an attempt by Gertrude to bless her son from which he recoiled.

Although Booth was quite tender with Gertrude earlier in the scene, placing his arms "shieldingly" about her, allowing her to sob "on his heart" as she declares her heart "cleft in twain" and stroking her hair as he bids her "good night," he returned at the end to an image of the traditional revulsion and separation, not only recoiling from her but "check[ing] the motion" to bless him. Henry Irving, in the 1870s, appears to have been the first nineteenth-century Hamlet to close the encounter with his mother on an image of reconciliation. Frequently, Hamlet delivered the closing couplet after Gertrude had left the stage, depriving her of whatever sympathy there might be in "I must be cruel only to be kind" (3.4.162) and focusing the scene's closing image on an isolated Hamlet.

Other nineteenth-century cuts stripped away the signals that Gertrude had been profoundly affected by the closet-scene exchange. The succeeding scene, in which Gertrude tries to shield Hamlet by asserting his madness (and by engaging in several rhetorical manipulations too complicated to discuss here), was cut in its entirety from about twenty per cent of the books, although it was printed in the majority of the most commonly used acting editions. However, even those printed editions (and all but three promptbooks) cut two crucial lines which suggest Gertrude's efforts to protect Hamlet. The Second Quarto's "Bestow this place on us a little while" (ĸɪʀ. line 11) is the first order Gertrude has issued in the play which does not reiterate an earlier order by Claudius; its effect is to delay the revelation of Hamlet's killing and, by removing Rosencrantz and Guildenstern, to deliver it privately to Claudius. ". . . a weeps for what is done" (4.1.26), Gertrude's first self-initiated lie, also shields Hamlet by making him appear more remorseful than anything in his own language would indicate. Neither of these lines appears in the standard editions and both are cut from all but a handful of the nineteenth-century books. Gertrude's only explicit expression of guilt after the closet scene is heard at the opening of the mad scene: "To my sick soul, as sin's true nature is, / Each toy seems prologue to some great amiss. / So full of artless jealously is guilt, / It spills itself in fearing to be spilt" (4.5.17–20). These lines do not appear in a single eighteenth-century book, and though Macready apparently restored them in 1842, they appear in only about twenty-two books before 1900. Thus little overt evidence remains in the nineteenth-century books to indicate that the closet scene had had any impact whatsoever on Gertrude.

With the most obvious indications of an association between Gertrude and Hamlet excised, it is not surprising that the more subtle should also be allowed to slip away. At times, however, the excisions seem amazingly systematic, as though the violation of the pattern had created intuitive recognition of it, prompting the removal of its remaining pieces. The best example of this occurs in the lines surrounding Gertrude's drinking of the poison (5.2). The conscious motive for cutting at this point may simply have been to reduce Gertrude's role to the minimum, but the effect is to weaken, indeed virtually eliminate, her association with Hamlet and her dissociation from Claudius. Like the cuts described above, these begin to appear in the mid-eighteenth century and become standard by the 1770s. Yet in this case, we have not only cuts, but overt revision. Lines 239 to 248 of the scene usually read as follows in nineteenth-century editions (stage directions are taken from the Modern Standard Drama edition and are typical):

> KING: Our son shall win.
> QUEEN: The Queen carouses to thy fortune, Hamlet. [*The Queen drinks, and returns the cup to Francisco.*]
> HAMLET: Good madam!
> KING: [*Aside to the Queen.*] Gertrude, do not drink.
> QUEEN: I have my lord—I pray you pardon me.
> KING: [*Turning aside from the Queen.*] It is the poisoned cup: it is too late.
> LAERTES: I'll hit him now.

The changes here are small but of great significance. The line which invites physical proximity of mother and son—"Here, Hamlet, take my napkin. Rub thy brows"—appears in only five nineteenth-century books; that which suggests physical intimacy—"Come, let me wipe thy face"—in only three. Missing with nearly equal frequency is Hamlet's "I dare not drink yet, madam, by and by"—a line which strongly suggests that she makes a direct offer of the poisoned cup. Nothing remains to invite the stage image associating Gertrude with Hamlet which is so powerfully implicit in the Folio and Second Quarto. At the same time, the revision of Gertrude's response to Claudius' order not to drink—from "I will" to "I have"—makes her speech to Claudius apologetic rather than defiant. She seems less estranged from Claudius' authority than excessively thirsty. The motivation for this revision may have been the difficulty of making credible Claudius' failure to stop Gertrude from drinking if she is still at his side—as the cut scene (and a good many promptbook notations) would suggest that she is. Its effect, however, is to deal a final blow to the controlling patterns of Gertrude's role, making her relationships at the end of the play quite different from those implicit in the Folio and Second Quarto texts.

Ironically, though no nineteenth-century promptbook I have consulted indicates that the Queen moves away from Claudius during his exchange and several make clear that she does not, the awkwardness of this arrangement is recognized in a number of attempts to mitigate it. This is most obvious in several of the Booth books which record something like the following. "While the Queen drinks, Osric and others approach the King" as though to provide him with a distraction from her act. Then "suddenly observing the Queen," Claudius cries "Gertrude do not drink." The Queen, of course, can only apologize by then.

One further set of cuts in this exchange deserves attention. Laertes says not "My lord, I'll hit him now" but only "I'll hit him now," as though to himself, and the King's response "I do not think't" is entirely omitted, suggesting that the visual association of the conspirators, like the association of Gertrude and Hamlet, is eliminated. A cut of this kind appears in about ninety percent of the nineteenth-century books. Thus Gertrude remains visually associated with Claudius to the end, apparently unaffected by her closet scene exchange with Hamlet.

This complex of nineteenth-century cuts eviscerated the textual patterns which give coherence—and even interest—to Gertrude's role—an effect which would be all the more striking had we space to examine her verbal patterns along with the visual. There too we find a complex of textual patterns, all of which shift markedly after the closet scene and call for a corresponding change in Gertrude's behavior. Although the post-closet-scene Gertrude may be many things, this patterning suggests that she cannot be unchanged. By obliterating those patterns, nineteenth-century cutting made of Gertrude an unresponsive, mindless figure, momentarily distraught by Hamlet's closet scene harangue, but ultimately unaffected by it.

It is hardly surprising that all these changes should have emerged in the mid-eighteenth century, become nearly universal between 1770 and 1800, and endured to the late nineteenth century. The Restoration introduction of changeable scenery necessitated cuts to make time for scene changes, and the habits of editing and performance tended to preserve cuts once they were made. Both editors and performers relied largely on previous editions rather than the Folio or Second Quarto in preparing new editions and promptbooks. Moreover, since many editions purported to give the play "as performed" by the major actors of the day, cuts were not only tolerated but expected. Similarly, actors performing in an age of tradition mastered their roles by learning the stage business of their predecessors. An innovation might be praised and imitated if audiences accepted it (as was Kemble's rejection of Gertrude's blessing), but could bring devastating criticism if rejected. Mills cites the story of an old critic who, in the reign of George III, refused to see any great merit in the performance of a new Hamlet, declaring, "He did not upset the chair, sir [upon seeing the Ghost in Gertrude's closet]. Now Mr. Betterton always upset the chair." Re-introducing previously cut material was equally risky. When Henry Irving restored "Now might I do it pat," many of the critics objected to the speech as "rather revolting." In such a milieu, cuts became quickly and thoroughly entrenched.

Yet the re-written Gertrude survived the changing performance practices of the first half of the twentieth century with startling frequency. Although the block cut (3.4.165–191) surrounding her closet scene vow is rare after 1925, the vow itself is missing from fully half the pre-World War II books. Indeed, despite a gradual restoration of Gertrude's text beginning around the turn of the century, it is only after World War II that the cuts which devastated Gertrude's role in the preceding century became the exception rather than the rule. Nearly all those cuts appear in about fifty percent of the books dated between 1900 and the war. Even after World War II, Olivier's 1948 film, the Globe Theatre Version published by French in 1951, a 1959 CBS television production, and Nicol Williamson's 1969 film preserve all of the crucial cuts—including the vow—and hence the nineteenth-century Gertrude. Given the impact of film and television and the wide circulation of an edition (as compared to a promptbook)—and particularly the impact of the Olivier film—these four have an influence far greater than their numbers would suggest. For many people who know *Hamlet* through these sources, the distorting lenses of the preceding age have still not been cast aside. Though her public appearances have become less frequent, the nineteenth-century Gertrude is not dead yet.

JUNE SCHLUETER AND JAMES P. LUSARDI

The Camera in Gertrude's Closet

Maurice Charney, in "*Hamlet* Without Words," points out that to an Elizabethan "closet" meant a private apartment, not a bedchamber. Yet modern stagings of the closet scene in *Hamlet* have included a conspicuous bed, inviting audiences to look upon the exchange between Gertrude and her son within the intimacy of the bedroom. Charney argues that the "ponderous marriage bed that usually dominates this scene is entirely out of place."[1] Literary purists, and even those with a stage orientation, might also feel that a television or film camera in Gertrude's closet, or in any part of a Shakespeare play, is similarly out of place. Yet in this century there have been a sizable number of television and film productions of Shakespeare. Moreover, the ready availability of videocassettes has not only directed unprecedented attention to the plays as theater but provided scholars with the luxury of repeated viewings and opportunities for comparative analyses.

Our own interest in camera-ready Shakespeare has guided us through the sequences and scenes of Shakespeare's plays in three stages: first through the consideration of problems inherent in a literary understanding of the scene, then through an identification of the signals the text provides for staging, and, finally, through a close look at the ways in which film and television productions have staged—and hence interpreted—the scene. Following is a literary and theatrical look at act 3, scene 4 of *Hamlet,* with the 1948 Olivier film camera and then the 1980 BBC television camera in Gertrude's closet.

THE ENIGMATIC TEXT

The closet scene in *Hamlet* is a drama of conflicting motives and frustrated intent. Gertrude has summoned Hamlet to the interview "in most great affliction of spirit,"[2] according to Guildenstern, and she assures the eavesdropping Polonius that she intends to be "round" with her son. If maternal concern could previously accommodate collaboration with the King and Polonius, it now been compounded with "amazement" at Hamlet's insulting behavior on the occasion of the play-within and with distress at her threatened husband's distress. Gertrude means to confront her son with his offense and to get to the bottom of it. She also means to reassert her claim on Hamlet's obedience. After all, the last time she did so, in act 1, scene 2, he had assented: "I shall in all my best obey you, madam." For Hamlet, of course, the "matter" of the meeting is not his own offense against Claudius but his mother's offense against his father and himself. He goes to Gertrude's chamber not to be probed but to probe, not to be instructed but to instruct. This is the first private moment Hamlet has had with his mother in the play, and, having just tested the Ghost and the King through the play-within, he is determined to expose her sin. As A. C. Bradley describes Hamlet's disposition in the closet scene, his "whole heart is in his horror at his mother's fall and in his longing to raise her."[3]

Neither Gertrude nor Hamlet intends that the closet be a place of death, but within moments of Hamlet's entrance, Gertrude cries out for help, fearing her son will murder her, and Polonius lies slain by an impulsive thrust of the sword that was earlier paralyzed. With the eavesdropper dead, Gertrude is without protection; condemning the "rash and bloody deed," she defends herself by twice challenging Hamlet to explain why he has treated her so unkindly. Hamlet's first response, an eloquent indictment of her infidelity, brings only her second defensive question; but his next reply, a comparison of the two husbands, humbles her, leaving her thrice begging that he speak no more. Her motive frustrated, Gertrude yields any claim to her position of dominance in the exchange. Hamlet's intention prevails.

But Hamlet's intention, to shame his mother into reform, becomes either too insistent or too elaborate for the Ghost to endure. Having counseled Hamlet to "Leave her to heaven," it reappears when Hamlet persists in his reproaches, even in the face of Gertrude's pleading. Hamlet immediately thinks it has come to chide a tardy son, which it still does do, but it has come as well to protect a wife for whom love still urges kindness: "O, step between her and her fighting soul! / Conceit in weakest bodies strongest works." Whether the Ghost's intervention is prompted by Hamlet's growing excitement or, as J. Dover Wilson proposes, by Hamlet's imminent disclosure of the particulars of the murder,[4] the Ghost succeeds in altering Hamlet's behavior and Gertrude's perception of it. Once the Ghost departs, Hamlet's counsel is that Gertrude confess herself to heaven, that she "Assume a virtue," avoiding Claudius's bed until use changes "the stamp of nature." Clearly Hamlet *has* cleft his mother's heart in twain, and she has acknowledged her fault.

But just as clearly Gertrude is prepared to yield to Hamlet's demands before the Ghost appears. Gertrude's original admission of the "black and grained spots" in her soul comes as the consequence of a drama as purposefully staged as Hamlet's more famous play-within-the play. Early in the closet scene, Hamlet instructs his mother to sit down and remain seated. As in *The Murder of Gonzago,* he plans to hold a mirror up to nature, this time to catch the conscience of the Queen. In this drama, Hamlet presents his mother with the "counterfeit presentment of two brothers" that she may see the difference between them. Even as he inserted a speech of "some dozen or sixteen lines" in the Gonzago play and interrupted the Players with explanatory notes, now he accompanies the images with an interpretive monologue, drawing the moral conclusion he wants his mother to draw. Acting on Hamlet's direction, Gertrude studies the godlike man who was her husband and the "mildew'd ear, / Blasting the wholesome brother," then pleads, "O Hamlet, speak no more! / Thou turn'st mine eyes into my very soul."

Despite the success of his second play-within, Hamlet is not content. The emotional intensity of this intimate scene in his mother's chamber once again urges him into overreaction. Earlier, hearing Polonius's echo of Gertrude's cry for help, Hamlet had run his sword through the curtain and the anonymous torso behind it. Now, though Gertrude admits she has seen her sinful soul and enjoins her son to speak no more, Hamlet elaborates his catalog of reproaches, forcing her to beg him to be silent—and forcing the Ghost to intervene.

On the one hand, the Ghost's appearance seems itself tardy, since Hamlet has already indicted his mother for her poor judgment in men and mentioned the murder. If the Ghost's injunction to leave Gertrude to heaven was intended to secure Hamlet's silence about her "o'erhasty marriage," Hamlet's "Such an act / That blurs the grace and blush of modesty" should have been sufficient cue for it to intrude. If the warning was meant to exclude her from implication in or knowledge of the murder, then the Ghost should have materialized even earlier, at Hamlet's pronouncement on Polonius's death: "A bloody deed—almost as bad, good mother, / As kill a king, and marry with his brother." On the other hand, the Ghost's appearance could not be more timely. For its intrusion deflects Hamlet from his headlong course, substituting a distraction that his unseeing mother thinks "the very coinage of [his] brain." Its appearance offers Hamlet a more acceptable tack: urging Gertrude not to excuse her own trespass as his madness but to confess herself to heaven. In effect, the Ghost saves both Gertrude and her son from Hamlet's excess and renews its injunction as well.

Ironically, Gertrude is left to implement her program of abstinence alone, for Hamlet, at Claudius's order, "must to England." The Ghost's reappearance may well have served to restore its injunction about Gertrude, but Hamlet's departure neutralizes its more potent command: Hamlet can hardly avenge the death of his father if Claudius has sent him from court. The final appearance of the Ghost signals the end of the long sequence of fits and starts that has defined Hamlet's reaction to the mandate for revenge. The visitations of act 1, scene 5 and act 3, scene 4 create a frame for the inaction and bungled action that have compromised the avenger and frustrated the Ghost's intent. Now Hamlet's threats are directed not at Claudius but at his schoolfellows, "Whom I will trust as I will adders fang'd, / . . . And blow them at the moon."

The Ghost's sudden entrance is, of course, a highly theatrical event, providing Hamlet with a terrifying reminder of his charge and the audience with a fourth encounter with the supernatural. But the presence of the Ghost in Gertrude's chamber also provides with a stage image of a family that has been fragmented by lust and murder. Though Gertrude does not see the Ghost, the audience does, and the tableau of husband, wife, and son in Gertrude's chamber, the Ghost (at least in Q1) in his nightgown, gives corporal form to the domestic trinity that for thirty years was Denmark's royal center. The audience has been presented with several stage images of the now prevailing three, with Hamlet sulking off to the side, as in act 1, scene 2, or scheming to undo the King, as in the play-within. But with Claudius wearing the crown, the audience does not see the compassion or the "piteous action" that, despite distraction and amazement, it sees in Gertrude's room. In a sense, the image of old Hamlet's family is being held up against the image of Claudius's family, in much the same way that Hamlet held up the "counterfeit presentment of two brothers" to Gertrude.

But the image of husband, wife, and son is for the audience's eyes, not Gertrude's, for, when the Queen looks upon the ghostly form, she sees only "th' incorporal air." Assuming the Ghost does have a physical presence, as entrance and exit lines urge, why does Gertrude not see it? Most critics accept or offer variations on the standard moral perspectives that the Ghost is sparing the Queen's feelings, Bradley's view, or that Gertrude is not worthy of the vision, Dover Wilson's view. Some endorse W. W. Greg's speculation that the Ghost is indeed the coinage of Hamlet's brain.[5] In act 1, though, the Ghost is visible not only to Hamlet but to Horatio and the sentries as well, suggesting that there are no moral—or psychological—prerequisites for the vision and that the Ghost is not simply Hamlet's invention. Still, the Ghost has not always assumed an individual corporal form or identity in production. In Tony Richardson's 1969 version, with Nicol Williamson, the presence of the Ghost was manifested by bright light and a disembodied voice. In the 1986 New York University production, in which five actors simultaneously played Hamlet, the entire supporting cast became the Ghost in act 1, positioning themselves in a grid formation before the frightened Hamlet to chant its admonitory lines, while the Hamlets themselves became the Ghost in the closet. In the 1985 American Shakespeare Repertory adaptation, Douglas Overtoom's Hamlet fell to the floor, contorting his body in a shaft of red light, and spoke the Ghost's part with a gravelly, unearthly voice, in a spectacular display of demon possession. Though exciting and imaginative theater, the commitment to any of these renderings in act 1—or to the position that, while the Ghost has physical presence in act 1, Hamlet hallucinates in act 3, scene 4, as in the 1964 Kozintsev film—neutralizes this domestic stage image in the closet scene and the corollary that Gertrude's failure to see is part of that image.

Gertrude, by Hamlet's account in his first soliloquy (1.2), was a devoted wife, and yet before "the salt of most unrighteous tears / Had left the flushing in her galled eyes," she married her husband's brother. Hamlet imputes this appalling reversal to "Frailty," by which he evidently means a failure not only in virtue but in judgment and even simple perception: "My father's brother, but no more like my father / Than I to Hercules. . . ." The shocked Hamlet's early reflections anticipate both the "counterfeit presentment of two brothers" and the stage image created by the appearance of the Ghost in the intimate atmosphere of the closet. Gertrude's inability to see that her devotion to this "Hyperion" should have kept her from the "incestuous sheets" of a "satyr" now finds a physical correlative in her inability to see the apparition of her husband at all. As Harley Granville-Barker points out, the visitation of the Ghost in act 3, scene 4, seen by Hamlet, unseen by Gertrude, presents a "picture of mother, father and son, united but divided, together, but in understanding curelessly apart,"[6] implying that Gertrude's inability to see the Ghost is emblematic of her spiritual blindness.

Certainly Gertrude is no moral giant. But, because Shakespeare is kinder to her than his sources are to her counterpart, the actual extent of her guilt remains in doubt. Interestingly, the Q1 version of the play is more generous and less elusive in its treatment of the Queen than the received version derived from Q2 and F.[7] In the Q1 closet scene, Hamlet is explicit in identifying Claudius as the murderer of old Hamlet: comparing the portraits of the two brothers, he asks, "can looke on him / That slew my father, and your deere husband, / To live in the incentuous pleasure of his bed?" (p. 602). And Gertrude, following the exit of the Ghost, is explicit in disavowing the deed: "I swear by heaven, / I never knew of this most horride murder" (p. 602). Moreover, she promises to support her son in his quest for revenge:

HAMLET: And mother, but assist me in revenge,
          And in his death your infamy shall die.
QUEENE: Hamlet, I vow by that majesty,
          That knowes our thoughts, and lookes into our hearts,
          I will conceale, consent, and doe my best,
          What stratagem soe're thou shalt devise.

                                                          (p. 602)

In the received text, there is no such clarification or confirmation of Gertrude's position. She remains a morally ambiguous figure. She may be merely obtuse and self-indulgent. She may be a servant of time and circumstance as shaped by Claudius. Or she may be worse.

The narrative of the Ghost, in making the revelations of act 1, scene 5, is so structured as to suggest that Gertrude's infidelity preceded her husband's death. Moreover, the specific language of the text reinforces that impression. The Ghost styles Claudius "that incestuous, that adulterate beast," and Hamlet reviles both his mother ("O most pernicious woman!") and his uncle ("O villain") in his response to the Ghost's story.[8] Hamlet's charge that Gertrude's behavior "makes marriage-vows / As false as dicers' oaths" may likewise be taken as evidence of her adultery. And yet the case against her is never really clinched. Hamlet's penchant for generalizing about his mother's betrayal of his father blurs distinctions among kinds of infidelity. And Gertrude herself proves to be an enigmatic commentator on her own guilt, admitting the "dark and grained spots" that infect and, in act 4, scene 5, the anxiety that afflicts her "sick soul" but never specifying the nature of her sins. Similarly, her reactions on other occasions fail to resolve the issue. Speaking to Claudius alone in act 2, scene 2 on the cause of Hamlet's distemper, she makes no apparent reference to an illicit liaison between them: "I doubt it is no other but the main, / His father's death, and our o'erhasty marriage." Her response to Hamlet's interruption of the play-within—"The lady doth protest too much, methinks"—seems simplicity itself: the Queen may be objecting to the redundancy of the dialogue, to the strident assertions of the Player Queen, or, perhaps embarrassed by her own recent history, to the devotion that death, she has learned, negates. When Claudius rises, calling for lights, she expresses interest only in the welfare of the King.

Nonetheless, as Hamlet prepares for the interview with his mother, he is in a violent mood. Pausing to soliloquize, he articulates his wrath: "Now could I drink hot blood, / And do such bitter business as the day / Would quake to look on." Though he fails to kill Claudius when he discovers him at prayer, his savage anger persists, expressed now in imaginings of Claudius in hell. Once in Gertrude's closet, he suggests what neither the Ghost nor Claudius nor Hamlet himself has spoken before: that Gertrude was an accomplice in the murder of the king. The killing of Polonius is "A bloody deed—almost as bad, good mother / As kill a king, and marry with his brother." In interpreting this line, critics have assumed, with Dover Wilson, that Hamlet is putting Gertrude to the test and that her "astonished" response "As kill a king!" "acquits" her.[9] It is, of course, also possible, as Harold Jenkins urges, that the testing is not deliberate but rather incident to Hamlet's "not distinguish[ing] the elements of killing and marrying in what he apparently regards as one composite crime."[10]

As the closet scene progresses, it is clear that Gertrude has seen her fault in Hamlet's mirror. Imploring Hamlet to be silent, she anguishes in shame—until the Ghost intervenes. Before the visitation, Hamlet had labored at getting Gertrude to see what he saw, and he was successful. Now, despite his excited descriptions of the apparition, Gertrude is unable to see what her son sees, and she concludes that Hamlet is mad. Whether she retains that opinion until the end of the scene or permits Hamlet to persuade her that "It is not madness / That I have utt'red" remains unclear. Hamlet closes the closet scene with three long speeches of counsel before his parting lines. The first of these, a defense of his sanity, ends with his urging his mother to repent. Gertrude's single line response is "O Hamlet, thou hast cleft my heart in twain." Are these the words of a still repentant Queen acknowledging the trespass shown her by one whose "pulse, as [hers], doth temperately keep time, / And makes as healthful music"? Or is this the expression of a deeply saddened mother who has witnessed the "ecstacy" of her son? Hamlet's second speech, which importunes Gertrude to repudiate Claudius's bed, is punctuated by three of Hamlet's four good nights and, finally, by "One word more, good lady." Gertrude's response to Hamlet's guidance in moral remediation and to his erratic attempts to leave is, simply, "What shall I do?" Is she so humbled at having provoked such a schooling from her son that she can say no more? Or is she protecting her own person by lending a seeming ear to Hamlet's preposterous counsel, daring to say no more? Hamlet's third speech is a tauntingly ironic injunction to secrecy, lest his mother reveal to the "bloat king" that "I essentially am not in madness, / But mad in craft." It secures Gertrude's cryptic promise: "Be thou assur'd, if words be made of breath, / And breath of life, I have no life to breathe / What thou hast said to me." Whether she follows Hamlet's instructions in reporting the interview remains questionable in act 4, scene 1, where she tells Claudius that Polonius is slain and that her son is mad. She may be keeping Hamlet's secret, or she may herself believe in Hamlet's distraction.

Nor is it certain after the encounter in the closet is over and Hamlet has departed for England that Gertrude no longer goes to Claudius's bed. The signals she gives are mixed. In act 4, scene 5, just before the entrance of Ophelia, she professes the chastened consciousness of sin that Hamlet has inspired, but, in the same scene, at the entrance of the incensed Laertes, she becomes the determined protector of Claudius, putting herself in danger to shield him from assault. When Laertes makes the demand for his father and the King replies that he is dead, Gertrude quickly adds, "But not by him." Such solicitous concern hardly seems the mark of a wife who has alienated herself from her husband. When Hamlet appears at Ophelia's grave, challenging Laertes to match his love for the dead girl, Gertrude speaks of her son's ranting as one privileged to know what is imports and what its course will be:

> This is mere madness,
> And thus awhile the fit will work on him;
> Anon, as patient as the female dove
> When that her golden couplets are disclos'd,
> His silence will sit drooping.

(5.1.284–288)

Does Gertrude believe her son mad, which neutralize his earlier counsel to her, or is she playing the protector once more?

Textually, Gertrude remains a mystery. She will appear one more time, in the final scene, to drink from the poisoned cup, knowingly or accidentally, and so die, leaving unanswered the questions concerning the extent of her guilt and the extent of her repentance. Yet these are questions that must be addressed in production and in some measure answered. Gertrude will become a compelling theatrical reality only when a coherent sequence of theatrical signals is associated with her presence on the stage, particularly in the pivotal closet scene.

THEATRICAL CUES

Before we turn to see how the Olivier and the BBC productions handle the character of Gertrude as well as other opportunities for interpretation, it is worth looking at some of the signals the text itself provides for playing the scene. The closet scene, like so much of Shakespeare's dramatic writing, is chary of stage direction, recording entrances and exits and an occasional action. But this scene (again, like so many others) is rich in verbal clues and cues that variously guide and prescribe the action that supplements, prompts, and validates words.

There is, for example, no stage direction that says Gertrude neither sees nor hears the Ghost. Yet Gertrude's language leaves no doubt that she does not. In response to Hamlet's sighting, she cries, "Alas, he's mad!" When, at the direction of the Ghost, Hamlet inquires after his mother's welfare, she replies, "Alas, how is 't with you, / That you do bend your eye on vacancy, / and with th' incorporal air do hold discourse?" Convinced of her son's distemper, she asks, "Whereon do you look?," then "To whom do you speak this?," and, finally, she confirms she sees "Nothing at all; yet all that is I see" and hears "nothing but ourselves."

The encounter with the Ghost is otherwise prescriptive in its language. Hamlet's words reflect fear and excitement and offer a description of the

Ghost's appearance and behavior: "look you how pale he glares? . . . Look, where he goes, even now, out at the portal!" Even without reference to the Q1 specification of a "night gowne," we still know from Hamlet that the Ghost is dressed "in his habit as he lived." While Hamlet is describing the Ghost to his mother, his mother is describing Hamlet, whose eyes are wild ("Forth at your eyes your spirits wildly peep") and whose hair "like life in excrements, / Start up and stand an end," the second a bit difficult to play.[11]

There are other moments in the scene in which dialogue clearly specifies action but any number of stagings could be managed. Hamlet's presentation to his mother of the two "counterfeit presentments," for example, must find its shape in production. On the New York University stage, one of the five Hamlets held up the palms of his hands in turn, providing no picture but verbal description. In the 1984–85 Royal Shakespeare Company's *Hamlet*, Roger Rees pointed to two imaginary paintings on the wall. Ian McKellan's Hamlet compared an oval framed picture of Claudius from a side table with one of his father that he pulled from his shirt. Nicol Williamson wore a locket containing the miniature portraiture of his father around his neck, which he held next to the likeness of Claudius around Gertrude's. How forcibly Hamlet imposes his lesson upon his mother remains a directorial decision as well. In the NYU production, Hamlet stood threateningly over his seated mother, forcing her head back so that her long red hair cascaded in the air. In ASR's contemporary staging, Hamlet held a pistol to Gertrude's forehead as he spoke of the act that "takes off the rose / From the fair forehead of an innocent love / And sets a blister there. . . ." As Gertrude pleaded with him to speak no more, Hamlet pinioned his mother, pressing his fingers into her neck.

Similarly, how Hamlet discovers that it is Polonius he has slain may also be variously staged. At line 27, Hamlet asks whether he has killed the King. By line 32, he knows it is Polonius: "Thou wretched, rash, intruding fool, farewell! / I took thee for thy better." Does Hamlet lift up the arras and see Polonius, as the editorial direction in several modern editions suggests, or does the falling body brush the curtain aside to lie within view as soon as Hamlet turns to discover it?

Throughout the closet scene, Shakespeare provides verbal cues for physical action, ranging from the prescriptive (Hamlet, about to wring his mother's heart, notices she is wringing her hands) to the suggestive (might Gertrude press her hands to her ears at "O, speak to me no more! / These words, like daggers, enter my ears. / No more, sweet Hamlet!," preventing her from hearing Hamlet's condemnation of Claudius as "A murderer and a villain"?). There is one moment in the closet scene, however, in which action prompts language and Shakespeare's text provides neither stage direction nor apparent cue. We are referring to Gertrude's cry early in act 3, scene 4: "What wilt thou do? Thou wilt not murder me? / Help, ho!" Textually, there seems to be little motivation for Gertrude's unfortunate presumption, the consequence of which is Polonius's death. But the Queen must have had cause to be afraid, and, in the absence of language signaling that cause, it is only in production that an audience can know why.

The sequence begins with the quick exchange between Hamlet and his mother, Hamlet challenging Gertrude's charges with barbed accusations of his own. Exhausted by her son's caustic cleverness and dismayed by his wish to deny her maternity, the Queen concludes, "Nay, then, I'll set those to you that can speak," to which Hamlet retorts, "Come, come, and sit you down; you shall not budge. / You go not till I set you up a glass / Where you may see the inmost part of you."

Action is clearly demanded here: Gertrude, moving away from Hamlet, either to recall Polonius or to fetch her husband and his attendants, is prevented from doing so by Hamlet, who insists she sit down and not budge until she has recognized her fault. His "Come, come" might at first appear to be an invitation to sit, albeit a firm one. But the Queen's extraordinary response demands that it be more. Q1 offers guidance. In her account to Claudius of Hamlet's behavior in her closet, Gertrude reports: "Whenas he came, I first bespake him faire, / But then he throwes and tosses me about, / As one forgetting that I was his mother" (p. 603).

That Hamlet is in a violent mood had already been established by his readiness to "drink hot blood" and by his wish to secure Claudius's damnation. Moreover, his swift slaying of Polonius immediately after Gertrude's cry at least confirms that mood and may even be taken to indicate that killing was on his mind. Traditionally, in production, Hamlet is rough, even brutal with his mother, pushing her down and restricting her movements with force, the assumption being that a sufficient show of Hamlet's physical superiority and of his intemperance will leave Gertrude fearing for her life.

Production may even provide a more tangible cue for Gertrude's cry. Hamlet tells his mother he plans to "set you up a glass" wherein she may see her fault. While no property is mandatory here since Hamlet's mirror is metaphorical, he might hold up an actual mirror or, in the absence of one, the reflective edge of a sword. Though offered as the glass that will expose her soul, the sword may terrify the Queen, who concludes that Hamlet has drawn it to slay her. Or Hamlet may draw his sword or rapier to restrain his mother from leaving. Either reading provides the ancillary benefit of an already drawn weapon with which to slay Polonius.

But even without the menacing weapon or the throwing and tossing that did not find its way into Q2 or F, Gertrude's cry might be explained in either of two ways. The first brings us back to the question of Gertrude's guilt. Her "What wilt thou do? Thou wilt not murder me?" may be prompted not by Hamlet's behavior but by his plan to undress his mother's soul. If the Queen knows the blackness within and fears that Hamlet knows or will soon know as well, her frightened cry may be the culmination of a mental drama in which she recalls her deeds and anticipates Hamlet's response. In such a reading, her readiness to conclude that Hamlet will murder may be presumptive evidence of the enormity of her guilt. Her "As kill a king!" need not be so astonished—nor exonerating—an exclamation as Dover Wilson assumes but, rather, a tentative expression of what she most fears Hamlet knows: that she was accomplice in her husband's murder. Her ensuing questions, imploring Hamlet to identify her deed, become a test of the extent of her son's knowledge. That Gertrude is not satisfied by Hamlet's reference to false marriage vows in his first response lends credibility to such a reading, for though she should now know what Hamlet accuses her of, she still seeks more: "Ay me, what act, / That roars so loud and thunders in the index?" In such a reading, Gertrude's response to Hamlet's comparison of the two brothers would leave her contrite but relieved that Hamlet was claiming no more.

But even if Gertrude is not guilty of the terrible crime Hamlet is about to suggest, her cry and the ensuing action have an arresting effect on an audience that previously did not associate Gertrude with her husband's death. The small but suggestive patch of drama begins with Gertrude's "Thou wilt not murder me?" and ends with her "As kill a king!" In between these outcries, the audience is provided with a stage image of death, in the form of the slain Polonius, whom Hamlet first thought the King. The drama would seem to be urging the audience into considering the possibility of Gertrude's complicity, a possibility that, while never made patent, invites more careful scrutiny of the Queen.

The second approach in effect renders gratuitous the psychological paradigm inherent in the first. But demanding psychological accountability or consistency in Shakespeare's characters may not always be warranted. Alan C. Dessen makes this point in his excellent book *Elizabethan Drama and the Viewer's Eye*. Taking care not to repudiate our traditional sense of dramatic character, he argues that our sense of character may at times be "superseded by some other principle we may not take into account." More specifically, he proposes that characters "can for a moment cease to be important as individuals but instead can participate in some larger, shared effect. . . ."[12] Gertrude's cry in act 3, scene 4 may well be a moment that is unjustifiable within a psychological matrix. Connecting as it does with the pent-up fury of Hamlet's soliloquy on his way to his mother's room, it may find its most resonant validation as one of Dessen's larger, shared effects. For an audience carrying the verbal images of Hamlet's self-appraisal with them into the closet, Gertrude's cry prompts and articulates its own astonishment and fear.

Hamlet, we know, has emotional warrant to kill as he approaches Gertrude's room. In his present mood, he is capable, by his own account, of terrifyingly "bitter business." Yet, in a prayer as potent as Lady Macbeth's plea that the spirits unsex her, he prays that the soul of Nero not enter his bosom, that he be "cruel, not unnatural," that he "speak daggers to her, but use none." This is the Hamlet who had advised the Players in act 3, scene 2 to "Suit the action to the word, the word to the action." Now he urges on himself a hypocritical division between "tongue and soul": "How in my words somever she be shent, / To give them seals never, my soul, consent!" An audience recognizing the pattern would, when it hears Gertrude's cry, fear that Hamlet's action will, after all, match his word; he will speak daggers to her and use one.

In Dessen's own analysis of the closet scene, he concentrates on Hamlet's rash and bloody frame of mind and on the way theatrical images may reflect on the state of Hamlet's soul rather than Gertrude's. The larger pattern he identifies consists of visual analogues linking the First Player as Pyrrhus brandishing his sword over the doomed Priam, Hamlet lifting his sword over the praying Claudius, and Hamlet thrusting his sword into the shrieking Polonius. Here the use and abuse of the revenging sword, as a symbolic stage property, becomes the focus of interest. "What would be the effect on an audience," asks Dessen, "if the director left Polonius's body, covered with blood, in full view and left the sword, also bloodied, in the hero's hand throughout much if not all of the scene?"[13] The suggested answer is that much of Hamlet's commentary on Gertrude's corruption would apply ironically to the commentator, for he "has himself been tainted with the disease and disorder of the world he has sought to cure, and the blood on the sword becomes an apt visual symbol for that stain or implication."[14] Dessen's recommended staging is, of course, a reading of the play, and that is just the point. An actor who lets the curtain fall on the dead Polonius and casts aside his weapon to turn his attention to Gertrude will create a different and probably more favorable impression of Hamlet, at Gertrude's expense. The given in the text is the stage property and its bloody use. How a director reads this textual signal will determine how the closet scene takes shape.

PRODUCTIONS

Since the Laurence Olivier film version of *Hamlet*[15] features the director in the role of the protagonist, the production is to an unusual degree under the control of a single creative personality. Olivier chose to film in black and white, for example, "to achieve through depth of focus a more majestic, more poetic image, in keeping with the stature of the verse."[16] While he managed to recruit a remarkable cast, including Eileen Herlie as Gertrude and Felix Aylmer as Polonius, he was still "prepared to take on the entire responsibility"[17] for the result.

It is an active camera that introduces us to the scene. The opening moments show Hamlet's shadow ascending a winding stairwell, Gertrude and Polonius conversing in the spacious chamber, Hamlet himself on the stair calling "Mother, mother, mother," and Gertrude rising to conceal Polonius in a curtained archway stage-right, then moving left to face the entranceway and the camera. With the frame fixed, Hamlet suddenly appears in it. In deep focus, we see Hamlet's back in the foreground as he enters the room and Gertrude in the distance standing in front of her bed. Having established the authority of the camera, Olivier makes bold use of it to shape the scene and to regulate both the perspective and the responses of the audience.

Thus, though Hamlet on the stairs calls quietly, even tentatively, to his mother, he moves steadily, inexorably toward the camera. When he enters the room for the first exchange with a self-possessed Gertrude, bareheaded but regal-looking in her elegant *robe de chambre,* the camera remains on his back as he pauses in the entranceway and then slowly bears down on her, reaching her on his wish that she were not his mother. When Gertrude attempts to come forward to get those that "can speak," Hamlet seizes her by the arm and throws her backward on the bed. The camera now makes a series of suggestive switches and movements. From behind the bed, it shows Hamlet in the act of throwing Gertrude down, follows her as she lands, her robe parting in the violence of the fall, and lifts to reveal Hamlet standing over her with his sword drawn. The angle is then reversed, with the camera looking at Gertrude over Hamlet's shoulder, the point of his sword poised at her naked throat, while he expresses his determination to expose her "inmost part." It is this gesture that motivates Gertrude's terrified "Thou wilt not murder me?" and Polonius's echoing "Help!" Viewed again from the front, Hamlet is exhilarated at the cry of the outsider who, he thinks, is the King. As he turns to Polonius's archway, the camera switches to that perspective for Hamlet's onrush, eyes wide and glaring, and his lunge with the sword almost into the camera's eye.

The manipulation of the camera in this opening sequence is clearly meant to dramatize the progressive violence of Hamlet's demeanor and his quick seizure, by force and terror, of the dominant position in the scene. For an audience primed by Hamlet's reflections in soliloquy in the two previous scenes, he is obviously yielding to his rash and bloody mood and seems ready to give it full scope. The camera invites the audience to share the shock of Gertrude and Polonius at Hamlet's towering excitement and precipitate actions.

When Hamlet stabs through the curtain and Gertrude screams behind him, his face is a mask of manic glee. Turning slowly toward the distraught Queen, he shouts defiantly, "Is it the King?" The camera switches angles, holding the weeping Gertrude in the foreground and her son, with head thrown back, by the archway. As Hamlet delivers his comment on the "bloody deed," he stands in his murderous pose, right arm outstretched, the sword in the curtain and in the body, now carefully watching his mother's startled reaction to "As kill a king. . . ." On "Ay, lady, it was my word," he withdraws the weapon and pulls the curtain, and Polonius topples into view. Casting his sword upon the body, Hamlet leans forward over the camera to utter a disappointed and contemptuous farewell to the "busy" old man. Though the body remains exposed, the camera will not return to it until late in the scene. Attention is fixed on Hamlet and Gertrude.

An unarmed Hamlet, but still a violent one, turns back to his sobbing mother, now in the center of the frame, her writhing hands folded as though in hysterical prayer. When Hamlet seizes her by the shoulders as she tries to rise, abruptly sitting her down again, she recovers from her weeping to shout angrily, "What have I done, that thou dar'st wag thy tongue / In noise so rude against me?" During Hamlet's indictment, she looks appalled, stifling sobs as she stares into his face; she starts her second question, "What act . . . ?," only to have it cut short when Hamlet grabs at the picture of his father hanging from his neck and that of Claudius hanging from hers to begin his comparison. Gertrude studies the image of old Hamlet as the son celebrates the virtues of his father. But, when Hamlet speaks of "An eye like Mars, to threaten and command," she raises her own languid eyes to gaze fixedly, lovingly on Hamlet's face. The spell is broken only when his disgust at his stepfather's image becomes disgust at her. This Hamlet's obsession and the sexuality of the woman who inspires it are made visually evident by the appearance of Gertrude as she sits on the bed, her robe open wide to reveal a full, firm body in a thin, clinging shift. In his pain and fury, Hamlet tears Claudius's picture from his mother's neck and stalks away, rounding on her with "O shame, where is thy blush?" Gertrude herself turns away at this reproach, into a closeup camera that frames her in a crouched position, the bottom portion of Hamlet's torso in the distance. Her contrite acknowledgment of her soul's "dark and grained spots" seems to solicit a tender response, but her son becomes only more incensed. Leaning forward on her bed, he assails his mother with images of corrupt sensuality. Holding her hand to her cheek, the beleaguered Queen turns back to Hamlet and throws her arms about his neck to beg "no more." His response is to grab her by the wrists and to deliver another verbal assault, which leaves her sobbing uncontrollably and screaming in anguish for relief. As a climax to the sequence, Hamlet seizes the panting Gertrude by the throat, but he is arrested in his physical assault by the ominous sounds of a drum.

With the drum pounding like a heartbeat, the camera rests on Hamlet's paralyzed face, then on the pleading face of Gertrude, whose lips move inaudibly. We are locked during an extended pause in the traumatized consciousness of Hamlet. Then, as abruptly as it stopped, the action resumes, with Hamlet roughly pushing his mother backward on the bed. She lies there mute, her arms outstretched, watching in amazement as her son turns away, looks upward, and prays to "heavenly guards" for protection, even as the sounds of the swelling winds accompany the ominous drum to signal the visitation of the Ghost.

This Ghost, however, does not assume corporal form. Though old Hamlet had appeared in his armor on the battlements, now he remains a disembodied voice. Here, as in act 1, Hamlet drops to the floor at its presence, as though felled by a blow, twisting his body and craning his neck to behold and address the apparition. Gertrude, sitting up to observe the spectacle of her son, concludes sadly, "Alas, he's mad!" The failure of the Ghost to materialize lends credibility to her judgment and eliminates the symbolic stage image of family reunion. But Olivier compensates for the loss of the Ghost as a physical presence and secures comparable effects by means of the camera. During most of the visitation, the camera becomes the Ghost. Hence, Gertrude no sooner reaches her conclusion than the prone Hamlet appears in a long shot, speaking and reaching toward the camera. When the father reminds the son of his "almost blunted purpose," the camera is fixed on the chastened Hamlet; but then it swings slowly stage-left to fix on Gertrude and returns to Hamlet for the Ghost's admonition, "But, look, amazement on thy mother sits." Never taking his eyes from the camera, Hamlet reaches toward Gertrude to ask, "How is it with you, lady?" When she counsels patience and questions him, "Whereon do you look?," Hamlet urgently points at the camera—"On him, on him!"—and describes the figure he sees. Finally, as Gertrude bows her head in weary conviction, he stretches toward the camera on his elbows to plead, "Do not look upon me, / Lest with this piteous action you convert / My stern [intents]."

As Olivier contrives the scene, it is difficult to disbelieve in the Ghost just because we don't actually see it. And Gertrude's perception of nothing but "vacancy" remains as fully a comment on her moral disability as it is on Hamlet's distress. Similarly, though the domestic stage image is sacrificed, the audience is invited to share the perspective of the dead father in his last encounter with the two people he loved most in life. The impact of this cinematic device, in contrast to the stage image, is psychological rather than symbolic, a poignant expression of alienation and loss. In the final moments of the visitation, the camera separates itself from the Ghost's perspective and then adopts it again to reassert the effect. In closeup, Gertrude asks, "To whom do you speak this?" We next see Hamlet and Gertrude in turn, now from behind the bed, each on the margin of the space where the Ghost presumably stands, Gertrude descrying nothing and Hamlet pointing at the archway. When woodwinds signal the departure of the Ghost, Hamlet, now in closeup, looks and lunges to his right, calling, "Why, look you there, look how it steals away!" The camera is already moving away from Hamlet as he lunges and crawls after it, pulling himself with one arm and reaching out with the other. The Ghost/camera retreats, holding the writhing Hamlet in sight until the darkness of the corridor closes it in.

In the aftermath of this extraordinary episode, Gertrude walks alone through the spacious chamber toward its empty archways, looking for "nothing." As she pauses to peer in the direction of the corridor, a peal of chimes indicates the return of ordinary reality, much as the knocking at the gate does in *Macbeth*. Coming back downstage, she looks and crosses left, where Hamlet is discovered sitting on the floor at the foot of the bed. "This," she comforts him, "is the very coinage of your brain."

At the imputation of madness, Hamlet rises to insist calmly on his own sanity and firmly on his mother's trespass. But this Gertrude is no longer interested in what Hamlet has to say. Consistent with this interpretation, Hamlet says a good deal less; Olivier makes his heaviest cuts here in the final panel of the scene, reducing Hamlet's lines by more than half (from nearly ninety to forty). Refusing to meet her son's eyes, she turns her head to the side and looks downward, then walks slowly away, saddened and resigned. As she reaches the bed, she sits down and weeps, not in terror as earlier and not for herself. These tears are for her distracted son, whose madness, not counsel, has cleft her heart. In the meantime, Hamlet comes up behind her, but the touching between mother and son is no longer cruel: Hamlet holds her tenderly at the shoulders, and she reaches her hand back to touch his. As he tells his mother to throw away the "worser part" of her divided heart, he rests his head on hers, then gently touches his lips to her forehead. Though his voice takes on an edge when he asks that she not return to Claudius's bed, Gertrude shows no resistance, turning to him afterward to hold his face and kiss him on the lips. This pair are like lovers making up rather than mother and son. Hamlet's "I must be cruel only to be kind" is gently said. It occasions a full embrace, after which Hamlet rests his head in Gertrude's lap, receiving her caresses. When he announces his imminent departure for England and his intention to remove Polonius's body, they once again face each other for a long meaningful look and a truly passionate kiss. For all that has happened in this remarkable encounter, the end of the scene recalls the beginning. In deep focus, we see Hamlet's back in the foreground as he drags out the body of Polonius and Gertrude in the distance standing by the richly draped bed. At last alone, she sits down for the fade-out.

The Oedipal suggestions in Olivier's rendering of this scene endorse the position popularized by Ernest Jones in *Hamlet and Oedipus.*[18] In 1937, ten years before he made the film, Olivier, in the company of Tyrone Guthrie and Peggy Ashcroft, went to visit Jones. According to Olivier:

> I have never ceased to think about Hamlet at odd moments, and ever since that meeting I have believed that Hamlet was a prime sufferer from the Oedipus complex—quite unconsciously, of course, as the professor was anxious to stress.[19]

It is the Oedipal premise that provides a coherent sequence of stage images. Even if this production were a *Hamlet* without words, the premise would be apparent. We could clearly discern the sexual energy in the closing embraces and kisses of mother and son, consummated on Gertrude's bed. Moreover, we could also see the external expression of the matricidal impulse, first examined in detail by Frederic Wertham[20] and accommodated in Jones's analysis: it is signaled in the escalation of Hamlet's violence when he grasps his mother's throat. The Ghost's intervention thwarts it. The Ghost may thus be taken as the correlative of a self-imposed restraint, appearing just as Hamlet is about to yield to his murderous urge and become "passion's slave."

Perhaps because the Oedipal pattern makes it clear that Gertrude will be guided by a son who has established his tacit right to demand the fidelity that she has betrayed, Hamlet's instructions to his mother about what she should tell Claudius are cut, as is the scene (4.1) in which Gertrude makes her report. Also cut is her anguished aside in act 4, scene 5 ("To my sick soul . . .") and her protection of Claudius from Laertes' wrath later in that scene. Yet here in act 4, scene 5, Gertrude twice rejects Claudius's touch, the second time poised at the base of a flight of stairs as the King laments, "O Gertrude, Gertrude, / When sorrows come, they come not single spies, / But in battalions. . . ." The messenger from act 4, scene 7 appears in a coda to act 4, scene 5, presenting separate letters from Hamlet to the King and to the Queen. As the Queen reads hers, she begins her ascent up one staircase; Claudius, pausing to look at the absorbed Queen, reads his as he ascends another. Olivier has extended the division suggested by Hamlet's separate letters to a potent theatrical image of the division between the pair engendered by Hamlet as Oedipal son.

The effect of Hamlet's lesson in the closet becomes fatally apparent in the final scene when Gertrude knowingly drinks the poisoned wine intended for her son. Starting at Claudius's dropping of the pearl into the drink, she sits in silence, the camera holding her and the hand that holds the cup in its frame. She looks to the cup repeatedly, as though planning her course. Then, before Claudius has a chance to intervene, she drinks. Olivier moves the Queen's toast—"The Queen carouses to thy fortune, Hamlet"—to a position following her apology to Claudius—"I will, my lord; I pray you pardon me"—diminishing further the possibility that Claudius's "Gertrude, do not drink" can come in time. Her farewell to Hamlet, abbreviated to "No, no, the drink, the drink! O my dear Hamlet," spoken gently and with a fragile smile, ignores the exclamation points of modern editions. This Gertrude knows what she has done and sees her own death as a gesture of atonement, of protection, and of love.

As in the Olivier film, the "ponderous marriage bed" that draws Charney's wry objection is a feature of the closet scene in Rodney Bennett's BBC *Hamlet*.[21] There is some difference, however, since the apartment of Claire Bloom's Gertrude is divided into two chambers, her closet and her bedroom, joined by a curtained opening. In the course of the scene, she moves between these spaces, first with Eric Porter as Polonius and then with Derek Jacobi as Hamlet. The movement is suggestive. Gertrude intends to conduct her interview with Hamlet in the closet, yet before long she finds herself being dragged into the bedroom, the more appropriate place for Hamlet's recriminations. Like Olivier's, Jacobi's Hamlet, in attempting to expose his mother's inner part, at the same time exposes his own; his moral disgust is also informed by sexual outrage. Still, despite this similarity and the presence of the marriage bed in both productions, there are important differences in the portrayal of this mother-son pair.

Bloom's Gertrude begins the scene by primping before an unseen mirror, removing her rings and touching her loose auburn hair, while Polonius in the doorway behind her adjures her to be firm with Hamlet. Turning, she sweeps past Polonius, from bedroom into closet, and sits in a chair facing the curtain at stage-right, where Polonius conceals himself at Hamlet's off-stage cries of "Mother." Dressed in a copper-colored robe over a white nightdress, she seems composed, though she breathes rapidly. When Hamlet enters from far upstage, he is disheveled. In contrast to the sober dignity of Olivier's mourning habit, even without his doublet, Jacobi's costume manifests neglect; with an open shirt tucked loosely into rust breeches and one boot drooping to his ankle, his appearance recalls Ophelia's account of his visit to her closet in act 2, scene 1. On this occasion, he carries under his left arm both sword and dagger.

Hamlet's first line cues the camera to begin the sequence of alternate closeups that accompanies the mother-son exchange. Hamlet is swift in his retorts, Gertrude sure but a bit hesitant in hers. At "Have you forgot me?," she stands to face her son, who responds with withering sarcasm: "You are the Queen, your husband's brother's wife." Stung by the insult, she angrily slaps Hamlet on the face and provokes him to a snarling conclusion, "And—would it were not so!—you are my mother." Gertrude immediately heads upstage to fetch assistance, but Hamlet crosses her path with his sword, preventing her progress. Backing away fearfully, she cries out, "Thou wilt not murder me?," and calls for help. Her astonished son, who despite his meanacing manner had no such intention, throws down his dagger on the instant and looks with bewilderment at his drawn sword. When he responds to Polonius's voice, he shouts "A rat?" as though he is frightened also and stabs frantically, then furiously thrice into the curtain. As Gertrude screams at him, he stands hugging the curtained form, asking doubtfully, "Is it the King?" There is no note of triumph in the question, as there was in Olivier's. Clearly, both Hamlets are dangerous, but they are so in different ways. While Olivier's Hamlet is actuated by a determined fury, which may overmaster him, Jacobi's acts on impulse and seems completely unpredictable. He responds, literally, to the moment, and if he terrifies Gertrude, he also terrifies himself.

Still hugging the unseen body, Hamlet becomes truculent again in response to Gertrude's condemnation of the deed—"almost as bad, good mother, / As kill a king"—yet he casts his eyes downward instead of studying Gertrude as she meekly repeats the charge. At "Ay, lady, it was my word," he pulls out the sword, stepping back, and when the dying Polonius falls out, he drops the sword and practically sings his surprise, "Thou wretched, rash, in-truu-ding fool. . . ." Then, kneeling over the body, he caps a gentle "farewell" with a contemptuous "too busy," while Gertrude stands behind him whimpering and clasping her hands before her face. So mercurial a Hamlet makes for a very uneasy audience.

To set up the "counterfeit presentment of two brothers," Hamlet backs his mother into the chair, leans over her, and inveighs against her fault. "What have I done?," she demands, and "Ay me, what act . . . ?" Both protests are vigorously spoken, with an angry sob, the camera singling her out for the second, but they represent the last vestige of defiance in Gertrude. When Hamlet kneels to show her the images, worn about their necks as in the Olivier production, his voice softens, and Gertrude breaks down, breathing painfully and weeping quietly. Unlike Herlie's Gertrude, this one does not look at the image of her dead husband or at her son; she closes her eyes and turns away toward the camera. Similarly, when Hamlet becomes vicious again, battering her with his words and moving behind her to shove the picture of Claudius in her face, she doesn't want to see it and throws back her head in agony. Finally, as her son rounds on her to display both images—"what judgment / Would step from this to this?"—she wails, leaps up, and runs from him out of the frame. Shouting reproaches, Hamlet pursues her, first as she stands fretfully and next as she paces erratically around the room, cupping her hands over her ears, trying to escape the wounding diatribe. There is no escape for Gertrude. At length, Hamlet catches her by the wrists, staring into her face for "O shame, where is thy blush?," then strides left dragging her to the inner chamber, where he throws her on the bed. The camera follows the pair through the opening, before it switches frames for Gertrude's rough landing.

On her back in the foreground, Hamlet standing over her, the rumpled Gertrude is especially vulnerable now, and Hamlet is intolerably cruel. In a sudden movement, he mounts the bed and his mother, his hips jerking in mock intercourse as he chides her "compulsive ardor." When he falls by her side, he is only apparently exhausted. For, when Gertrude begs that he speak no more and, wracked by sobs, confesses her fault, he resumes in near frenzy his verbal and physical pummeling of the thrashing woman for her corrupt sexuality. At her second plea for mercy—"These words, like daggers, enter in my ears"—he pulls himself up over her head and shouts directly into her ear, "A murderer and a villain." As he continues, he yanks her from behind into a sitting position, her skirts around her thighs, and pinions her arms at her back, her long hair spread over her weeping face and wrenched shoulders. Had Gertrude concluded here that her son was about to kill her, she could not be accused of overreacting. An audience is as relieved as Hamlet is amazed and shaken at the Ghost's intervention.

The figure of the Ghost, framed by the open curtains at the entrance to the bedroom, seems nearly translucent in sharp blue light, shimmering as though in an aura. In this manifestation, played by Patrick Allen, the Ghost's "habit as he lived" is not a nightgown but the armor of the earlier visitations, only now it bears helmet in hand. A strain of music in muted monotone accompanies its appearance. The camera, as it did early in the scene, again alternates shots, switching between the Ghost and the mother-son pair, never showing all three in tableau. Pushing away his mother with a gasp, Hamlet comes to the foot of the bed and drops to his knees to address the apparition. Seated behind him, Gertrude witnesses her son's distress and, frowning in her pity for him, concludes that he is mad. Meanwhile, reacting to Gertrude's concern, the Ghost steps farther into the run to admonish Hamlet to speak to her. Still looking up, eyes fixed on the shade of his father, Hamlet does so quietly and draws an affectionate but incredulous response. Though the camera documents Hamlet's insistent claims with shots of the Ghost looking down at him, Gertrude perceives nothing. Then a curious thing happens. In a long shot, the kneeling Hamlet turns from the Ghost to his mother and, imploring her to see and hear, points to vacancy. It is just enough to create an ambiguity about the Ghost. A moment later, as Gertrude rises to comfort her son and Hamlet turns back to the Ghost with "Why, look you there," the camera shows the steel blue form backing away. When the frantic Hamlet finally identifies "My father," the effect on Gertrude is stunning: she screams in horror, pressing her hand to her mouth, and collapses in tears. A final glimpse of the Ghost's retreating figure leaves Hamlet downstage staring after it and his mother on the floor behind him sobbing hysterically, "This is the very coinage of your brain."

Just as Bloom's convulsive outcry contrasts with Herlie's tender reading of the line, so the reconciliation of mother and son proceeds on rather different terms. It is a seemingly pensive Hamlet who swings on his knees toward the distraught Gertrude to confute the charge of madness. Alerted by the change in tone, she looks up with a quizzical expression. Calmly and deliberately, Hamlet remonstrates with her, slowly closing the distance between them. When he brings his face up to hers, the camera focuses on Gertrude as he counsels her to confess and repent. Looking searchingly into her son's eyes, for the first time, she shows pain and sadly tells him that he has cleft her heart. Then, with Hamlet in closeup, he clenches her hands and, for the first time in the scene, speaks lovingly to his mother, joyfully urging her to throw away the "worser part." The moment ends with the camera on Gertrude, winding her arms around her son and clasping him tightly, her head cradled in the recess of his shoulder.

The reconciliation is interrupted, however, when Hamlet enjoins Gertrude to avoid Claudius's bed. Her expression sobers, and she draws back, looking hurt. Although Hamlet becomes openly persuasive, she looks away, at which he becomes vehement: "And when you are desirous to be bless'd, / I'll blessing beg of you." Ironically, it is Hamlet's reaction, on reentering the closet, to the sight of Polonius that wins her over. Starting, his hand to his mouth, he turns back to his mother, repentant but also resigned to his role as "scourge." Explaining that he "must be cruel only to be kind," he reaches out his hands to her; responding eagerly, she cries out softly when he suddenly withdraws them from her grasp. Returning to the closet to retrieve his sword and dagger, Hamlet pauses as Gertrude follows him in, and, dropping the weapons on the body, he remarks, "One word more, good lady," and sits in the chair. Her "What shall I do?" is unresisting. Indeed, throughout his bitterly snide injunctions to secrecy and his conspiratorial revelation of his plans for Rosencrantz and Guildenstern, she kneels by his side, stroking, embracing, and caressing him. She firmly assures him of her silence and shows distress when reminded of his departure for England. Only at the end of his discourse, when Hamlet seems strangely exhilarated by his uncertain prospects, does her face cloud; but even this may be expressive of tender concern. As Hamlet pronounces his benediction over Polonius, trying to be clever but stifling a sob, and drags the body off, uttering his final good nights, Gertrude stands silently, touching his chair.

At the end of the closet scene, this Gertrude does not know for certain whether her Hamlet "essentially [is] not in madness, / But mad in craft." Still, she has been powerfully moved to accept her marital shame and to reaffirm her maternal love. If emotionally exhausted, she remains morally resolved to abide by the lesson of Hamlet's "mirror" and to act in the interest of her son. Hence, in act 4, scene 1, her voice is strained near weeping yet controlled when she tells the King of Polonius's death at the hand of the maddened Hamlet. When Claudius speaks of his own danger, she is non-committal, and when he touches her shoulder, she brushes past him to sit in the chair. Although at the end of the scene Claudius appeals to her, "O, come away! / My soul is full of discord and dismay," she remains seated in the place where she sealed her submission to Hamlet.

In the case of this Gertrude, however, the lesson does not hold. While she speaks her guilty aside in act 4, scene 5, later in the scene, when the mad Ophelia enters, Gertrude embraces Claudius and then clings to him as the Messenger reports that the mob is backing the returned Laertes. Her fierce comment on "false Danish dogs" is prelude to her defense of Claudius from Laertes' assault. Though Laertes' weapon is drawn when he enters, she approaches him directly placing a hand on his shoulder in an effort to pacify him. Claudius must twice tell her to let the furious young man go before she tentatively steps away, to interject firmly that it was not Claudius who killed his father. For Ophelia's second mad scene, Gertrude stands by Claudius again, showing no signs of the separation her son had advised.

Bloom sits on the throne next to Patrick Stewart in the final scene, holding onto his arm as Hamlet and Laertes duel. When Claudius drops the poisoned pearl into the cup, her face shows no suspicion. It is in the spirit of a toast that she picks up the cup and drinks, wanting to celebrate the prowess of her son, and it is in this same spirit that she ignores as inconsequential Claudius's instruction not to drink. Having wiped Hamlet's face, she even offers the cup to him, although he refuses it. In fact, this Claudius might have made a gesture to save his Queen; instead, he stands idly by. Only when the drugged Queen slumps to the floor does she realize that the drink was poisoned. She leaves this life clinging to Hamlet, aware of the treachery of her husband, but unreformed.

In the Olivier production, Gertrude seems incapable of the perfidy attached to the killing of a king. Hamlet may not have been far from the truth when he cynically told Horatio in act 1, scene 2 that it was "thrift" that seduced his mother into a hasty remarriage. This Gertrude is a weak, yielding woman who, as the consequence of Hamlet's traumatizing counsel in the closet, alters the poor judgment that allowed her to move with apparent ease from a Hyperion to a satyr. Though her final fatal tribute to Hamlet risks sentimentality, it completes the sequence of theatrical images—the intimate closet scene, the separate letters, the drinking of the poisoned cup—that together endorse the psychological paradigm of a morally unstructured woman whose Oedipal love for her son reconstructs her. For this Gertrude, Malcom's epitaph for Cawdor might serve: "Nothing in his life / Became him like the leaving it."

The BBC Gertrude, by contrast, might well have assented to the killing of a king, not because she was in the habit of initiating evil but because, with Edmund in *King Lear*, she believed "that men / Are as the time is." The chief quality of this Gertrude is malleability: she adjusts readily to circumstance, assuming the virtue or the vice appropriate to the occasion. In the Queen's closet, Gertrude is emotionally involved in her son's anguish and in the recognition of her sin. But virtue readily abandoned is cheaply earned. With Hamlet away from court, Gertrude's fawning on Claudius continues. Amid the carnage of the final scene, her death, like Edmund's, is "but a trifle here."

NOTES

[1] Maurice Charney, "*Hamlet* without Words," in *Shakespeare's More Than Words Can Witness: Essays on Visual and Nonverbal Enactment in the Plays,* ed. Sidney Homan (Lewisburg, Pa.: Bucknell University Press, 1980), p. 33.

[2] Quotations are from *The Complete Works of Shakespeare,* 3d ed., ed. David Bevington (Glenview, Ill.: Scott, Foresman, 1980).

[3] A. C. Bradley, *Shakerspearean Tragedy: Lectures on Hamlet, Othello, King Lear, Macbeth* (London: Macmillan, 1929), p. 138.

[4] J. Dover Wilson, *What Happens in Hamlet,* 3d ed. (Cambridge: At the University Press, 1960), p. 252.

[5] See Bradley, *Shakespearean Tragedy,* pp. 139–40; Dover Wilson, *What Happens,* pp. 353–55; W. W. Greg, "Hamlet's Hallucination," *Modern Language Review,* 12 (1917): 393–421.

[6] Harley Granville-Barker, *Prefaces to Shakespeare: Hamlet* (Princeton: Princeton University Press, 1946), p. 230.

[7] Quotations from the first quarto (referred to as Q1) are from *Shakespeare's Plays in Quarto: A Facsimile Edition of Copies Primarily from the Henry E. Huntington Library,* ed. Michael J. B. Allen and Kenneth Muir (Berkeley: University of California Press, 1981). Quotations from the first folio (referred to as F) are from *The First Folio of Shakespeare: The Norton Facsimile,* ed. Charlton Hinman (New York: Norton, 1968).

[8] It is worth noting that in Q1 the Ghost omits the epithet "adulterate" from its imprecation and Hamlet expresses contempt only for Claudius: "Yes, yes, by heaven, a damnd pernitious villaine, / Murderous, bawdy, smiling damned villaine" (p. 588). The implication that Q1 absolves Claudius and Gertrude of the blot of adultery is contravened, however, by Claudius's admission in the prayer scene (3.3) of "the adulterous fault I have committed" (p. 601).

9 Dover Wilson, *What Happens*, p. 248.

10 Harold Jenkins, ed., *The Arden Shakespeare: Hamlet* (London: Methuen, 1982), p. 320n. Jenkins invites comparison with the Player Queen's lines: "A second time I kill my husband dead, / When second husband kisses me in bed" (3.2.182–83).

11 Charney, in "*Hamlet* without Words," is amused by the prospect of staging the biological feature of the pilomotor response, the same reaction predicted by the Ghost in act 1, scene 5, when it warns Hamlet that a description of its postdeath experiences would make part his "knotted and combined locks," causing "each particular hair to stand on end." Charney notes that the one literal rendering, reported by Arthur Colby Sprague (*Shakespeare and the Actors: The Stage Business in His Plays (1660–1905)* [Cambridge: Harvard University Press, 1944], p. 382), was Garrick's: the famous eighteenth-century actor accomplished the effect with a mechnical wig (pp. 40–41).

12 Alan C. Dessen, *Elizabethan Drama and the Viewer's Eye* (Chapel Hill: University of North Carolina Press, 1977), p. 163.

13 Ibid., p. 98.

14 Ibid., p. 100.

15 *Hamlet* (1948), produced and directed by Laurence Olivier. With Laurence Olivier (Hamlet), Basil Sydney (Claudius), Eileen Herlie (Gertrude), Jean Simmons (Ophelia), Felix Aylmer (Polonius), Terence Morgan (Laertes), Norman Wooland (Horatio), Peter Cushing (Osric), Anthony Quayle (Marcellus), Esmond Knight (Bernardo), John Laurie (Francisco), Harcourt Williams (First Player), Patrick Troughton (Second Player), Tony Tarver (Third Player), Stanley Holloway (Gravedigger), Russel Thorndike (Priest).

16 Laurence Olivier, *Confessions of an Actor: An Autobiography* (New York: Penguin, 1984), p. 151.

17 Ibid., p. 183.

18 Ernest Jones, *Hamlet and Oedipus* (Garden City, N.Y.: Doubleday, 1949).

19 Olivier, *Confessions*, p. 102.

20 Frederic Wertham, "The Martricidal Impulse: Critique of Freud's Interpretation of Hamlet," *Journal of Criminal Psychopathology* (April 1944): 455–64.

21 *Hamlet* (1980), produced by Cedric Messina, directed by Rodney Bennett. With Derek Jacobi (Hamlet), Claire Bloom (Gertrude), Eric Porter (Polonius), Patrick Stewart (Claudius), Patrick Allen (Ghost), Emrys James (First Player), Lalla Ward (Ophelia), Robert Swann (Horatio), David Robb (Laertes), Christopher Baines (Francisco), Niall Padden (Bernardo), Paul Humpoletz (Marcellus), John Humphry (Voltemand), John Sterland (Cornelius), Raymond Mason (Reynaldo), Jonathan Hyde (Rosencrantz), Geoffrey Bateman (Guildenstern), Jason Kemp (Second Player), Geoffrey Beevers (Third Player), Bill Homewood (Prologue and Mime King), Peter Richards (Mime Queen), Terence McGinty (Mime Murderer), Peter Burroughs, Styart Fell (Other Players), Ian Charleson (Fortinbras), Dan Meaden (Norwegian Captain), Iain Blair (Sailor), Reginald Jessup (Messenger), Tim Wylton (First Gravedigger), Peter Benson (Second Gravedigger), Michael Poole (Priest), Peter Gale (Osric), David Henry (English Ambassador).

Sample Student Research Paper

Afton Stinnett

Dr. Douglass

EN 235-55

19 June 1997

Reclaiming Shakespeare's Gertrude:

Rejecting Role Revisions on Stage and in Film

Literary scholars agree that <u>Hamlet</u> is the
greatest play by the world's foremost playwright.
But we need not be scholarly types to realize
that <u>Hamlet</u> is part of our lives. Ask anyone to
quote a line--any line--from a Shakespeare play,
and the majority will respond, "To be, or not to
be" (3.1.56). A glance at the library's shelves
reveals that William Shakespeare's <u>Hamlet</u> has
received a substantial amount of attention. Although the vast majority of this critical writing
has justifiably focused on Hamlet himself, the
character of Gertrude warrants attention as well.
In countless stage and film productions, Gertrude
has traditionally been played as a shallow, deceitful, and adulterous woman in whom "reason
panders will" (3.4.89). But this depiction of
Gertrude is contrary to Shakespeare's textual intentions. In fact, a close examination of the
text finds a Gertrude whose words and deeds reflect a caring, devoted, sensitive mother. This
change in attitude toward Gertrude is apparent
when the text Shakespeare created is compared

Thesis
statement

Stinnett 2

with nineteenth-century stage productions and popular twentieth-century film versions.

Although Gertrude is distinguished because she is Queen of Denmark, she is important to the play principally through her role as Hamlet's caring mother. In her efforts to console her son, she tenderly speaks--"Good Hamlet, cast thy nighted colour off" (1.2.68)--and imparts her wisdom about life: "Thou know'st 'tis common,-- all that live must die, / Passing through nature to eternity" (1.2.72-73). Gertrude confirms to Hamlet that it is indeed her wish that he stay in Denmark. Her statements are concise, positive and exactly what a grieving son should hear. She is also an intuitive parent. For example, in offering her explanation for Hamlet's behavior, Gertrude demonstrates a clear-sighted and accurate analysis: "I doubt it is no other but the main,-- / His father's death and our o'er hasty marriage" (2.2.56-57).

Gertrude's role in Shakespeare's text

In the "closet scene" (3.4), more importantly, we witness a conversation that reveals Gertrude's devotion to Hamlet. Gertrude's principal purpose in having summoned Hamlet is to confront him about his recent offensive behavior and to demand an explanation for it. Hamlet, however, has a far different design. His concern is his mother's offense against his father--her "o'er hasty marriage"--so he goes to her chamber intending to rebuke her. In his anger and

Gertrude's role in Shakespeare's text, continued

Stinnett 3

rage, Hamlet insults Gertrude, murders Polonius,
and then accuses his mother of incest, haste,
and poor judgment in her marriage to Claudius.
Gertrude's attempts to avoid further confrontation are unsuccessful until the Ghost appears,
interrupts Hamlet, and protects her through
an admonition to Hamlet concerning his "almost
blunted purpose" (3.4.112). As the scene concludes, Gertrude agrees to keep Hamlet's secret
that he is "essentially . . . not in madness, /
But mad in craft" (3.4.189-190). At this important juncture, Gertrude realizes that her son's
life is at stake and she pledges to act on his
behalf.

Following the closet scene, Gertrude demonstrates her renewed devotion to Hamlet in several
instances, but her concern for her son is most
evident in the play's final scene, in which she
displays her sensitivity to Hamlet's needs. A
second "touch" in Hamlet's favor prompts Gertrude
to ease his physical discomfort and to encourage
him as he prepares to continue the fencing contest: "Here, Hamlet, take my napkin, rub thy
brows: / The queen carouses to thy fortune . . ."
(5.2.262-263). Only moments later, Hamlet's com-
ment--"I dare not drink yet, madam; by and by"
(5.2.267)--indicates that she has offered him the
poisoned cup from which she has just drunk, un-
aware of Claudius's treachery. Hamlet declines
her offer, but Gertrude persists in her desire

Gertrude's role in
Shakespeare's text,
continued

Stinnett 4

to provide a token of comfort before Hamlet resumes the contest: "Come, let me wipe thy face"
(5.2.268). Clearly, Gertrude demonstrates a keen
sensitivity to her son's needs and an intense desire to meet them.

These, then, are distinguishing characteristics of the Gertrude whom Shakespeare created,
but they are not necessarily displayed by the
Gertrude who appears on the stage or the screen
today. Ellen J. O'Brien notes that the revision
of Gertrude's role for the stage began as early
as 1755 and became "nearly universal" between
1770 and 1800 ([34] 208). The "rewriting" process
continued well into the twentieth century, with
the most extensive changes occurring during the
nineteenth century ([27] 199). Gertrude's role
has been modified so extensively, in fact, that
an actress who assumes the part in a contemporary
stage or film production is presented with a role
far different from that which Shakespeare originally designed.

Specific examples of changes in Gertrude's
role are found in the play's final scene, where
some lines have been omitted and others revised,
resulting in the elimination of evidence of the
relationship between Gertrude and Hamlet. Virtually all nineteenth-century versions of the play
in print omit Gertrude's attempts to comfort
Hamlet during the fencing match: her offer of
a napkin so that he might wipe his brow, her

Margin annotations:

Transition to modifications in Gertrude's role

Changes in Gertrude's role during the nineteenth century

Stinnett 5

willingness to wipe it for him, and her offer of
a drink from the "poisoned cup" (O'Brien 207).
Deprived of these lines, Gertrude is also denied
the opportunity that Shakespeare provided her
to display signs of her sensitivity to Hamlet's
needs, and her role as a caring, devoted mother
diminishes.

To gain further insight regarding the inconsistencies imposed upon Gertrude's character,
we should return to the closet scene. After a
thorough study of the manner in which this crucial scene is frequently scripted by writers
adapting <u>Hamlet</u> for the stage or for the screen,
O'Brien has concluded that the closet scene
suffered the "most devastating" cuts. With overwhelming consistency, nineteenth-century acting
editions and promptbooks eliminate Hamlet's appeal to Gertrude not to reveal that his madness
is feigned and Gertrude's promise to do so--evi-
dence of her devotion to Hamlet. Instead, these
versions of the play conclude the scene with
Hamlet's couplet: "I must be cruel only to be
kind: / Thus bad begins, and worse remains behind" (3.4.162-163) (O'Brien [31-32]). Of the
182 nineteenth-century promptbooks collated in
<u>Shakespeare as Spoken</u>, she notes, only six retain
Gertrude's promise to keep Hamlet's secret. In
fact, according to O'Brien, the overwhelming
majority of <u>Hamlet</u> stage productions from 1755
to 1900 did not include these details in the

Changes in Gertrude's role during the nineteenth century, continued

Stinnett 6

closet scene (O'Brien 205). Having made no promise, Gertrude emerges from the closet scene unaffected by her encounter with Hamlet—a character quite different from the one Shakespeare created.

Further revision of the closet scene occurred during the intervening years, notably in two significant modifications introduced in the twentieth century's best-known film production of Hamlet. For his 1948 film version, Laurence Olivier interpreted the Queen's closet as a bedroom. In Shakespeare's day, however, Gertrude's closet would not have been a bedroom but a small, private chamber used for prayer or study. This modification facilitates the second distortion: a passionate embrace and kiss between Hamlet and Gertrude on her bed, mistakenly presenting the pair as "lovers making up rather than [as] mother and son" (Schlueter and Lasardi 226).

Changes in Gertrude's role present in twentieth-century film versions, particularly Olivier's

The degree to which the Olivier production has influenced subsequent film versions is evident in their continued interpretation of the closet as a bedroom. In the 1980 BBC Hamlet production (which features Derek Jacobi and Claire Bloom), Gertrude's bedroom is connected to (though divided from) her closet, where she intends for their conversation to take place. During Hamlet's most violent outbursts, however, the action occurs in the bedroom. Eventually, Hamlet throws Gertrude on the bed and, in a "sudden

Further examples of revisions in twentieth-century films

Stinnett 7

movement, he mounts the bed and his mother, his
hips jerking in mock intercourse as he chides her
'compulsive ardor'" (Schlueter and Lasardi 229).
Shakespeare's stage directions, of course, do not
include this action. In a more recent film version, the enduring influence of Olivier's modifications is also present. Five decades after
Olivier's version first appeared, Mel Gibson's
1990 film version preserves the bedroom and the
inappropriate kisses. Unquestionably, an entire
generation of theatre patrons has been influenced
by the Olivier production, and Gibson's film version seems destined to have a similar effect on
future audiences.

Evidence presented here indicates that Shakespeare created Gertrude as a caring, devoted,
sensitive mother whose role has undergone modification during the four intervening centuries. In
examining Gertrude's role, one must be aware of
these revisions, most notably those introduced by
nineteenth-century stage productions and by twentieth-century film versions. Not heeding this
caution risks an evaluation of Gertrude based on
inaccurate representations of Shakespeare's intentions. Clearly, Gertrude warrants attention,
but such notice should be based strictly upon the
dialogue Shakespeare created for her.

Conclusion—
summarizes major
points discussed in
essay

Stinnett 8

Works Cited

Douglass, Scott, ed. <u>Hamlet</u>. Harcourt Brace Casebook Series in Literature. Ft. Worth: Harcourt, 1998.

<u>Hamlet</u>. [BBC/Time-Life's Shakespeare Plays
Ser.] Dir. Rodney Bennett. Perf. Derek
Jacobi, Patrick Stewart, Claire Bloom, Lalla
Ward, and Eric Porter. BBC Television/Time-
Life, 1980.

<u>Hamlet</u>. Dir. Laurence Olivier. Perf. Olivier,
Basil Sydney, Eileen Herlie, Jean Simmons,
and Felix Aylmer. Two Cities, 1948.

<u>Hamlet</u>. Dir. Franco Zeffirelli. Perf. Mel Gib-
son, Glenn Close, Alan Bates, Paul Scofield,
Ian Holm, and Helena Bonham-Carter. Warner
Bros., 1989.

O'Brien, Ellen J. "Revision by Excision: Rewriting Gertrude." Douglass 199-209.

Schlueter, June, and James P. Lusardi. "The Camera in Gertrude's Closet." Douglass 209-34.

Shakespeare, William. <u>Hamlet, Prince of Denmark</u>.
Douglass 19-139.

Bibliography

SHAKESPEAREAN BIOGRAPHY

Alexander, Peter. *Shakespeare's Life and Art.* Westport, CT: Greenwood, 1979.

Andrews, John F., ed. *William Shakespeare: His World, His Work, His Influence.* New York: Scribner's, 1985. 3 vols.

Baldwin, T. W. *William Shakspere's Petty School.* Urbana: U of Illinois P, 1943.

---. *William Shakspeare's Small Latine and Lesse Greeke.* 2 vols. Urbana: U of Illinois P, 1944.

Bentley, Gerald Eades. *Shakespeare: A Biographical Handbook.* New Haven: Yale UP, 1974.

Brown, Ivor. *How Shakespeare Spent the Day.* London: Bodley Head, 1963.

Brown, John Russell, and Bernard Harris, eds. *Early Shakespeare.* New York: Schocken, 1966.

Burgess, Anthony. *Nothing Like the Sun: A Story of Shakespeare's Love Life.* New York: Norton, 1964.

Dutton, Richard. *William Shakespeare: A Literary Life.* New York: St. Martin's, 1989.

Eccles, Mark. *Shakespeare in Warwickshire.* Madison: U of Wisconsin P, 1963.

Edwards, Philip. *Shakespeare: A Writer's Progress.* Oxford: Oxford UP, 1987.

Fraser, Russell. *Young Shakespeare.* New York: Columbia UP, 1988.

Halliday, F. E. *The Life of Shakespeare.* London: Duckworth, 1961.

---. *Shakespeare in His Age.* London: Duckworth, 1956.

Harbage, Alfred. *Conceptions of Shakespeare.* Cambridge: Harvard UP, 1966.

Harrison, George Bagshawe. *Shakespeare at Work.* London: Routledge, 1933.

Holderness, Graham, ed. *The Shakespeare Myth.* Manchester: Manchester UP, 1988.

Johnson, Samuel. *The Lives of the English Poets.* 3 vols. Ed. George Birkbeck Hill. Oxford, 1905. Rpt. New York: Octagon, 1967.

Jones, Emrys. *The Origins of Shakespeare.* Oxford: Clarendon, 1977.

Knight, W. Nicholas. *Shakespeare's Hidden Life: Shakespeare at the Law 1585–1595.* New York: Mason, 1973.

McClellan, Kenneth. *Whatever Happened to Shakespeare?* London: Vision, 1978.

Mortimer, John. *William Shakespeare: The Untold Story.* New York: Delacorte, 1978.

Ogburn, Charlton. *The Mysterious William Shakespeare: The Myth and the Reality.* New York: Dodd, 1984.

Quennell, Peter. *Shakespeare: A Biography.* New York: World, 1963.

Ribner, Irving. *William Shakespeare: An Introduction to His Life, Times and Theatre.* Waltham, MA: Blaisdell, 1969.

Schoenbaum, S. *Shakespeare's Lives.* New. ed. Oxford: Oxford UP, 1991.

---. *William Shakespeare: A Compact Documentary Life.* Oxford: Oxford UP, 1977.

Smart, John Semple. *Shakespeare: Truth and Tradition.* Oxford: Clarendon, 1966.

Wilson, J. Dover. *The Essential Shakespeare.* New York: Haskell, 1977.

COMPLETE WORKS

Greenblatt, Stephen, et al., eds. *The Norton Shakespeare: Based on the Oxford Edition.* New York: Norton, 1997.

Bevington, David, ed. *The Complete Works of Shakespeare.* 4th ed. New York: Longman-Addison, 1997.

Evans, G. Blakemore, et al., eds. *The Riverside Shakespeare.* 2nd ed. Boston: Houghton, 1997.

Farrow, Matty. *The Works of the Bard.* Online. Internet. 10 July 1997. Available http://www.gh.cs.su.oz.au/~matty/Shakespeare/Shakespeare.html# othersites.

Hylton, Jeremy. *The Complete Works of William Shakespeare.* 9 Dec. 1996. Online. Internet. 10 July 1997. Available http://the-tech.mit.edu/Shakespeare/works.html.

Text of Shakespeare's Plays. Online. Internet. 10 July 1997. Available http://www.pixi.com/~pchs/shakes/text2.htm.

SHAKESPEARE'S EARLY EDITORS

Black, Matthew W., and Matthias A. Shaaber. *Shakespeare's Seventeenth-Century Editors 1632–1685.* New York: MLA, 1937.

Capell, Edward, ed. *Mr. William Shakespeare: His Comedies, Histories, and Tragedies.* 10 vols. London, 1767. New York: AMS, 1968.

De Grazia, Margreta. *Shakespeare Verbatim: The Reproduction of Authenticity and the Apparatus of 1790.* Oxford: Clarendon, 1991.

Douglass, Terry Scott. "Nicholas Rowe's Edition of Shakespeare." Diss. Florida State Univ., 1982.

Ford, H. L. *Shakespeare, 1700–1740: A Collation of the Editions and Separate Plays.* 1935. New York: Blom, 1968.

Gray, Terry A. *Nicholas Rowe's Preface to His 1709 Edition of Shakespeare's Works.* 3 Jan. 1997. Online. Internet. 10 July 1997. Available http://www.palomar.edu/Library/ROWE.HTM.

Greg, W. W. *The Editorial Problem in Shakespeare: A Survey of the Foundations of the Text.* Oxford: Clarendon, 1942.

---. "Principles of Emendation in Shakespeare." *Aspects of Shakespeare.* Oxford: Clarendon, 1933.

Hanmer, Thomas, ed. *The Works of Shakespear.* 6 vols. Oxford, 1744. New York: AMS, 1969.

Hinman, Charlton, ed. *The First Folio of Shakespeare: The Norton Facsimile.* New York: Norton, 1968.

Jaggard, William. *Shakespeare Bibliography: A Dictionary of Every Known Issue of the Writings of the Poet and of Recorded Opinion Thereon in the English Language.* New York: Ungar, 1959.

Johnson, Samuel. *Johnson on Shakespeare.* Ed. Arthur Sherbo. Vols. 7 and 8. New Haven: Yale UP, 1968.

---. *The Plays of William Shakespeare.* 8 vols. London, 1765. New York: AMS, 1968.

Lounsbury, Thomas R. *The First Editors of Shakespeare.* London: Nutt, 1906.

---. *The Text of Shakespeare: Its History from the Publication of the Quartos and Folios down to and Including the Publication of the Editions of Pope and Theobald.* New York: Scribner's, 1906.

Lynch, Kathleen M. *Jacob Tonson: Kit-Cat Publisher.* Knoxville: U of Tennessee P, 1971.

Malone, Edmond, ed. *The Plays and Poems of William Shakespeare.* 10 vols. London, 1790. New York: AMS, 1968.

---, ed. *The Plays and Poems of William Shakespeare.* 21 vols. Rev. by James Boswell. London, 1821.

Marder, Louis. *His Exits and His Entrances: The Story of Shakespeare's Reputation.* Philadelphia: Lippincott, 1963.

McAfee, Helen. *Pepys on the Restoration Stage.* 1916. New York: AMS, 1963.

McKerrow, R. B. "The Treatment of Shakespeare's Text by His Earlier Editors, 1709–1768." *Ronald Brunlees McKerrow: A Selection of His Essays.* Comp. John Phillip Immroth. Metuchen, NJ : Scarecrow, 1974. 159–88.

Mills, Robert John. "Eighteenth-Century Editors of Shakespeare." Diss. U of Alberta, 1979.

Nicoll, Allardyce. "The Editors of Shakespeare from First Folio to Malone." *Studies in the First Folio.* Ed. Israel Gollancz. London: Oxford UP, 1924. 157–78.

Papali, G. F. *Jacob Tonson, Publisher: His Life and Work (1656–1736).* Auckland: Tonson, 1968.

Pope, Alexander, ed. *The Works of Shakespear.* 6 vols. London, 1725. New York: AMS, 1969.

Pope, Alexander, and William Warburton, eds. *The Works of Shakespear.* 8 vols. London, 1747. New York: AMS, 1968.

Rowe, Nicholas, ed. *The Works of Mr. William Shakespear.* 6 vols. London, 1709. New York: AMS, 1967.

Smith, D. Nichol, ed. *Eighteenth-Century Essays on Shakespeare.* 2nd ed. Oxford: Clarendon, 1963.

---. *Shakespeare in the Eighteenth Century.* Oxford: Clarendon, 1928.

Taylor, Gary. *Reinventing Shakespeare: A Cultural History, from the Restoration to the Present.* New York: Weidenfeld, 1989.

Theobald, Lewis. *The Works of Shakespeare.* 7 vols. London, 1733. New York: AMS, 1968.

SHAKESPEARE'S PUBLICATION HISTORY

Blayney, Peter. *The First Folio of Shakespeare.* Hanover, MD: Folger, 1991.

Chambers, E. K. *William Shakespeare: A Study of Facts and Problems.* 2 vols. Oxford: Clarendon, 1930.

De Grazia, Margreta. *Shakespeare Verbatim: The Reproduction of Authenticity and the Apparatus of 1790.* Oxford: Clarendon, 1991.

Ford, H. L. *Shakespeare, 1700–1740: A Collation of the Editions and Separate Plays.* 1935. Rpt. New York: Blom, 1968.

Greg, W. W. *The Editorial Problem in Shakespeare: A Survey of the Foundations of the Text.* Oxford: Clarendon 1954.

---. *The Shakespeare First Folio.* Oxford: Clarendon, 1955.

Hinman, Charlton. *The Printing and Proof-Reading of the First Folio of Shakespeare.* 2 vols. Oxford: Clarendon, 1963.

---, ed. *The First Folio of Shakespeare: The Norton Facsimile.* New York: Norton, 1968.

Honingmann, E. A. J. *The Stability of Shakespeare's Text.* London: Arnold, 1965.

Jaggard, William. *Shakespeare Bibliography: A Dictionary of Every Known Issue of the Writings of the Poet and of Recorded Opinion Thereon in the English Language.* New York: Ungar, 1959.

Kirschbaum, Leo. *Shakespeare and the Stationers.* Columbus: Ohio State UP, 1955.

Lounsbury, Thomas R. *The Text of Shakespeare: Its History from the Publication of the Quartos and Folios down to and Including the Publication of the Editions of Pope and Theobald.* New York: Scribner's, 1906.

Marder, Louis. *His Exits and His Entrances: The Story of Shakespeare's Reputation.* Philadelphia: Lippincott, 1963.

McKerrow, R. B. "The Treatment of Shakespeare's Text by His Earlier Editors, 1709–1768." *Ronald Brunlees McKerrow: A Selection of His Essays.* Comp. John Phillip Immroth. Metuchen, NJ: Scarecrow, 1974. 159–88.

Nicoll, Allardyce. "The Editors of Shakespeare from First Folio to Malone." *Studies in the First Folio.* Ed. Israel Gollancz. London: Oxford UP, 1924. 157–78.

Smart, John Semple. *Shakespeare: Truth and Tradition.* Oxford: Oxford UP, 1966.

Smith, D. Nichol, ed. *Eighteenth-Century Essays on Shakespeare.* 2nd ed. Oxford: Clarendon, 1963.

---. *Shakespeare in the Eighteenth Century.* Oxford: Clarendon, 1928.

Taylor, Gary. *Reinventing Shakespeare: A Cultural History, from the Restoration to the Present.* New York: Weidenfeld, 1989.

Walder, Ernest. *Shakesperian Criticism: Textual and Literary, from Dryden to the End of the Eighteenth Century.* Bradford, 1895. Rpt. New York: AMS, 1972.

Walker, Alice. *Textual Problems of the First Folio.* Cambridge: Cambridge UP, 1953.

Williams, George Walton. *The Craft of Printing and the Publication of Shakespeare's Works.* Washington: Folger, 1985.

GENERAL REFERENCE SOURCES

Boyce, Charles. *Shakespeare A to Z: The Essential Reference to His Plays, His Poems, His Life and Times, and More.* New York: Dell-Doubleday, 1990.

Campbell, Oscar James, and Edward G. Quinn. *The Reader's Encyclopedia of Shakespeare.* New York: Crowell, 1966.

Jenkins, Harold, ed. *Hamlet.* By William Shakespeare. Arden Edition of the Works of William Shakespeare. New York: Methuen, 1982.

McDonald, Russ. *The Bedford Companion to Shakespeare: An Introduction with Documents.* Boston: Bedford-St. Martin's, 1996.

Mowat, Barbara A., and Paul Werstine, eds. *The Tragedy of Hamlet, Prince of Denmark.* By William Shakespeare. New Folger Library Shakespeare. New York: Washington Square-Pocket, 1992.

Naylor, Edward Woodall. *Shakespeare and Music.* London: Dent, 1931.

Onions, C. T., and Robert D. Eagleson. *A Shakespeare Glossary.* Rev. ed. Oxford: Clarendon, 1986.

Palmer, Alan, and Veronica Palmer. *Who's Who in Shakespeare's England.* New York: St. Martin's, 1981.

Schoenbaum, Marilyn, ed. *A Shakespeare Merriment: An Anthology of Shakespearean Humor.* New York: Garland, 1988.

Sobran, Joseph. *Alias Shakespeare: Solving the Greatest Literary Mystery of All Time.* New York: Free, 1997.

SHAKESPEARE'S ENGLAND

Andrews, John F., ed. *William Shakespeare: His World, His Work, His Influence.* 3 vols. New York: Scribner's, 1985.

Beier, A. L., and Roger Finlay, eds. *London 1500–1800: The Making of the Metropolis.* New York: Longman, 1986.

Black, J. B. *The Reign of Elizabeth, 1558–1603.* 2nd ed. Oxford: Oxford UP, 1959.

Bruster, Douglas. *Drama and the Market in the Age of Shakespeare.* Cambridge: Cambridge UP, 1992.

Byrne, Muriel St. Clare. *Elizabethan Life in Town and Country.* 8th ed. Boston: Houghton, 1961.

Cressy, David. *Education in Tudor and Stuart England.* London: Arnold, 1975.

Frye, Roland M. *Shakespeare and Christian Doctrine.* Princeton: Princeton UP, 1963.

Ordish, T. Fairman. *Shakespeare's London: A Study of London in the Reign of Queen Elizabeth.* Williamstown, MA: Corner, 1975.

Reese, Max Meredith. *Shakespeare: His World and His Work.* New York: St. Martin's, 1980.

Stone, Lawrence. *The Crisis of the Aristocracy, 1558–1641.* Oxford: Oxford UP, 1965.

Tillyard, E. M. W. *The Elizabethan World Picture.* New York: Random, 1959.

Underdown, David. *Revel, Riot, and Rebellion: Popular Politics and Culture in England, 1603–1660.* Oxford: Oxford UP, 1985.

Woodbridge, Linda. *Women and the English Renaissance.* Urbana: U of Illinois P, 1984.

Wright, Louis B. *Middle Class Culture in Elizabethan England.* New York: Hippocrene, 1978.

Wright, Louis B., and Virginia A. LaMar, eds. *The Folger Guide to Shakespeare.* New York: Washington Square-Pocket, 1969.

SHAKESPEARE'S LANGUAGE AND STYLE

Abbott, E. A. *A Shakespearian Grammar.* New York: Haskell, 1972.

Blake, N. F. *Shakespeare's Language: An Introduction.* New York: St. Martin's, 1983.

Boyce, Charles. *Shakespeare A to Z: The Essential Reference to His Plays, His Poems, His Life and Times, and More.* New York: Facts on File, 1990.

Brown, John Russell. *Shakespeare's Dramatic Style.* London: Heinemann, 1970.

Charney, Maurice. *Style in* Hamlet. Princeton: Princeton UP, 1969.

Clemen, Wolfgang H. *The Development of Shakespeare's Imagery.* Cambridge: Harvard UP, 1951.

Danson, Lawrence. *Tragic Alphabet: Shakespeare's Drama of Language.* New Haven: Yale UP, 1974.

De Grazia, Margreta. *Shakespeare Verbatim.* Oxford: Clarendon, 1990.

De Grazia, Margreta, and Peter Stallybrass. "The Materiality of the Shakespearean Text." *Shakespeare Quarterly* 44 (1993): 255–83.

Evans, Ifor. *The Language of Shakespeare's Plays.* 2nd ed. London: Methuen, 1959.

Fisch, Harold. Hamlet *and the Word.* New York: Ungar, 1971.

Houston, John Porter. *Shakespearean Sentences: A Study in Style and Syntax.* Baton Rouge: Louisiana State UP, 1988.

Kokeritz, Helge. *Shakespeare's Pronunciation.* New Haven: Yale UP, 1953.

Lanham, Richard A. *The Motives of Eloquence: Literary Rhetoric in the Renaissance.* New Haven: Yale UP, 1976.

Levin, Harry. "An Explication of the Player's Speech." *William Shakespeare's* Hamlet. Ed. Harold Bloom. Modern Critical Interpretations. New York: Chelsea, 1986. 29–44.

Onions, C. T., and Robert D. Eagleson. *A Shakespeare Glossary.* Rev. ed. Oxford: Clarendon, 1986.

Partridge, Eric. *Shakespeare's Bawdy.* New York: Routledge, 1991.

Rubinstein, Frankie. *A Dictionary of Shakespeare's Sexual Puns and Their Significance*. Basingstoke: Macmillan, 1989.

Schoenbaum, Marilyn, ed. *A Shakespeare Merriment: An Anthology of Shakespearean Humor*. New York: Garland, 1988.

Spurgeon, Caroline F. E. *Shakespeare's Imagery and What It Tells Us*. Cambridge: Cambridge UP, 1935.

Wells, Stanley. *Shakespeare: An Illustrated Dictionary*. Oxford: Oxford UP, 1986.

SHAKESPEARE'S THEATRE, HIS AUDIENCE AND THE ACTORS

Adams, John Cranford. *The Globe Playhouse*. New York: Barnes, 1966.

Adams, Joseph Quincy. *Shakespearean Playhouses: A History of English Theatres from the Beginning to the Restoration*. Magnolia, MA: Smith, 1959.

Avery, Emmett L. "The Shakespeare Ladies Club." *Shakespeare Quarterly* 7 (1956): 153–58.

Baldwin, Thomas Whitfield. *The Organisation and Personnel of the Shakespearean Company*. Princeton: Princeton UP, 1927.

Barber, Frances. "Ophelia in *Hamlet*." *Players of Shakespeare 2: Further Essays in Shakespearean Performance by Players with the Royal Shakespeare Company*. Ed. Russell Jackson and Robert Smallwood. Cambridge: Cambridge UP, 1988. 137–49.

Barton, John. *Playing Shakespeare*. London: Methuen, 1984.

Beckerman, Bernard. *Shakespeare at the Globe*. New York: Columbia UP, 1962.

Bentley, G. E. *The Profession of Player in Shakespeare's Time, 1590–1642*. Princeton: Princeton UP, 1986.

Berry, Herbert. *Shakespeare's Playhouses*. AMS Studies in the Renaissance 19. New York: AMS, 1987.

Bradbrook, Muriel C. *Elizabethan Stage Conditions*. Hamden, CT: Archon, 1962.

---. *The Rise of the Common Player*. Cambridge: Cambridge UP, 1979.

Cook, Ann Jennalie. *The Privileged Playgoer of Shakespeare's London, 1576–1642*. Princeton: Princeton UP, 1981.

Crowl, Samuel. *Shakespeare Observed: Studies in Performance on Stage and Screen*. Athens: U of Ohio P, 1992.

Day, Barry. *This Wooden "O": Shakespeare's Globe Reborn*. London: Oberon, 1996.

Dessen, Alan C. *Elizabethan Stage Conventions and Modern Interpreters*. Cambridge: Cambridge UP, 1984.

Draper, John W. *The* Hamlet *of Shakespeare's Audience*. New York: Octagon, 1966.

Foakes, R. A. *Illustrations of the English Stage 1580–1642*. Stanford, CA: Stanford UP, 1985.

Franks, Philip. "Hamlet." *Players of Shakespeare 3: Further Essays in Shakespearian Performance by Players with the Royal Shakespeare Company*. Ed. Russell Jackson and Robert Smallwood. Cambridge: Cambridge UP, 1993. 189–200.

Gielgud, John, and John Miller. *Acting Shakespeare*. New York: Scribner's, 1992.

Greg, W. W. *Dramatic Documents from the Elizabethan Playhouses.* 2 vols. Oxford: Clarendon, 1931.

Gurr, Andrew. *Playgoing in Shakespeare's London.* 2nd ed. Cambridge: Cambridge UP, 1996.

---. *The Shakespearean Stage, 1574–1642.* 3rd ed. Cambridge: Cambridge UP, 1992.

Gurr, Andrew, and John Orrell. *Rebuilding Shakespeare's Globe.* New York: Routledge, 1989.

Harbage, Alfred. *Shakespeare's Audience.* New York: Columbia UP, 1961.

Harrison, George Bagshawe. *Elizabethan Plays and Players.* Ann Arbor: U of Michigan P, 1956.

Hattaway, Michael. *Elizabethan Popular Theatre: Plays in Performance.* London: Routledge, 1982.

Hill, Errol. *Shakespeare in Sable: A History of Black Shakespearean Actors.* Amherst: U of Massachusetts P, 1986.

Hodges, Cyril W. *The Globe Restored.* New York: Somerset, 1973.

Hotson, Leslie. *Shakespeare's Wooden O.* London: Hart, 1959.

Jackson, Russell, and Robert Smallwood, eds. *Players of Shakespeare 2: Further Essays in Shakespearean Performance by Players with the Royal Shakespeare Company.* Cambridge: Cambridge UP, 1988.

---, eds. *Players of Shakespeare 3: Further Essays in Shakespearian Performance by Players with the Royal Shakespeare Company.* Cambridge: Cambridge UP, 1993.

Joseph, B. L. *Elizabethan Acting.* 2nd. ed. Oxford: Oxford UP, 1964.

Kennedy, Dennis. *Foreign Shakespeare: Contemporary Performance.* Cambridge: Cambridge UP, 1993.

---. *Looking at Shakespeare: A Visual History of Twentieth-Century Performance.* Cambridge: Cambridge UP, 1993.

Levine, Laura. *Men in Women's Clothing.* Cambridge: Cambridge UP, 1993.

Miller-Schutz, Chantal. *Shakespeare's Globe.* 9 July 1997. Online. Internet. 13 Aug. 1997. Available http://www.rdg.ac.uk/AcaDepts/ln/Globe/Globe.html.

Nagler, Alois M. *Shakespeare's Stage.* New Haven: Yale UP, 1981.

Nevo, Ruth. "Acts III and IV: Problems of Text and Staging." *William Shakespeare's* Hamlet. Ed. Harold Bloom. Modern Critical Interpretations. New York: Chelsea, 1986. 45–64.

Olivier, Laurence. *Confessions of an Actor.* New York: Simon, 1986.

---. *On Acting.* New York: Simon, 1982.

Orrell, John. *The Quest for Shakespeare's Globe.* Cambridge: Cambridge UP, 1983.

Rose, Mark. "Reforming the Role." *William Shakespeare's* Hamlet. Ed. Harold Bloom. Modern Critical Interpretations. New York: Chelsea, 1986. 117–28.

Shattuck, Charles H. *Shakespeare on the American Stage.* 2 vols. Washington: Folger Shakespeare Library, 1976–1987.

Shaw, George Bernard. *Shaw on Shakespeare.* Ed. Edwin Wilson. New York: Dutton, 1961.

Smith, Irwin. *Shakespeare's Blackfriars Playhouse.* New York: New York UP, 1964.

---. *Shakespeare's Globe Playhouse.* New York: Scribner's, 1956.

Speaight, Robert. *Shakespeare on the Stage: An Illustrated History of Shakespearean Performance.* Boston: Little, 1973.

Sprague, Arthur Colby. *Shakespeare and the Actors.* New York: Russell, 1963.

Styan, J. L. *Shakespeare's Stagecraft.* Cambridge: Cambridge UP, 1967.

Thompson, Peter W. *Shakespeare's Theatre.* London: Routledge, 1983.

Trewin, John Courtenay. *Shakespeare on the English Stage 1900–1964.* London: Barrie, 1964.

Weimann, Robert. *Shakespeare and the Popular Tradition in the Theater: Studies in the Social Dimension of Dramatic Form and Function.* Baltimore: Johns Hopkins UP, 1978.

SHAKESPEARE'S SOURCES

Bullough, Geoffrey. *Narrative and Dramatic Sources of Shakespeare.* 8 vols. New York: Columbia UP, 1957–1975.

Gollancz, Israel. *The Sources of* Hamlet. London: Cass, 1967.

Muir, Kenneth. *The Sources of Shakespeare's Plays.* New Haven: Yale UP, 1978.

Taylor, Marion A. *A New Look at the Old Sources of* Hamlet. The Hague: Mouton, 1968.

HAMLET: PSYCHOLOGICAL PERSPECTIVE

Fleming, Keith. "Hamlet and Oedipus Today: Jones and Lacan." *Hamlet Studies* 4 (1982): 54–71.

Holland, Norman N. *Psychoanalysis and Shakespeare.* New York: McGraw, 1966.

Jenkins, Harold. *Hamlet and Ophelia.* Oxford: Oxford UP, 1964.

Jones, Ernest. *Hamlet and Oedipus.* New York: Norton, 1976.

Kirsch, Arthur. "Hamlet's Grief." *Hamlet.* Ed. Harold Bloom. Modern Literary Characters. New York: Chelsea, 1990. 122–38.

Knight, G. Wilson. "The Embassy of Death: An Essay on *Hamlet.*" *Hamlet.* Ed. Harold Bloom. Modern Literary Characters. New York: Chelsea, 1990. 80–94.

Lenz, Carolyn Ruth Swift, Gayle Greene, and Carol Thomas Neely, eds. *The Woman's Part: Feminist Criticism of Shakespeare.* Urbana: U of Illinois P, 1980.

Levin, Harry. *The Question of Hamlet.* Oxford: Oxford UP, 1959.

Neely, Carol Thomas. "'Documents in Madness': Reading Madness and Gender in Shakespeare's Tragedies and Early Modern Culture." *Shakespeare Quarterly* 42 (1991): 315–38.

Rosenberg, Marvin. *The Masks of Hamlet.* Newark: U of Delaware P, 1992.

Schowalter, Elaine. "Representing Ophelia: Women, Madness, and the Responsibilities of Feminist Criticism." *Shakespeare and the Question of Theory.* Ed. Patricia Parker and Geoffrey Hartman. London: Methuen, 1985.

Schwartz, Murry M., and Coppelia Kahn, ed. *Representing Shakespeare: New Psychoanalytic Essays.* Baltimore: Johns Hopkins UP, 1980.

Taylor, Mark. *Shakespeare's Darker Purpose: A Question of Incest.* New York: AMS, 1982.

Zhang, Siyang. "Hamlet's Melancholy." *Shakespeare and the Triple Play: From Study to Stage to Classroom.* Ed. Sidney Homan. Toronto: Associated UP, 1988. 76–81.

HAMLET: MODERN CRITICAL OPINION

Adelman, Janet. *Suffocating Mothers: Fantasies of Maternal Origin in Shakespeare's Plays,* Hamlet *to* The Tempest. New York: Routledge, 1992.

Biggs, Murray. "'He's Going to His Mother's Closet': Hamlet and Gertrude on Screen." *Shakespeare Survey* 45 (1993): 53–62.

Bligh, John. "The Women in the Hamlet Story." *Dalhousie Review* 53 (1973): 275–85.

Bloom, Harold, ed. *Hamlet.* Modern Literary Characters. New York: Chelsea, 1990.

---, ed. *William Shakespeare's* Hamlet. Modern Critical Interpretations. New York: Chelsea, 1986.

Bradley, A. C. *Shakespearean Tragedy: Lectures on* Hamlet, Othello, King Lear, Macbeth. New York: St. Martin's, 1985.

Calderwood, James. *To Be and Not to Be: Negation and Metadrama in* Hamlet. New York: Columbia UP, 1983.

Camden, Carroll. "On Ophelia's Madness." *Shakespeare Quarterly* 15 (1964): 247–55.

---. "Hamlet's 'Cruelty' in the Nunnery Scene: The Actors' Views." *Shakespeare Quarterly* 18 (1967): 129–40.

Charney, Maurice. *Hamlet's Fictions.* London: Routledge, 1987.

Clayton, Thomas, ed. *The* Hamlet *First Published (Q1, 1603): Origins, Form, Intertextualities.* Newark: U of Delaware P, 1992.

Clemen, Wolfgang H. *The Development of Shakespeare's Imagery.* Cambridge: Harvard UP, 1951.

Coleridge, Samuel Taylor. *Coleridge's Criticism of Shakespeare.* Ed. R. A. Foakes. Detroit: Wayne State UP, 1989.

Cox, Lee Sheridan. *Figurative Design in* Hamlet: *The Significance of the Dumb Show.* Columbus: Ohio State UP, 1973.

De Grazia, Margreta. *Shakespeare Verbatim: The Reproduction of Authenticity and the Apparatus of 1790.* Oxford: Clarendon, 1991.

Dean, Leonard Fellows, ed. *Shakespeare: Modern Essays in Criticism.* New York: Oxford UP, 1967.

Drakakis, John, ed. *Alternative Shakespeares.* New York: Routledge, 1985.

Draper, John W. *The* Hamlet *of Shakespeare's Audience.* New York: Octagon, 1966.

Dusinberre, Juliet. *Shakespeare and the Nature of Women.* London: Macmillan, 1975.

Edwards, Philip. *Shakespeare's Styles: Essays in Honour of Kenneth Muir.* Cambridge: Cambridge UP, 1980.

Eliot, T. S. *Selected Essays.* New ed. New York: Harcourt, 1950.

Elsom, John, ed. *Is Shakespeare Still Our Contemporary?* London: Routledge, 1989.

Empson, William. *Essays on Shakespeare.* Cambridge: Cambridge UP, 1986.

Felperin, Howard. "O'erdoing Termagant." *William Shakespeare's* Hamlet. Ed. Harold Bloom. Modern Critical Interpretations. New York: Chelsea, 1986. 99–115.

Flatter, Richard. *Hamlet's Father.* London: Heinemann, 1949.

Fowler, Gene. *Good Night, Sweet Prince.* New York: Viking, 1944.

Frye, Northrop. *Fools of Time: Studies in Shakespearean Tragedy.* Toronto: U of Toronto P, 1967.

Gielgud, John, and John Miller. *Acting Shakespeare.* New York: Scribner's: 1992.

Girard, Rene. "Hamlet's Dull Revenge." *Hamlet.* Ed. Harold Bloom. Modern Literary Characters. New York: Chelsea, 1990. 166–85.

Goddard, Harold C. "Hamlet." *Hamlet.* Ed. Harold Bloom. Modern Literary Characters. New York: Chelsea, 1990. 95–121.

---. "Hamlet: His Own Falstaff." *William Shakespeare's* Hamlet. Ed. Harold Bloom. Modern Critical Interpretations. New York: Chelsea, 1986. 11–28.

---. *The Meaning of Shakespeare.* Chicago: U of Chicago P, 1973.

Goldberg, Jonathan. "Hamlet's Hand." *Shakespeare Quarterly* 39 (1988): 307–27.

Gottschalk, Paul. *The Meanings of* Hamlet. Albuquerque: U of New Mexico P, 1972.

Granville-Barker, Harley. *Prefaces to Shakespeare.* 2 vols. Princeton: Princeton UP, 1978.

Heilbrun, Carolyn. "The Character of Hamlet's Mother." *Shakespeare Quarterly* 8 (1957): 201–6.

Honigmann, E. A. J. *Myriad-Minded Shakespeare: Essays, Chiefly on the Tragedies and Problem Comedies.* New York: St. Martin's, 1989.

Hopkins, Lisa. "'That's Wormwood': Hamlet Plays His Mother." *Hamlet Studies* 16 (1994): 83–5.

Jump, John, ed. *Hamlet: A Casebook.* London: Macmillan, 1968.

King, Walter N. *Hamlet's Search for Meaning.* Athens: U of Georgia P, 1982.

Knights, L. C. *An Approach to* Hamlet. Stanford: Stanford UP, 1961.

---. *Hamlet and Other Shakespearean Essays.* Cambridge: Cambridge UP, 1979.

---. "*Hamlet* and the Perplexed Critics." *Sewanee Review* 92 (1984): 225–38.

Lenz, Carolyn Ruth Swift, Gayle Greene, and Carol Thomas Neeley, eds. *The Woman's Part: Feminist Criticism of Shakespeare.* Urbana: U of Illinois P, 1980.

Levin, Harry. *The Question of* Hamlet. Oxford: Oxford UP, 1965.

Lyons, Bridget Gellert. "The Iconography of Ophelia." *English Literary History* 44 (1977): 60–74.

Mack, Maynard. *Everybody's Shakespeare: Reflections Chiefly on the Tragedies.* Lincoln: U of Nebraska P, 1993.

Mack, Maynard, Jr. *Killing the King: Three Studies in Shakespeare's Tragic Structure.* Yale Studies in English 180. New Haven: Yale UP, 1973.

MacKenzie, Agnes Mure. *The Women in Shakespeare's Plays: A Critical Study from the Dramatic and the Psychological Points of View and in Relation to the Development of Shakespeare's Art.* London: Heinemann, 1924.

McGee, Arthur. *The Elizabethan* Hamlet. New Haven: Yale UP, 1987.

McKewin, Carole. "Shakespeare Liberata: Shakespeare, The Nature of Women, and the New Feminist Criticism." *Mosaic* 10.3 (1977): 157–64.

Mowat, Barbara A. "Images of Woman in Shakespeare's Plays." *Southern Humanities Review* 11 (1977): 145–57.

Nardo, Anna K. "Hamlet, 'A Man to Double Business Bound.'" *Shakespeare Quarterly* 34 (1983): 181–99.

Nevo, Ruth. *Tragic Form in Shakespeare.* Princeton: Princeton UP, 1972.

O'Brien, Ellen J. "Revision by Excision: Rewriting Gertrude." *Shakespeare Survey* 45 (1993): 27–35.

Prosser, Eleanor. *Hamlet and Revenge.* Stanford: Stanford UP, 1971.

Putzel, Rosamond. "Queen Gertrude's Crime." *Renaissance Papers, 1961.* Ed. George Walton Williams. Durham, NC: Southeastern Renaissance Conference, 1962. 37–46.

Rose, Jacqueline. "Hamlet—The *Mona Lisa* of Literature." *Hamlet.* Ed. Harold Bloom. Modern Literary Characters. New York: Chelsea, 1990. 186–99.

Rose, Mark. "*Hamlet.*" *Homer to Brecht: The European Epic and Dramatic Traditions.* Ed. Michael Seidel and Edward Mendelson. New Haven: Yale UP, 1977. 238–254.

Rosenberg, Marvin. "The Stage and *Hamlet.*" *Hamlet Studies* 1 (1979): 51–53.

Rosenblatt, Jason P. "Aspects of the Incest Problem in Hamlet." *Shakespeare Quarterly* 29 (1978): 349–364.

Schlueter, June, and James P. Lusardi. "The Camera in Gertrude's Closet." *Shakespeare and the Triple Play: From Study to Stage to Classroom.* Ed. Sydney Homan. Toronto: Associated UP, 1988. 150–74.

Seidel, Michael, and Edward Mendelson, eds. *Homer to Brecht: The European Epic and Dramatic Traditions.* New Haven: Yale UP, 1977.

Smith, Rebecca. "A Heart Cleft in Twain: The Dilemma of Shakespeare's Gertrude." *The Woman's Part: Feminist Criticism of Shakespeare.* Ed. Carolyn Ruth Swift Lenz, Gayle Greene, and Carol Thomas Neeley. Urbana: U of Illinois P, 1980. 194–210.

Summers, Joseph H. "The Dream of a Hero: *Hamlet.*" *Hamlet.* Ed. Harold Bloom. Modern Literary Characters. New York: Chelsea, 1990. 139–55.

Taylor, Marion A. *A New Look at the Old Sources of* Hamlet. The Hague: Mouton, 1968.

Turner, Robert Y. *Shakespeare's Apprenticeship*. Chicago: U of Chicago P, 1974.

Wagner, Linda Welshimer. "Ophelia: Shakespeare's Pathetic Plot Device." *Shakespeare Quarterly* 14 (1965): 94–7.

Waldock, A. J. A. *Hamlet: A Study in Critical Method*. Cambridge: Cambridge UP, 1931.

Watterson, William Collins. "Gertrude the Poet." *Hamlet Studies* 13 (1991): 92–7.

Watts, Cedric. *Hamlet*. Twayne's New Critical Introductions to Shakespeare. Boston: Twayne, 1988.

Wells, Stanley, ed. *The Cambridge Companion to Shakespeare Studies*. Cambridge: Cambridge UP, 1986.

HAMLET: ANALYSIS OF FILM VERSIONS

Ashworth, John. "Olivier, Freud, and Hamlet." *Atlantic Monthly* 183 (May 1949): 30–3.

Ball, Robert Hamilton. *Shakespeare on Silent Film: A Strange Eventful History*. London: Allen, 1968.

Booth, Stephen. "On the Value of Hamlet." *Reinterpretations of Elizabethan Drama*. Ed. Norman Rabkin. New York: Columbia UP, 1969. 137–76.

Brook, Peter. "Finding Shakespeare on Film." *Focus on Shakespearean Films*. Film Focus Ser. Ed. Charles W. Eckert. Englewood Cliffs: Prentice, 1972.

Brown, John Russell. *Shakespeare's Plays in Performance*. New York: St. Martin's, 1967.

———. "The Study and Practice of Shakespeare Production." *Shakespeare Survey* 18 (1965): 59.

Buchman, Lorne. *Still in Movement: Shakespeare on Screen*. Oxford: Oxford UP, 1991.

Bulman, James C., and Herbert Coursen. *Shakespeare on Television: An Anthology of Essays and Reviews*. Hanover, NH: UP of New England, 1988.

Cary, Cecile Williamson, and Henry S. Limouze, eds. *Shakespeare and the Arts: A Collection of Essays from the Ohio Shakespeare Conference, 1981 Wright State University, Dayton, Ohio*. Washington: UP of America, 1982.

Charney, Maurice. *Style in Hamlet*. Princeton: Princeton UP, 1969.

Coursen, H. R. "Shakespeare and Television: The BBC-TV *Hamlet*." *Shakespeare and the Arts: A Collection of Essays from the Ohio Shakespeare Conference, 1981 Wright State University, Dayton, Ohio*. Ed. Cecile Williamson Cary and Henry S. Limouze. Washington: UP of America, 1982. 127–33.

Crowl, Samuel. "Hamlet 'Most Royal': An Interview with Kenneth Branagh." *Shakespeare Bulletin* 12.4 (Fall 1994): 5–8.

———. *Shakespeare Observed: Studies in Performance on Stage and Screen*. Athens: U of Ohio P, 1992.

Dehn, Paul. "The Filming of Shakespeare." *Talking of Shakespeare*. Ed. John Garrett. London: Hodder, 1954. 49–72.

Dent, Alan, ed. *Hamlet: The Film and the Play*. London: World Film, 1948.

Eckert, Charles W., ed. *Focus on Shakespearean Films.* Film Focus Ser. Englewood Cliffs: Prentice, 1972.

Gielgud, John, and John Miller. *Acting Shakespeare.* New York: Scribner's, 1992.

Hurtgen, Charles. "The Operatic Character of Background Music in Film Adaptations of Shakespeare." *Shakespeare Quarterly* 20 (1969): 53.

Jensen, Michael P. "Mel Gibson on Hamlet." *Shakespeare on Film Newsletter* 15.2 (1991): 1+.

Jorgens, Jack J. *Shakespeare on Film.* Bloomington: Indiana UP, 1977.

Kitchin, Laurence. "Shakespeare on the Screen." *Shakespeare Survey* 18 (1965): 70–4.

Kliman, Bernice W. "The BBC *Hamlet,* a Television Production." *Hamlet Studies* 4 (1982): 99–105.

---. *Hamlet: Film, Television and Audio Performance.* Rutherford, NJ: Fairleigh Dickinson UP, 1988.

---. "Kozintsev's *Hamlet,* a Flawed Masterpiece." *Hamlet Studies* 1.2 (1979): 118–28.

---. "Olivier's *Hamlet:* A Film-Infused Play." *Literature Film Quarterly* 5.4 (1977): 305–14.

---. "The Spiral of Influence: One Defect in *Hamlet.*" *Literature/Film Quarterly* 11.3 (1983): 159–66.

Manvell, Roger. *Shakespeare and the Film.* New York: Barnes, 1979.

Morris, Peter. "Shakespeare on Film." *Films in Review* 24 (Mar. 1973): 132–63.

Olivier, Laurence. "An Essay in Hamlet." *The Film* Hamlet: *A Record of Its Production.* Ed. Brenda Cross. 3rd ed. London: Saturn, 1948. 11–15.

Rothwell, Kenneth S., and Annabelle Henkin Melzer. *Shakespeare on Screen: An International Filmography and Videography.* New York: Schuman, 1990.

Shaltz, Justin. "Three *Hamlet*s on Film." *Shakespeare Bulletin* 11.1 (Winter 1993): 36–7.

Shirley, Frances. *Shakespeare's Use of Off-Stage Sounds.* Lincoln: U of Nebraska P, 1963.

Skoller, Donald. "Problems of Transformation in the Adaptation of Shakespeare's Tragedies, From Play-Script to Cinema." Diss. New York U, 1968.

Sprague, Arthur Colby. *Shakespeare and the Actors.* Cambridge: Harvard UP, 1944.

Sprague, Arthur Colby, and J. C. Trewin. *Shakespeare's Plays Today.* London: Sidgwick, 1970.

Styan, J. L. *Shakespeare's Stagecraft.* Cambridge: Cambridge UP, 1967.

HAMLET: FILM VERSIONS

More than eighty films related to Hamlet *and produced from 1900–1989 are listed along with commentary and analysis in*
Rothwell, Kenneth S., and Annabelle Henkin Melzer. *Shakespeare on Screen: An International Filmography and Videography.* New York: Schuman, 1990.

FULL-LENGTH VERSIONS

Hamlet. Dir. Laurence Olivier. Perf. Olivier, Basil Sydney, Eileen Herlie, Jean Simmons, and Felix Aylmer. Two Cities, 1948.

Hamlet. Dir. Albert McCleery and George Schaefer. Perf. Maurice Evans, Joseph Schildkraut, Ruth Chatterton, Sarah Churchill, and Barry Jones. Hallmark Hall of Fame, 1953.

Hamlet. Dir. Ralph Nelson. Perf. John Neville, Oliver Neville, Margaret Courtenay, Barbara Jefford, and Joseph O'Connor. Dupont Show of the Month, 1959.

Hamlet: Prinz von Danemark. Dir. Franz Peter Wirth. Perf. Maximilian Schell, Hans Caninenberg, Wanda Rotha, Dunja Movar, and Franz Schafheitlin. Bavaria Attelier, 1960.

Gamlet. [*Hamlet.*] Dir. Grigori Kozintsev. Perf. Innokenti Smokhtunovski, Mikhail Nazwanov, Eliza Radzin-Szolkonis, Anastasia Vertinskaya, and Yuri Tolubeyev. Lenfilm, 1964.

Hamlet. Dir. John Gielgud and Bill Colleran. Perf. Richard Burton, Alfred Drake, Eileen Herlie, Linda March, and Hume Cronyn. Electronovision, 1964.

Hamlet at Elsinore. Dir. Philip Saville. Christopher Plummer, Robert Shaw, June Tobin, Jo Maxwell Muller, Alec Clunes, and Michael Caine. BBC Television/Danmarks Radio, 1964.

Hamlet. Dir. Tony Richardson. Perf. Nicol Williamson, Anthony Hopkins, Judy Parfitt, Marianne Faithfull, and Mark Dignam. Woodfall, 1969.

Hamlet. Dir. Peter Wood. Perf. Richard Chamberlain, Richard Johnson, Margaret Leighton, Ciaran Madden, Michael Redgrave. Hallmark Hall of Fame, 1970.

Hamlet. [BBC/Time-Life's Shakespeare Plays Ser.] Dir. Rodney Bennett. Perf. Derek Jacobi, Patrick Stewart, Claire Bloom, Lalla Ward, and Eric Porter. BBC Television/Time-Life, 1980.

Den Tragiska Historien om Hamlet, Prinz av Danmark. Dir. Ragnar Lyth. Perf. Stellan Skarsgaard, Frej Lindquist, Mona Malm, Pernella Wallgren, and Sven Lindberg. SVT 1, 1984.

Hamlet. Dir. Franco Zeffirelli. Perf. Mel Gibson, Glenn Close, Alan Bates, Paul Scofield, Ian Holm, and Helena Bonham-Carter. Warner Bros., 1990.

Hamlet. Dir. Kenneth Branagh. Perf. Kenneth Branagh, Derek Jacobi, Julie Christie, Richard Briers, Kate Winslet. Castle Rock, 1996.

CRITICISM AND ANALYSIS ON FILM

Hamlet: The Age of Elizabeth. [*Encyclopaedia Britannica's* The Humanities Ser. 1] Dir. Michael Langham, John Barnes, Douglas Campbell, Floyd Rinker, and Angelo McDermott. Perf. Maynard Mack [lecturer], Peter Donat, Tony Van

Bridge, Donald Davis, Douglas Campbell, and William Needles. Encyclopaedia Britannica Educational Corporation, 1959.

What Happens in Hamlet? [*Encyclopaedia Britannica*'s The Humanities Ser. 2.] Dir. Michael Langham, John Barnes, Floyd Rinker, and Angelo McDermott. Perf. Maynard Mack [lecturer], Peter Donat, Max Helpmann, and Charmion King. Encyclopaedia Britannica Educational Corporation, 1962.

Hamlet: The Poisoned Kingdom. [*Encyclopaedia Britannica*'s The Humanities Ser. 3.] Dir. Michael Langham, John Barnes, Douglas Campbell, Floyd Rinker, and Angelo McDermott. Perf. Maynard Mack [lecturer], Peter Donat, Max Helpmann, and Charmion King. Encyclopaedia Britannica Educational Corporation, 1962.

Hamlet IV: The Readiness Is All. [*Encyclopaedia Britannica*'s The Humanities Ser. 4.] Dir. Michael Langham, John Barnes, Douglas Campbell, Floyd Rinker, and Angelo McDermott. Perf. Maynard Mack [lecturer], Peter Donat, Max Helpmann, and Charmion King. Encyclopaedia Britannica Educational Corporation, 1962.

Hamlet: The Trouble with Hamlet. [Explorations in Shakespeare Ser. 4.] Dir. Robert Nelson. Perf. Briain Petchey, Dawn Greenhalgh, Bernard Behrens, and Jackie Burroughs. Ontario Educational Communications Authority, 1969.

Hamlet *Revisited: Approaches to* Hamlet. Prod. Ron Hobin. Perf. John Gielgud [host], Tom Courtenay, Richard Chamberlain, Nicol Williamson, Maximilian Schell, Innokenti Smoktunovsky, and John Barrymore. WNET, 1970.

Hamlet. [Shakespeare in Perspective Ser.] Dir. David Wilson. Perf. Clive James [commentator]. BBC / Time-Life, 1980.

Mel Gibson Goes Back to School. Dir. Mel Gibson. Icon, 1990.

ELECTRONIC SOURCES

Bate, Jonathan, ed. *The Arden Shakespeare CD-ROM: Texts and Sources for Shakespeare Studies.* Ver. 1.0. CD-ROM. Surrey, Kent: Nelson, 1997.

Beowulf-Hamlet. British Literature Ser. CD-ROM. Dallas: Zane, 1995.

Barton, Anne, et al., eds. *Editions and Adaptations of Shakespeare.* CD-ROM. Alexandria, VA: Chadwyck, 1997.

Exploring Shakespeare. CD-ROM. Detroit: Gale, 1996.

Hamlet. Vers. 1.0. CD-ROM. Shakespeare Interactive Ser. New York: Hall, 1997.

Rose, Mark, ed. *The Norton Shakespeare Workshop CD-ROM.* CD-ROM. New York: Norton, 1997.

Shakespeare. CD-ROM. Pleasant Grove, UT: Creative Multimedia, 1989.

The Shakespeare Quartet. CD-ROM. Knoxville, TN: Communication and Information Technologies, 1994.

Shakespeare Study Guide. CD-ROM. Irvine, CA: World Library, 1993.

Shakespeare's London. British Literature Ser. CD-ROM. Dallas: Zane, 1995.
Shakespeare's Theater. British Literature Ser. CD-ROM. Dallas: Zane, 1995.
William Shakespeare (1564–1616). British Literature Ser. CD-ROM. Dallas: Zane, 1995.
The World Shakespeare Bibliography on CD-ROM. CD-ROM. Cambridge: Cambridge UP, 1996.

WEB SITES

Starting Spots

Garzik, Jeff. *Selected Shakespearean Plays.* Online. Internet. 10 July 1997. Available http://www.spinne.com/shakespeare/.
---. *William Shakespeare and the Internet.* 17 Mar. 1997. Online. Internet. 10 July 1997. Available http://www.palomar.edu/Library/shake.htm.
Internet Movie Database: William Shakespeare. Online. Internet. 10 July 1997. Available http://us.imdb.com/M/person-exact?+Shakespeare,%20William.
Kollenbrandt, Peter. *Shakespeare Database Home Page.* 28 Feb. 1996. Online. Internet. 10 July 1997. Available http://ves101.uni-muenster.de/.
Ricker, Julie. *Selected Resources on Shakespeare.* Online. Internet. 10 July 1997. Available http://rodent.lib.rochester.edu/ref/shakes.htm.
Shakespeare Sites. Online. Internet. 10 July 1997. Available http://hamlet-movie.com/cmp/shakespeare.html.
The Shakespeare Web. 31 May 1997. Online. Internet. 10 July 1997. Available http://www.shakespeare.com/.
Ulin, Amy. *Surfing with the Bard.* 2 June 1997. Online. Internet. 10 July 1997. Available http://www.ivgh.com/amy/.
The Yahoo William Shakespeare Page. Online. Internet. 10 July 1997. Available http://www.yahoo.com/Arts/Performing_Arts/Theater/Plays/Playwrights/Shakespeare_William_1564_1616_/.

Hamlet Sites

Hamlet the Movie [Kenneth Branagh Version]. Online. Internet. 10 July 1997. Available http://hamlet-movie.com/.
Lupo, G. M. *The Tragedy of Hamlet, Prince of Denmark.* 8 May 1997. Online. Internet. 10 July 1997. Available http://www.lupo.com/~hamlet/hamlet/hamlet.html.
The Hamlet *Home Page.* 7 June 1997. Online. Internet. 10 July 1997. Available http://www.hamlet.edmonton.ab.ca.

Texts of Shakespeare's Plays

Farrow, Matty. *The Works of the Bard.* Online. Internet. 10 July 1997. Available http://www.gh.cs.su.oz.au/~matty/Shakespeare/Shakespeare.html# othersites.

Hylton, Jeremy. *The Complete Works of William Shakespeare.* 9 Dec. 1996. Online. Internet. 10 July 1997. Available http://the-tech.mit.edu/Shakespeare/works.html.

Text of Shakespeare's Plays. Online. Internet. 10 July 1997. Available http://www.pixi.com/~pchs/shakes/text2.htm.

Miscellaneous Information

Bickerton, Matthew. *The Bringing to Life of Stratford-upon-Avon.* Online. Internet. 10 July 1997. Available http://www.marketingnet.com/stratford/tourint.html.

Folger Shakespeare Library. Online. Internet. 10 July 1997. Available http://www.folger.edu/.

Gray, Terry A. *Nicholas Rowe's Preface to His 1709 Edition of Shakespeare's Works.* 3 Jan. 1997. Online. Internet. 10 July 1997. Available http://www.palomar.edu/Library/ROWE.HTM.

Miller-Schutz, Chantal. *Shakespeare's Globe.* 9 July 1997. Online. Internet. 13 Aug. 1997. Available http://www.rdg.ac.uk/AcaDepts/ln/Globe/Globe.html.

Massi, J. M. *The Shakespeare Classroom.* 2 Mar. 1997. Online. Internet. 10 July 1997. Available http://www.jetlink.net/~massij/shakes.html.

Rusche, Harry. *Shakespeare Illustrated.* 13 June 1997. Online. Internet. 10 July 1997. Available http://www.cc.emory.edu/ENGLISH/classes/Shakespeare_Illustrated/Shakespeare.html.

Schlenger, Andreas. *International Shakespeare Globe Centre, Germany.* 14 Mar. 1996. Online. Internet. 10 July 1997. Available http://www.rrz.uni-koeln.de/phil-fak/englisch/shakespeare/engl/shaknete.html.

Shakespeare Queries and Replies from Web Surfers. 31 May 1997. Online. Internet. 10 July 1997. Available http://www.shakespeare.com/qandr.html.

Today in Shakespeare History. Online. Internet. 10 July 1997. Available http://www.shakespeare.com/Today/todayinsh.cgi.

Shakespeare Acting Companies

Bickerton, Matthew. *Royal Shakespeare Company.* Online. Internet. 10 July 1997. Available http://www.marketingnet.com/stratford/toursc.html.

Cohen, Amy R. *The Shenandoah Shakespeare Express.* 10 Apr. 1997. Online. Internet. 10 July 1997. Available http://www.shakespeare.com/Shenandoah Express/.

Lee, Chester. *Alabama Shakespeare Festival.* 6 July 1997. Online. Internet. 10 July 1997. Available http://www.asf.net/.

The Shakespeare Theatre in the Nation's Capital. Online. Internet. 10 July 1997. Available http://shakespearedc.org/.

Shakespeare Authorship Controversy

Kathman, Dave, and Terry Ross. *The Shakespeare Authorship Page: Dedicated to the Proposition that Shakespeare Wrote Shakespeare.* Online. Internet. 10 July 1997. Available http://www.bcpl.lib.md.us/~tross/ws/will.html.

Boyle, William E. *Shakespeare Oxford Society Home Page.* 5 July 1997. Online. Internet. 10 July 1997. Available http://www.shakespeare-oxford.com/.

Appendix: Documenting Sources

A Guide to MLA
Documentation Style

Documentation is the acknowledgment of information from an outside source that you use in a paper. In general, you should give credit to your sources whenever you quote, paraphrase, summarize, or in any other way incorporate borrowed information or ideas into your work. Not to do so—on purpose or by accident—is to commit **plagiarism,** to appropriate the intellectual property of others. By following accepted conventions of documentation, you not only help avoid plagiarism, but also show your readers that you write with care and precision. In addition, you enable them to distinguish your ideas from those of your sources and, if they wish, to locate and consult the sources you cite.

Not all ideas from your sources need to be documented. You can assume that certain information—facts from encyclopedias, textbooks, newspapers, magazines, and dictionaries, or even from television and radio—is common knowledge. Even if the information is new to you, it need not be documented as long as it is found in several reference sources and as long as you do not use the exact wording of your source. Information that is in dispute or that is the original contribution of a particular person, however, *must* be documented. You need not, for example, document the fact that Arthur Miller's *Death of a Salesman* was first performed in 1949 or that it won a Pulitzer Prize for drama. (You could find this information in any current encyclopedia.) You would, however, have to document a critic's interpretation of a performance or a scholar's analysis of an early draft of the play, even if you do not use your source's exact words.

Students of literature use the documentation style recommended by the Modern Language Association of America (MLA), a professional organization of more than twenty-five thousand teachers and students of English and other languages. This method of documentation, the one that you should use any time you write a literature paper, has three components: *parenthetical references in the text, a list of works cited,* and *explanatory notes.*

Parenthetical References in the Text

MLA documentation uses references inserted in parentheses within the text that refer to an alphabetical list of works cited at the end of the paper. A typical **parenthetical reference** consists of the author's last name and a page number.

```
Gwendolyn Brooks uses the sonnet form to create
poems that have a wide social and aesthetic range
(Williams 972).
```

If you use more than one source by the same author, include a shortened title in the parenthetical reference. In the following entry, "Brooks's Way" is a shortened form of the complete title of the article "Gwendolyn Brooks's Way with the Sonnet."

```
Brooks not only knows Shakespeare, Spenser, and
Milton, but she also knows the full range of
African-American poetry (Williams, "Brooks's Way"
972).
```

If you mention the author's name or the title of the work in your paper, only a page reference is necessary.

```
According to Gladys Margaret Williams in "Gwendolyn
Brooks's Way with the Sonnet," Brooks combines a
sensitivity to poetic forms with a depth of emotion
appropriate for her subject matter (972-73).
```

Keep in mind that you use different punctuation for parenthetical references used with *paraphrases and summaries,* with *direct quotations run in with the text,* and with *quotations of more than four lines.*

Paraphrases and Summaries

Place the parenthetical reference after the last word of the sentence and before the final punctuation:

```
In her works Brooks combines the pessimism of Mod-
ernist poetry with the optimism of the Harlem Re-
naissance (Smith 978).
```

Direct quotations run in with the text

Place the parenthetical reference after the quotation marks and before the final punctuation:

> According to Gary Smith, Brooks's A Street in Bronzeville "conveys the primacy of suffering in the lives of poor Black women" (980).

> According to Gary Smith, the poems in A Street in Bronzeville, "served notice that Brooks had learned her craft . . ." (978).

> Along with Thompson we must ask, "Why did it take so long for critics to acknowledge that Gwendolyn Brooks is an important voice in twentieth-century American poetry?" (123)

Quotations set off from the text

Omit the quotation marks and place the parenthetical reference one space after the final punctuation.

> For Gary Smith, the identity of Brooks's African-American women is inextricably linked with their sense of race and poverty:
>> For Brooks, unlike the Renaissance poets, the victimization of poor Black women becomes not simply a minor chord but a predominant theme of A Street in Bronzeville. Few, if any, of her female characters are able to free themselves from a web of poverty that threatens to strangle their lives. (980)

[Quotations of more than four lines are indented ten spaces (or one inch) from the margin and are not enclosed within quotation marks. The first line of a single paragraph of quoted material is not indented further. If you quote two or more paragraphs, indent the first line of each paragraph three additional spaces (one-quarter inch).]

SAMPLE REFERENCES

The following formats are used for parenthetical references to various kinds of sources used in papers about literature. (Keep in mind that the parenthetical reference contains just enough information to enable readers to find the source in the list of works cited at the end of the paper.)

An entire work

> August Wilson's play <u>Fences</u> treats many themes frequently expressed in modern drama.

[When citing an entire work, state the name of the author in your paper instead of in a parenthetical reference.]

A work by two or three authors

> Myths cut across boundaries and cultural spheres and reappear in strikingly similar forms from country to country (Feldman and Richardson 124).

> The effect of a work of literature depends on the audience's predispositions that derive from membership in various social groups (Hovland, Janis, and Kelley 87).

A work by more than three authors

> Hawthorne's short stories frequently use a combination of allegorical and symbolic methods (Guerin et al. 91).

[The abbreviation *et al.* is Latin for "and others."]

A work in an anthology

> In his essay "Flat and Round Characters" E. M. Forster distinguishes between one-dimensional characters and those that are well developed (Stevick 223–31).

[The parenthetical reference cites the anthology (edited by Stevick) that contains Forster's essay; full information about the anthology appears in the list of works cited.]

A work with volume and page numbers

> In 1961 one of Albee's plays, <u>The Zoo Story</u>, was
> finally performed in America (Eagleton 2:17).

An indirect source

> Wagner observed that myth and history stood before
> him "with opposing claims" (qtd. in Winkler 10).

[The abbreviation *qtd. in* (quoted in) indicates that the quoted material was not taken from the original source.]

A play or poem with numbered lines

> "Give thy thoughts no tongue," says Polonius,
> "Nor any unproportioned thought his act"
> (<u>Ham</u>. 1.3.59-60).

[The parentheses contain the act, scene, and line numbers, separated by periods. When included in parenthetical references, titles of the books of the Bible and well-known literary works are often abbreviated—*Gen.* for *Genesis* and *Ado* for *Much Ado about Nothing,* for example.]

> "I muse my life-long hate, and without flinch / I
> bear it nobly as I live my part," says Claude McKay
> in his bitterly ironic poem "The White City" (3-4).

[Notice that a slash [/] is used to separate lines of poetry run in with the text. The parenthetical reference cites the lines quoted.]

The List of Works Cited

Parenthetical references refer to a **list of works cited** that includes all the sources you refer to in your paper. (If your list includes all the works consulted, whether you cite them or not, use the title *Works Consulted.*) Begin the works cited list on a new page, continuing the page numbers of the paper. For example, if the text of the paper ends on page six, the works cited section will begin on page seven.

Center the title *Works Cited* one inch from the top of the page. Arrange entries alphabetically, according to the last name of each author (or the first word of the title if the author is unknown). Articles—*a, an,* and *the*—at the beginning of a title are not considered first words. Thus, *A Handbook of Critical Approaches to Literature* would be alphabetized under *H.* In order to conserve space, publishers' names are abbreviated—for example, *Harcourt* for Harcourt Brace College Publishers. Double-space the entire works cited list between and within entries. Begin typing each entry at the left margin, and indent subsequent lines five spaces or one-half inch. The entry itself generally has three divisions—author, title, and publishing information—separated by periods.*

A book by a single author

> Kingston, Maxine Hong. <u>The Woman Warrior: Memoirs of a Girlhood among Ghosts</u>. New York: Knopf, 1976.

A book by two or three authors

> Feldman, Burton, and Robert D. Richardson. <u>The Rise of Modern Mythology</u>. Bloomington: Indiana UP, 1972.

[Notice that only the *first* author's name is in reverse order.]

A book by more than three authors

> Guerin, Wilfred, et al., eds. <u>A Handbook of Critical Approaches to Literature</u>. 3rd. ed. New York: Harper, 1992.

[Instead of using *et al.,* you may list all the authors' names in the order in which they appear on the title page.]

Two or more works by the same author

> Novoa, Juan-Bruce. <u>Chicano Authors: Inquiry by Interview</u>, Austin: U of Texas P, 1980.

---

* The fourth edition of the *MLA Handbook for Writers of Research Papers* (1995) shows a single space after all end punctuation.

---. "Themes in Rudolfo Anaya's Work." Address
    given at New Mexico State University, Las
    Cruces. 11 Apr. 1987.

[List two or more works by the same author in alphabetical order by title.
Include the author's full name in the first entry; use three unspaced hyphens
followed by a period to take the place of the author's name in second and
subsequent entries.]

An edited book

Oosthuizen, Ann, ed. Sometimes When It Rains: Writ-
    ings by South African Women. New York: Pandora,
    1987.

[Note that the abbreviation *ed.* stands for *editor.*]

A book with a volume number

Eagleton, T. Allston. A History of the New York
    Stage. Vol. 2. Englewood Cliffs: Prentice.
    1987.

[All three volumes have the same title.]

Durant, Will, and Ariel Durant. The Age of Napoleon:
    A History of European Civilization from 1789 to
    1815. New York: Simon, 1975.

[Each volume has a different title, so you may cite an individual book without referring to the other volumes.]

A short story, poem, or play in a collection of the author's work

Gordimer, Nadine. "Once upon a Time." "Jump" and
    Other Stories. New York: Farrar, 1991. 23-30.

A short story in an anthology

Salinas, Marta. "The Scholarship Jacket." Nosotros:
    Latina Literature Today. Ed. Maria del Carmen

Boza, Beverly Silva, and Carmen Valle. Binghamton: Bilingual, 1986. 68-70.

[The inclusive page numbers follow the year of publication. Note that here the abbreviation *Ed.* stands for *Edited by*.]

A poem in an anthology

Simmerman, Jim. "Child's Grave, Hale County, Alabama." <u>The Pushcart Prize, X: Best of the Small Presses</u>. Ed. Bill Henderson. New York: Penguin, 1986. 198-99.

A play in an anthology

Hughes, Langston. <u>Mother and Child</u>. <u>Black Drama Anthology</u>. Ed. Woodie King and Ron Miller. New York: NAL, 1986.399-406.

An article in an anthology

Forster, E. M. "Flat and Round Characters." <u>The Theory of the Novel</u>. Ed. Philip Stevick. New York: Free, 1980. 223-31.

More than one selection from the same anthology

If you are using more than one selection from an anthology, cite the anthology in one entry. In addition, list each individual selection separately, including the author and title of the selection, the anthology editor's last name, and the inclusive page numbers.

Kirszner, Laurie G., and Stephen R. Mandell, eds. <u>Literature: Reading, Reacting, Writing</u>. 3rd ed. Fort Worth: Harcourt, 1997.
Rich, Adrienne. "Diving into the Wreck." Kirszner and Mandell 874-76.

A translation
Carpentier, Alejo. <u>Reasons of State</u>. Trans. Francis Partridge. New York: Norton, 1976.

An article in a journal with continuous pagination in each issue

LeGuin, Ursula K. "American Science Fiction and the
    Other." <u>Science Fiction Studies</u> 2 (1975):
    208-10.

An article with separate pagination in each issue

Grossman, Robert. "The Grotesque in Faulkner's
    'A Rose for Emily.'" <u>Mosaic</u> 20.3 (1987): 40-55.

[20.3 signifies volume 20, issue 3.]

An article in a magazine

Milosz, Czeslaw. "A Lecture." <u>New Yorker</u> 22 June
    1992: 32.
"Solzhenitsyn: An Artist Becomes an Exile." <u>Time</u>
    25 Feb. 1974: 34+.

[34+ indicates that the article appears on pages that are not consecutive; in
this case the article begins on page 34 and then continues on page 37. An
article with no listed author is entered by title on the works cited list.]

An article in a daily newspaper

Oates, Joyce Carol. "When Characters from the Page
    Are Made Flesh on the Screen." <u>New York Times</u>
    23 Mar. 1986, late ed.: C1+.

[C1+ indicates that the article begins on page 1 of Section C and continues
on a subsequent page.]

An article in a reference book

"Dance Theatre of Harlem." <u>The New Encyclopaedia
    Britannica: Micropaedia</u>. 15th ed. 1987.

[You do not need to include publication information for well-known reference books.]

Grimstead, David. "Fuller, Margaret Sarah." <u>Encyclo-
    pedia of American Biography</u>. Ed. John A. Gar-
    raty. New York: Harper, 1974.

[You must include publication information when citing reference books that are not well known.]

A CD-ROM: Entry with a print version

> Zurbach, Kate. "The Linguistic Roots of Three
> Terms." <u>Linguistic Quarterly</u> 37 (1994): 12-47.
> <u>Infotrac: Magazine Index Plus</u>. CD-ROM. Informa-
> tion Access. Jan. 1996.

[When you cite information with a print version from a CD-ROM, include the publication information, the underlined title of the database (<u>Infotrac: Magazine Index Plus</u>), the publication medium (CD-ROM), the name of the company that produced the CD-ROM (Information Access), and the electronic publication date.]

A CD-ROM: Entry with no print version

> "Surrealism." <u>Encarta 1996</u>. CD-ROM. Redmond: Micro-
> soft, 1996.

[If you are citing a part of a work, include the title in quotation marks.]

> <u>A Music Lover's Multimedia Guide to Beethoven's 5th</u>.
> CD-ROM. Spring Valley: Interactive, 1993.

[If you are citing an entire work, include the underlined title.]

An online source: Entry with a print version

> Dẹkoven, Marianne. "Utopias Limited: Post-sixties
> and Postmodern American Fiction." <u>Modern Fic-
> tion Studies</u> 41.1 (Spring 1995): 121-34. On-
> line. Internet. 17 Mar. 1996. Available
> http://muse.jhu.edu/journals/MFS/v041/41.1
> dekoven.html.

[When you cite information with a print version from an online source, include the publication information for the printed source, the number of pages (*n. pag.* if no pages are given), the publication medium (Online), the name of the computer network (Internet), and the date of access. If you wish, you may also include the electronic address, preceded by the word *Available*. Information from a commercial computer service—America Online, Prodigy, and CompuServ, for example—will not have an electronic address.]

O'Hara, Sandra. "Reexamining the Canon." *Time* 13 May
1994: 27. Online. America Online. 22 Aug. 1994.

An online source: Entry with no print version

"Romanticism." *Academic American Encyclopedia*. Online. Prodigy. 6 Nov. 1995.

[This entry shows that the material was accessed on November 6, 1996.]

An online source: Public Posting

Peters, Olaf. "Studying English through German."
29 Feb. 1996. Online Posting. Foreign Language
Forum, Multi Language Section. CompuServe.
15 Mar. 1996.
Gilford, Mary. "Dog Heroes in Children's Literature." 4 Oct. 1996. Newsgroup alt.animals.dogs.
America Online. 23 Mar. 1996.

[**WARNING:** Using information from online forums and newsgroups is
risky. Contributors are not necessarily experts, and frequently they are
incorrect and misinformed. Unless you can be certain that the information you are receiving from these sources is reliable, do not use it in your
papers.]

An online source: Electronic Text

Twain, Mark. *The Adventures of Huckleberry Finn*.
From *The Writing of Mark Twain*. Vol. 13.
New York: Harper, 1970. Online. Wiretap.
spies. Internet. 13 Jan. 1996. Available
http.//www.sci.dixie.edu/DixieCollege/Ebooks/
huckfin.html.

[This electronic text was originally published by Harper. The name of the
repository for the electronic edition is Wiretap.spies.]

An online source: E-Mail

Adkins, Camille. E-Mail to the author. 8 June 1995.

An interview

Brooks, Gwendolyn. "Interviews." <u>Triquarterly</u> 60
(1984): 405-10.

A lecture or address

Novoa, Juan-Bruce. "Themes in Rudolfo Anaya's Work."
New Mexico State University, Las Cruces,
11 Apr. 1987.

A film or videocassette

"<u>A Worn Path</u>." By Eudora Welty. Dir. John Reid and
Claudia Velasco. Perf. Cora Lee Day and Con-
chita Ferrell. Videocassette. Harcourt, 1994.

[In addition to the title, the director, and the year, include other pertinent information such as the principal performers.]

Explanatory Notes

Explanatory notes, indicated by a superscript (a raised number) in the text, may be used to cite several sources at once or to provide commentary or explanations that do not fit smoothly into your paper. The full text of these notes appears on the first numbered page following the last page of the paper. (If your paper has no explanatory notes, the works cited page follows the last page of the paper.) Like works cited entries, explanatory notes are double-spaced within and between entries. However, the first line of each explanatory note is indented five spaces (or one-half inch), with subsequent lines flush with the left-hand margin.

TO CITE SEVERAL SOURCES

In the paper

Surprising as it may seem, there have been many
attempts to define literature.[1]

In the note

¹ For an overview of critical opinion, see Arnold 72; Eagleton 1–2; Howe 43–44; and Abrams 232–34.

TO PROVIDE EXPLANATIONS

In the paper

In recent years gothic novels have achieved great popularity.³

In the note

³ Gothic novels, works written in imitation of medieval romances, originally relied on supernatural occurrences. They flourished in the late eighteenth and early nineteenth centuries.

Credits